PHILOSOPHY AS PASSION

PHILOSOPHY
AS
PASSION

THE

THINKING OF

SIMONE DE BEAUVOIR

KAREN VINTGES

*Indiana
University
Press*

BLOOMINGTON AND INDIANAPOLIS

Originally published in 1992 as *Filosofie als passie. Het denken van Simone de Beauvoir* (Prometheus, Amsterdam). Translated by Anne Lavelle. This translation was made possible by the Netherlands Organization for Scientific Research.

Library of Congress Cataloging-in-Publication Data
Vintges, Karen.
[Filosofie als passie. English]
Philosophy as passion : the thinking of Simone de Beauvoir / Karen Vintges.
p.   cm.
Includes bibliographical references and index.
ISBN 0-253-33059-9 (cl : alk. paper).—
ISBN 0-253-21070-4 (pa : alk. paper)
1. Beauvoir, Simone de, 1908–   .   I. Title.
B2430.B344V5513   1996
194—dc20
95-51748
1 2 3 4 5   01 00 99 98 97 96

To Vincent

CONTENTS

ACKNOWLEDGMENTS

During the course of writing this book, I long pondered the use of the personal pronoun "he" when women are (also) referred to. The—by this time—well-known problem is that using "he/she" seems forced: it disturbs the reading process and suggests an overly fussy political correctness. For this reason, and following Beauvoir's own lead, I opted to express emancipatory feminist content through the mutual connection of words, rather than through the words themselves.

The research from which this book results was supported by the Belle van Zuyleninstitute of the University of Amsterdam. I want to thank its board and members for their moral support and encouragement. Special thanks go to my supervisor, Theo de Boer. I have benefited greatly from his philosophical knowledge and wisdom. I would also like to thank the philosophers who were the members and students of the Social Philosophy Department of the Philosophy Faculty of the University of Amsterdam during the course of writing this book: Hans Achterhuis, Veit Bader, Nel van den Haak, Josef Keulartz, Harry Kunneman, Barbara Noske, and Ton Salman.

Warm thanks go to my colleagues within the Amsterdam Philosophical Women's Society: Ineke van der Burg, Angela Grooten, Annemie Halsema, Joke Hermsen, Chris van der Hoek, Veronica Vasterling, Desirée Verweij, and Hannie van Wijk. Each and every one of them gave me the utmost practical support.

For their comments, assistance, and advice, I would also like to mention Mieke Aerts, Tjitske Akkerman, Renate Bartsch, Hans Beentjes, J. Bommeljé, Rosi Braidotti, Françoise Collin, Sandra Harding, Willy Jansen, David Jopling, Sarah Kofman, Helma Lutz, Baukje Prins, Brita Rang, Marian Schwegmann, Margaret Simons, Martha Vicinus, Coos Vink, and Marianne van den Wijngaarden. Ton Dekker's astute critical reading of the manuscript was indispensable.

Thanks are also due to many of the librarians of the University of Amsterdam's libraries, but I would like to mention specially Marleen

Houpt, Inge Sol, and Susan Schoute, as well as Nicoline Meiners of Antiquariaat Lorelei. My family and friends provided encouragement and dinners with equal liberality and gave me loving support.

Finally, I want to thank my translator, Anne Lavelle, who taught me the correct usage of the verb "to get" along with many other things about the English language; the linguistic idiosyncrasies in this work are all mine.

Roland Noske gave me loving support all along, and through difficult times. It is to our newborn son Vincent that I dedicate this book.

ABBREVIATIONS

Quotations and references are drawn where possible from current English editions of Beauvoir's work. Translations have been revised only where necessary. This is apparent when reference is made to the French original.

AFS	*Adieux, A Farewell to Sartre*
Am	*L'Amérique au jour le jour*
ASD	*All Said and Done*
BN	*Being and Nothingness*
EA	*The Ethics of Ambiguity*
EH	*Existentialism and Humanism*
EN	*L'être et le néant*
FA	*La force de l'âge*
FbS	*Faut-il brûler Sade?*
FoC	*Force of Circumstance*
Hc	*Huis clos*
Imrp	"Idéalisme moral et réalisme politique"
JG	*Journal de guerre*
LDS	*Le deuxième sexe*
LE	*Les écrits de Simone de Beauvoir*
LL	*Lucifer and the Lord*
LM	"Littérature et métaphysique"
LS	*Letters to Sartre*
M	*The Mandarins*
MBS	*Must We Burn De Sade?*
MDD	*Memoirs of a Dutiful Daughter*
ME	"Mon expérience d'écrivain"
MPps	"Merleau-Ponty et le pseudo-sartrisme"
OA	*Old Age*
OO	"Oeil pour oeil"

PC	*Pyrrhus et Cinéas*
PMA	*Pour une morale de l'ambiguïté*
PoL	*The Prime of Life*
QL	*Que peut la littérature?*
TM	*Les temps modernes*
TSS	*The Second Sex*
VED	*A Very Easy Death*
W	*Words*

PHILOSOPHY AS PASSION

1

INTRODUCTION

 "Thinking again?" the Duchess asked, with another dig of her sharp little chin. "I've a right to think," said Alice sharply, for she was beginning to feel a little worried. "Just about as much right," said the Duchess, "as pigs have to fly."

—Louis Carroll,
Alice's Adventures in Wonderland

The problem

"It was the first time in my life that I had felt intellectually inferior to anyone else. . . . Day after day, and all day long I set myself up against Sartre, and in our discussions I was simply not in his class" (MDD: 343–44). Simone de Beauvoir continually assured us that her life's companion, Jean-Paul Sartre, was her intellectual superior. Time and again, she reiterated her view of their division of labor: Sartre was the philosopher; she the literary writer. Sartre had independence of thought; she lacked "originality" (PoL: 221). Sartre's "exaggerations" would be more fruitful for philosophy than her own "scrupulous precision" (p. 42).

However, Beauvoir's teachers did not share this view when she passed her "*agrégation*" in philosophy at age twenty-one. She had prepared for this tough examination leading to a teaching diploma while still a final-year philosophy student—no mean feat, given the fact she was the youngest entrant and took second place in the lists. First place went to her lover Jean-Paul Sartre, who was making his second attempt. In her biography of Sartre, Annie Cohen-Solal quotes a fellow student of Beauvoir and Sartre's:

As two members of the jury, Davy and Wahl, told me later, it had not been easy to decide whether to give the first place to Sartre or to her. If Sartre already showed great intelligence and a solid, if at times inexact, culture, everybody agreed that, of the two, she was the real philosopher. (Cohen-Solal, 1987: 74)

But is Beauvoir's work philosophical in itself? This question is now raised increasingly and is central to the present volume. Studies on Beauvoir tend to concentrate on her person, and often take a personal tone, thus making impossible an objective view of her work.[1] On the rare occasions when they make Beauvoir's oeuvre the main focus, they approach it from a literary-theoretical point of view. It is only recently that such works as *The Second Sex* and her moral-philosophical essays have been explored from a philosophical perspective (see Hatcher, 1984; Simons, 1987, 1995; Singer, 1985; Butler, 1986; Kruks, 1990). However, no study has yet examined the philosophical merits of Beauvoir's *total* oeuvre. Feminist theoreticians usually consider *The Second Sex* as a sociological study and the rest of her work as meritorious literary writing. In other intellectual circles, Beauvoir is seen primarily as the writer of a kind of superior romances; her work is labeled first as literature, and then, through lack of real literary merit, as bad literature.

In academic-philosophical circles, Beauvoir's work is seldom read. Her name does not appear in philosophical handbooks or introductions to existentialism. At best, she is mentioned as a pupil of Sartre's or as his biographer (for an overview, see Simons, 1990: 493). Today's philosophers, usually men who are not particularly *au fait* with feminism and related subjects, still consider Beauvoir's work as lacking philosophical content. The fact of the matter is that, unlike the literary sciences, cultural anthropology, and psychoanalytic theory, academic philosophy to date has proved inhospitable to feminist theory and its critical probing of the boundaries of different academic disciplines. This is hardly surprising, as academic philosophers have traditionally focused on pure logic and abstract thought, and thus thought themselves above gender differences or other empirical phenomena.

This study shows that Beauvoir, like some other philosophers before her, attacked the assumed irreconcilability of thinking and empirical matters, thus questioning the boundaries and breadth of philosophy. Yet, she never claimed the philosophical label for her own oeuvre, but chose to go through life as literary author. In my view, this should be seen in the context of her time, and particularly in the context of a tradition that saw women and philosophy as each other's antitheses. Since time out of mind, we find the notion of the incompatibility of womanhood and rational thinking; the tradition of philosophy itself has made no mean contribution to the maintenance of this concept. Can women be rational? This question has been answered with a resounding "No" by philosophers from Aristotle to Rousseau, from Thomas Aquinas to Hegel: woman represents nature and the body; she is sex.[2] As sexual ascesis has generally been considered a precondition for rational thought since the time of Plato, the intellectual woman was considered a contradiction in terms; she simply could not exist. Women were not suited to the higher arts, science, or philosophy (according to Hegel), but at best were able to write superficial verse (according to Rousseau). Poetry and literature could be compatible with femininity, but the logic, rationality, power of thought, and analytic capacity required by the sciences and philosophy were the exclusive preserve of men.[3] The rise of universities played a considerable role in the dissemination of this idea because women were excluded from participation in the research and education these institutions undertook.[4] Beauvoir herself, who majored in philosophy at the Sorbonne, was still a product of the university tradition of excluding women. As a female student, she was not allowed to register at the École Normale Superieure where her male counterparts in the *agrégation* examination enjoyed their elite training.

Of course, there were many women who were able to get around all of the barriers and who still managed to develop intellectually. But those women usually worked alongside an erudite man, although rarely on an equal basis. Of the well-known intellectual male-female teams in history, the woman is always (seen as) the helpmate of the intellectually "superior" man. There was no place for the individual, intellectual woman working alone, as she would have been continually confronted with all manner of social obstacles, such as the prohibition against women speaking in public or teaching (see Alic, 1986; Labalme, 1984; Schiebinger, 1989). Only the woman doctor has been able to practice her profession independently during most of history. On the whole, the learned woman was relegated to the marginal areas of intellectual life.

Women themselves used their pens to attack the notion that female intellectuals had no right of existence, and a number of men defended them.[5] In the early Renaissance, Christine de Pisan opened the debate that has gone down in history as the *Querelle des femmes*. In fact, this debate is still ongoing, and Beauvoir's *The Second Sex* can be seen as a contribution to it. In this study of women, she challenges a variant of the notion that the intellectual woman is a contradiction in terms—a variant through which Freud made great strides in this century; he represented the creative woman as an essentially phallic woman and the thinking woman as a masculine woman. But this notion was already well entrenched and is evident from the traditional derogatory terms for learned women, varying from "bluestockings" and "*précieuses*" to "*savantes.*"

The Dutch writer Carry van Bruggen fulminated against this representation in the early 1920s. Van Bruggen, who had philosophical aspirations and was intensely involved in the discourse on the matter of intellectual women,[6] characterized the then-prevalent male reaction to intellectual women as follows: "The man says, with that inimitable, childlike naivety which is his innate exceptional charm: That woman has a Male Intellect." She added crossly, "Isn't it sweet? It is so self-evident that Logic is the preserve, the inheritance, the prerogative of the Man, that without the merest shred of evidence, the woman who attempts to practice it is equated with the woman who 'attempts to masculinize herself' " (van Bruggen, 1925: 218, 220). Beauvoir's *The Second Sex* vigorously attacked the notion of real and unreal women, and criticized explicitly the representation of the intellectual woman as bluestocking and *précieuse* (see e.g., TSS I: 138). To Beauvoir, a woman is a being who creates herself and who does not have to fit certain criteria in advance.

Intellectual women in history have certainly resisted their so-called exceptionality, but this does not alter the fact they have been hindered by their exceptional status. They have suffered from continual criticism from men and women: "they jeer at me throughout the city, the women mock me. . . . I cannot find a quiet stable to hide in, and the donkeys tear me with their teeth, the oxen stab me with their horns," sighs an intellectual woman of the Italian Renaissance (in King, 1984: 72–73). Not surprisingly, learned women in history usually lacked an unequivocally positive self-image, and this has only recently begun to change. Being both a woman and an intellectual has caused so much friction that the learned woman often defined herself in terms of failure (failed woman, failed man), or in negative terms, either as sexless being (not a man and not a woman), or as an extension of men. Beauvoir also opted for this latter, safe path by presenting herself as the helpmate of the intellectually superior Sartre. Her self-image was thus rooted in a long tradition. As a woman, it was hard for Beauvoir to identify with academic philosophy, the preserve par excellence of Rational Thought. In her time, there was no question of the kind of debate on the possible gendered presuppositions of the academic disciplines that is current today in the form of academic women's studies, or of a general rejection of the notion that men and women were rational and irrational respectively. Differences among women and among men are now often considered greater than those between women and men, and the strict rational-irrational distinction has come under question. Science and philosophy are no longer considered purely rational. The gulf between rationality and other forms of consciousness is gradually being closed by more and more research material from science historians, sociologists, and theoreticians.[7]

This study attempts to contribute to closing that gulf but represents an attempt from a different point of departure—an examination of the rational thinking of the "writer" Simone de Beauvoir. Despite Beauvoir's self-image, I am searching for her philosophy.[8] In doing so, I will concentrate on those works which, according to Beauvoir herself, form the core of her oeuvre: the moral-philosophical treatises written in the 1940s and 1950s; her study of *The Second Sex*; her novel *The Mandarins*; and her autobiographical work (see Bair, 1990a: 269; Jeanson, 1966: 286–87; Schwarzer, 1986: 125).

The independence of her thinking will be revealed through a comparison with that of the early Sartre. The reason for limiting this comparison is that Beauvoir's work is usually seen as a footnote to or an expansion of Sartre's original existentialist philosophy in *L'être et le néant* (1943: *Being and Nothingness*). It is often assumed Beauvoir was unable to "follow" Sartre's later philosophical development and continued stubbornly to defend his earlier thinking—including against Sartre himself (see Bair, 1990a: 381, 452). Thus, research on Beauvoir's own thinking requires a comparison with Sartre's original existentialist philosophy.[9] If Beauvoir's thinking turns out to be strikingly different from Sartre's, we will have a basis for an approach to her work as an independent philosophical oeuvre.[10]

It is remarkable that philosophic interest in Sartre's existentialism has ebbed away almost completely over recent decades. To my knowledge, Sartre's work is now the subject of only marginalized interest among professional philosophers. This is all the more striking in view of the major similarities between it and what has been dubbed "postmodernist" thinking. Those who still remember the proverbial black polo-neck sweaters and melancholy discussions that, under the collective name existentialism, made the philosophical running not too long ago, may also have remarked these similarities—postmodernism's same penchant for black and bohemian style. But both cults had or have their serious exponents, and both are based on a serious body of ideas, which also demonstrate major parallels. Existentialism and postmodernism share the idea of the impossibility of universal moral theories. God and Truth are dead, and thus the foundations of morality have disappeared. Both philosophical movements attempt to think through this notion to its extreme consequences.

Simone de Beauvoir wholeheartedly supported the existentialist philosophical view of the impossibility of a moral theory, but in marked contrast to Sartre, she never actually departed from the terrain of ethics as such. We will attempt to discover how she tried to conceive a morality without foundations, which nevertheless can provide answers to the question of how to live, a contribution that is relevant in the light of the present-day debates on ethics and postmodernism's failure to present alternatives.

For explanatory reasons, our presentation of the philosophic thinking of Beauvoir does not follow the chronological order of her oeuvre. After chapter 2's exploration of the biographical context of her oeuvre, chapter 3 examines *The Second Sex*, Beauvoir's most important philosophical work, showing how it breaks with Sartre's dualistic ontology. In chapter 4 we turn to her essay on Sade and her moral philosophical treatises, to show how Beauvoir developed her own philosophy, creating a place for existentialist ethics. In chapter 5, we look at the forms of her ethics in the different phases of her work. So again, her moral philosophical treatises, but also her novel *The Mandarins*, are discussed here, as is also the case in chapter 6, where we once more compare her ideas on ethics with Sartre's philosophy. In chapter 7, we go into the content of Beauvoir's personal positive ethics. Here her two earliest autobiographical works are examined, using an approach distilled from the foregoing chapters. In chapters 8 and 9, we give an inventory of the practical expression of Beauvoir's personal positive ethics, by looking closely at the two last volumes of her autobiography. Chapter 8 treats her daily lifestyle as an intellectual woman. Chapter 9 explores the type of intellectuality she developed, going into some of the details of the philosophical tradition from which she came and discussing the genre of her novels. Finally, chapter 10 takes stock of the life and work of Beauvoir. The reader who is primarily interested in the thematic content of Beauvoir's thinking rather than in the academic bases of this study could, perhaps, skip the now-following section on heuristics.

Heuristics

In my search for Simone de Beauvoir's own thinking, French philosopher Michel Foucault's final work was an important source of inspiration. His broadening of ethics to include the concept of "aesthetics of existence" gave me a tool to elucidate what, in my view, forms the core of Beauvoir's oeuvre. I outline here some of the main themes in Foucault's concept to provide insight into the theoretical backgrounds to my research.

Under the name "aesthetics of existence" or "self-practices," Foucault ranges texts on sexuality from classical antiquity "whose main object, whatever their form (speech, dialogue, treatise, collection of precepts, etc.) is to suggest rules of conduct." Foucault goes on to explain that these documents were

> texts written for the purpose of offering rules, opinions, and advice on how to behave as one should: "practical" texts, which are themselves objects of a "practice" in that they were designed to be read, learned, reflected upon, and tested out, and they were intended to constitute the eventual framework of everyday conduct. These texts thus served as functional devices that would enable individuals to question their own conduct, to watch over and give shape to it, and to shape themselves as ethical subject. (Foucault, 1986a: 12–13)

The most important characteristic of these ethical texts was their autonomy; they were separate from religion, state, and law, but also separate from theoretical texts containing doctrines, or a general morality. In his books *The Use of Pleasure* (1986a) and *The Care of the Self* (1986b), Foucault uses theoretical texts from antiquity, such as works by Plato and Aristotle, as the background against which the questioning and stylization of one's own behavior using 'practical' texts could take place.

These practical texts may be aimed at the concrete shaping of one's own existence, but according to him, they should still count as ethics because the relationship with one's self always implies a relationship with others: care of the self is aimed at man's ability to occupy a place in society in a competent and adequate manner, whether this consists of fulfilling a public trust or having friendly relationships. "Thus, the problem of relationship with others is present all along this development of care for self" (Foucault, 1988a: 7).

This conclusion is not superfluous. Traditionally, ethics is concerned with the question of a good society, i.e., the question of how we should behave toward our fellow human beings. The traditional question originated by Socrates on "the good life" does not mean we are striving for this as the goal of some egotistical or solipsistic project, but that we ask ourselves how we can pursue a good life in relation to and with our fellow human beings. The history of ethics comprises reflection on this question (see also Williams, 1985: 12). Foucault locates his "aesthetics of existence" in this tradition, arguing that care of the self serves relationships with others.

In *The Use of Pleasure* and *The Care of the Self*, Foucault not only wants to reveal a specific type of ethics, he accompanies his analysis with a general framework of concepts and a set of analytical tools to enable the study of the history of ethics as such. Each moral system has a number of general prescriptive rules, a cohesive body of precepts we can call a moral code. But each system also encompasses specific forms of subjectivity that one must adopt in order to be able to act according to that moral code. This means that every moral system embodies a specific relationship of the individual to himself (*un rapport à soi*) which is necessary for compliance with the moral code. Foucault suggests reserving the term "ethos" for this subjective dimension. Subsequently, he argues that the level to which the moral code and the ethos respectively dominate in moral systems is variable in history.

In classical antiquity, the ethos held most sway, and even functioned independently, with moral codes working only in the background (see Foucault, 1986a: 25 ff). This relationship between ethos and moral code is not always possible, but should be preferred in principle. Moral systems should offer as much room as possible for subjective space. As the moral code increases its dominance, or even absorbs the ethos completely, we are confronted with more moralistic systems and therefore more rigid types of morality. Foucault preferred a reintroduction of Greek ethics as "art of living." He was not concerned here with its content—it was focused too strongly on the master-slave concept—but with the readmission of the *type* of ethics he characterized as aesthetics of existence.

Foucault also launched a set of analytical tools to study and chart the ethos side of moral systems. He distinguishes four aspects of the ethos, or rather the relationship of the self to itself. First is the part of the self that is at issue in our ethical actions (e.g., desires, intentions, feelings). For this aspect, Foucault introduces the term "ethical substance." The second aspect of the ethos answers the question, in whose or what's behalf do we want to act morally (e.g., divine law, a natural law, rationale, or a life that is as beautiful as possible)? In this respect, Foucault talks about the "*mode d'assujettissement*," or mode of subjection. The third aspect is the "*pratique de soi*": this concerns self-forming activities, i.e., the self-techniques and self-practices we employ to shape ourselves into ethical individuals. Finally, Foucault distinguishes the "telos," the ethos goal for which we strive: do we want to become free or wise or, for example, immortal (for the foregoing, see Dreyfus and Rabinow, 1983, pp. 229–52). In my view, these four aspects can be stated in plain English as answers to the questions: what, why, how, and to what purpose?

Foucault's concepts and distinctions put me on the track of a specific developmental process in Beauvoir's thinking on ethics. It is usually assumed that her involvement in ethics was short-lived because, following in Sartre's footsteps, she ultimately traded them in definitively for politics. However, using Foucault's distinctions, I discovered that moral themes were undoubtedly central to Beauvoir's work, including her later writings, but then in the form of a moral system oriented to the ethos. I found morality in Beauvoir took the form of an independent "art of living" against the backdrop of a so-called negative moral code. By means of the analytical tools developed by Foucault to analyze and unravel the diverse forms of the ethos (the questions, what, why, how, and to what purpose), the various aspects of the ethos in Beauvoir could then be grasped. Not only did a specific logic in her oeuvre become visible (e.g., the transition to the autobiographical genre), on closer inspection, it appeared Beauvoir herself had actually plotted and conceptualized this development. It also appeared that her type of ethics had certain advantages over Foucault's; his plea for the reintroduction of the Greek form of aesthetics of existence could be questioned through Beauvoir's thinking.

In making visible Beauvoir's work as philosophical oeuvre, I found the perceptions of Martha Nussbaum were working in the background. In *The Fragility of Goodness* (1986), she shows the literary tradition is ideally suited to dealing with ethical choice, because that choice is located at the level of concrete human existence, a level which Nussbaum believes can only be done justice by the literary genre. In the course of my researches, I discovered a similar perception in Beauvoir. According to her, the meaning human beings give to their lives can only be fully expressed through the literary genre. For this reason, she calls a literature that attempts to show the subjective truth of human existence "philosophical literature," as distinct from pure literature. Again, Beauvoir's own body of ideas proved to justify my approach to her work as philosophical oeuvre. Her own concepts also inspired my determination of the central theme in Beauvoir's ethos or art of living—her belief that if we are to understand what truly motivates him, man has to be placed in the context of his time. This led to an elucidation of what Beauvoir was about, but could not say in so many words. As a result, the aim of her personal art of living became visible, namely the stylization of herself into an intellectual woman. Based on this analysis, Beauvoir's specific art of living as intellectual woman could then be charted. At the conclusion of this study, I explore the content of this art of living and its relevance for our thinking today.

2

THE LIFE OF A THINKING WOMAN

Who was Simone de Beauvoir?

Simone de Beauvoir is rarely mentioned outside the context of Jean-Paul Sartre. No twentieth-century intellectual relationship is so busily discussed as that of these two writers who were both interlocuters and lovers. For a long time, it appeared as if public interest was focused more on their relationship—which has been labeled the romance of the century—than on their lives as separate individuals. It is only recently that a shift has taken place, primarily as a result of Annie Cohen-Solal's biography of Sartre (1987), Bair's biography of Beauvoir (1990a), *and* through the publication in 1990 of Beauvoir's letters to Sartre and her war diary covering the period 1939 to 1941.

If Sartre's extensive love life was already well known, the publication of Beauvoir's letters and diary caused a real scandal. She was painted in the mass media as a true schemer, specializing in *liaisons dangereuses*: Beauvoir was "elevated" to a modern-day Marquise de Merteuilh, with Sartre as Valmont. From the total of around 1,200 pages now added to Beauvoir's complete oeuvre, it appeared that when she was around thirty she had a very active sex life, and her letters are detailed reports to Sartre on her activities. According to her adopted daughter, Sylvie Le Bon, who published the material after Beauvoir's death, Beauvoir believed the letters had been lost. But biographer Deirdre Bair claimed Beauvoir kept the 321 letters within reach at all times.[1] Apparently, she did not want to reveal their full contents during her lifetime.

The material certainly provides a revealing picture of a specific period in her lie. In minute detail, Beauvoir describes her daily routines, and her (bi)sexual relationships occupy a major place in them. Her preoccupations with physical love are surprisingly amoral. She had no scruples about starting an affair with Bost, the boyfriend of Sartre's lover Olga. She secretly read the diaries of Wanda, Sartre's mistress, and conspired with Sartre against one of her own lovers. And she continually tried to turn both Sartre and Bost against Olga.[2]

During a period of some years, she pursued a number of relationships with women, on which she reported to Sartre in a rather unfeeling and disparaging way. Sorokine, Védrine, and Kosakiewitch are only ever referred to by their surnames, and are otherwise used as objects. She was bitchy about her sister Hélène, nicknamed Poupette, who emerged as a lachrymose, aggrieved type, whose only aim was to make claims on Simone and ape everything she did. Beauvoir portrayed her female lovers in exactly the same terms. They all made demands on her; they all hung on her, crying and begging for five minutes of her precious time. The women all wanted to share Sartre with her, and to "copy exactly" her relationship with him, Beauvoir notes in her diary (JG: 283). With Bost and Sartre at the front, she says her women lovers are *surrogates* (p. 276). She only experienced real passion with Sartre and Bost. But the women needed her, and that "touched my heart at its one vulnerable point" (PoL: 230). If in her autobiography Beauvoir termed her feelings for her sister a "mixture of authority and affection" (ASD: 15), in fact they appear to have been more a combination of charmed condescension and irritation, a combination that characterized her relationships with younger women in this period of her life.

The fact that Beauvoir censored her autobiography extensively also becomes clear when the war diary is compared to the version included in *The Prime of Life*. All relationships with women have been expunged, and her sexual escapades during this period are completely suppressed. Admittedly, her behavior at that time ensued from the amoral, individualistic life-style she and her friends led before World War II. Relationships in the small, enclosed world in which she lived then could reach a point where they became explosive. But as their social commitment grew, and with it the broadening of their social contacts, the sexual intrigues declined. During the course of the war, Beauvoir began to perceive the existence of her fellow human beings and the social dimension of the world. For example, in a letter to Sartre written in 1945, she is able to conclude that they had really hurt Védrine (LS: 389). World War II finally put an end to a period in her life that was characterized by a purely individualistic and amoral resistance to bourgeois values and norms, a resistance expressed primarily through experiments in sexuality, and which as such forms a precursor to the so-called sexual revolution of the 1960s. Beauvoir's opposition to the bourgeoisie's inability "to assume their bodies" (FoC: 478) was one of the factors that generated her need to fill her days and letters with *liaisons dangereuses*. However, the specific form of her love life in this period—a number of relationships simultaneously, in which her female lovers are termed "surrogates"—also tells us something about a personal problem of Beauvoir's. If we examine this period closely, what is striking in her life-style was her inability to be alone. Her busy love life in the years preceding World War II was one of her strategies against loneliness. For example, when Bost departed to spend a few days of his leave with Olga, Beauvoir's desperation hurled her into the arms of one of her female lovers: "not unpleasant" she notes in her diary (JG: 289).

We again find this pattern in her habit of writing in cafes during this period. She herself wrote, "to sit facing a blank sheet of paper all alone is an austere experience, whereas here I could always glance up and reassure myself humanity existed" (PoL: 279–80). But it seems more as though Beauvoir was trying to convince herself of her own existence; she only felt she existed when others saw her.

Because she needed the other to exist, her relationship with the other was problematic. "Perhaps it is hard for anyone to learn the art of peaceful coexistence with somebody else: certainly I had never been capable of it. Either I reigned supreme or sank into the abyss" (p. 61). An early crush on school-friend Zaza had already introduced her to the shameful experience of self-loss: "During my subjugation by Zaza I plumbed the black depths of humility" (p. 61). She talked of this as her "most serious problem": "how was I to reconcile my longing for independence with the feelings that drove me so impetuously towards another person" (p. 153). For Beauvoir, finding balance in a relationship with the other was not easy and the "serious problem" was thus destined to become *the* subject of her oeuvre. Within the framework of existentialist philosophy, she designed an ethics in which reciprocal and equal relationships with the other are conceivable. But if we now look at Beauvoir's life as a whole, it appears the relationship with the other remained her critical problem throughout life.

Simone was born to a Catholic bourgeois family in Paris's Montparnasse in 1908. It was a family for whom respectability was everything. Her father, a bourgeois lover of culture, compensated for a boring job as legal secretary with amateur dramatics. The young Simone was fascinated by this father, who took her intellectual development in hand at an early age. Her mother, who came from a petit-bourgeois, provincial family, ensured a strict Catholic upbringing for Simone and her sister Poupette who was two years younger. Maman de Beauvoir sacrificed herself completely to her daughters' upbringing. She never left them alone for a moment and allowed them no space. In her account of her mother's death, Beauvoir quotes her mother's adage, "I have lived for others," adding for her readers' benefit, "yes, but also through others" (VED: 34).

If Simone began as the family showpiece, her role changed in puberty as Father de Beauvoir's attention shifted to the younger daughter. From this time, Simone began increasingly to resist her parents, although secretly at first. Because her father was not well off and could not afford a dowry, Simone was allowed to attend university and train as a teacher of philosophy. In her years at the University of Paris, she became increasingly alienated from her Catholic, bourgeois milieu, and especially from the strict rules and norms imposed on "the weaker sex." The story of her school-friend Zaza played a significant role here. She died of an illness following a period of emotional exhaustion: predestined for an arranged marriage, she could not obtain her parents' consent to marry the man of her choice.[3] All her life, Simone would continue to blame the bourgeoisie for its stifling attitudes on the role of women.

While Simone was still studying philosophy, she was accepted into the teacher-training program and was therefore attending a number of lectures at the École Normale Supérieure. It was here she met her beloved Jean-Paul Sartre. Her final exams—at twenty-one, Simone was France's youngest philosophy teacher ever—coincided with the beginning of their relationship. At the end of *Memoirs of a Dutiful Daughter*, Beauvoir describes in lyrical terms the future she envisaged with Sartre:

> Sartre corresponded exactly to the dream-companion I had longed for since I was fifteen: he was the double in whom I found all my burning aspiration raised to the pitch of incandescence. I should always be able to share everything with him. When I left him at the beginning of August, I knew that he would never go out of my life again. (MDD: 345)

But from the very beginning, Sartre made it clear that monogamy wasn't for him. Besides their "essential" relationship, there would be other, "contingent" relationships (p. 22). Simone agreed, but had difficulty with Sartre's continual affairs for the rest of her life.[4] When, a few years into their relationship, she realized she was concentrating too much on

Sartre and was losing sight of her own life, she accepted a job teaching philosophy in Marseilles, hundreds of kilometers away from him. When he offered to marry her so that they could both get jobs in the same place, she rejected his offer and packed her bags, in tears. She wanted to put a permanent end to the tendency she had identified, of losing herself in a relationship and giving up her own plans and projects. In Marseilles she rediscovered herself, partly through long, solitary walks in the country-side, and became adept at being alone. The necessity for women to retain or achieve their independence as individuals was to become a recurrent theme in her work, not only in *The Second Sex*, but also in her novels.

When Simone was offered a job in Paris some years later, she im-mersed herself in the French capital's intellectual and cultural life. With friends, she rebelled against bourgeois morality in the name of art, cul-ture, and freedom. Both Simone and Sartre hated the so-called respect-able masses, the genteel ladies and gentlemen, life in the provinces, the family, children, and the pervasive humanist message. Beauvoir charac-terizes their attitude during this period as "anti-bourgeois anarchism." She describes both of them as like "elves," lacking a sense of reality, shielded as they were from material cares and responsibilities (see p. 362).[5]

When World War II broke out, Beauvoir was forced to accept that she was bound to the world and to the fate of others by a thousand threads. Sartre's internment and the chaos and misery around her made her realize the existence of the world and her fellow human beings. During the course of the war, her increasing social awareness was translated into the development of an ethics within the framework of existentialism. The recognition of the other as fellow being, and of the self as socially anchored creature formed its point of departure.

In addition, her political engagement increased during the course of the war and subsequently began to take on clearer forms. Her novel *The Blood of Others* (1945), written from 1941 through 1943, on the French resistance movement against German occupation, was a portent. After the war and until 1956, Beauvoir was a fellow traveler of the commu-nists'. She then became an active anti-Gaullist and sympathized with the Algerian cause. From 1968 onward, she gave her support to the leftist movement in France and was an active advocate of feminism.

When she was dismissed from teaching in 1943 (Sorokine's mother had filed a complaint against her for corrupting her daughter), to sup-port herself she took a job with French radio compiling programs on the Middle Ages.[6] But she quickly decided to devote herself to writing. After a failed attempt—her first novel *Quand prime le spirituel* (*When Things of the Spirit Come First*), which describes the bourgeois milieu and

Zaza's story, was rejected by Gallimard—her novel *She Came to Stay* was published in 1943 (with approval from the illegal *Comité des Écrivains*) and was immediately well received. Based on its reception, Beauvoir decided to pursue a full-time career in writing and from that time onward produced novels, essays, and autobiographical works with great regularity and reasonable success. After the war, she shared increasingly in the fame that fell to "the existentialists"—and especially to Sartre.

In 1947, she departed for a lecture tour of the United States, where she became involved in a stormy love affair with writer Nelson Algren that was to last four years in spite of the distance. The relationship would end miserably because Beauvoir continued to make Sartre her priority. A subsequent love affair with Claude Lanzmann followed the same pattern, and this relationship also failed to give her peace of mind. Beauvoir frequently suffered from depression and was subject to nervous crises. She took sleeping pills and abused alcohol. This would remain the case during her intimate friendship with Sylvie Le Bon in the final twenty years of her life. At seventy-eight, Beauvoir died of pulmonary edema, probably exacerbated by her chronic alcohol abuse. At no time in her life had she found emotional peace in her relationships with others; her love life remained turbulent because she continued to see her relationship with Sartre as "essential." At the end of this study, we will see the nature of this necessity.

The relationship between life and work

Why all this focus on Beauvoir's life, and especially on her love life? Haven't the details been dragged up all too often? Toril Moi remarked that people tend to have interest only in the personal side of intellectual women and not in their work. No matter what a woman says, writes, or thinks, the only important element is what she *is*, and Beauvoir is a prime example of this tendency (see Moi, 1990: 27). Biographer Deirdre Bair also observed that Beauvoir's life generated more interest than her work. When she and Sartre's biographer, Annie Cohen-Solal, were part of a panel discussion, Bair was asked only about Beauvoir's life, while Cohen was questioned solely on Sartre's work (see Bair, 1990a: 18).

However, in my view, both Beauvoir and Sartre aroused excessive interest in their private lives. In Sartre's case, his personality, and specifically his love life are often the focus. I asked myself, what generates this need to scrutinize the (bedroom) secrets of both? The answer appears to lie partially in the term *la volonté de savoir* (the will to know), coined by Michel Foucault to typify a dominant trait in Western culture: the greedy fascination with sexual detail. He points out that this "will to know" is itself a form of lust experience, and the term would seem to characterize neatly the recent storm of reports on Beauvoir's private life. The glee of the world's press following the "revelations" in her letters to Sartre had only just died down when a new flood of sensational reports hit the head-lines. This time it was the publication of Deirdre Bair's biography that generated copy on Beauvoir's sex life.

Foucault objected to the "will to know," because he believed it leads to a reduction of people to no more than a sexual identity through which they are easily stereotyped. In Beauvoir, we see a classic example of someone who has been snowed under by an avalanche of labels. To give just one example, was she a lesbian, or wasn't she? When I wrote a news-paper article on Beauvoir and failed to label her as lesbian or heterosex-ual, the editors asked specifically for clarification.

The fact that Beauvoir and Sartre especially evoke this "will to know" is probably because they were always open about their private lives. However, this was sparked by their belief that everything, and truly everything, in a person's life was important, because only someone's total situation can shed light on the uniqueness of his existence. But their em-phasis on the total situation implied they were also concerned with the mutual connection and interplay of a myriad of factors required to make someone's life comprehensible, and which have to be taken into consid-eration if the individuality of a person is to be "synthesized" (PoL: 128). The work of an author is not least such a factor, and it is therefore essen-tial to see and interpret the connections between life and work.

In the present volume, the focus on Beauvoir's life, and specifically on her personal relationships, is in line with this approach and as such is distinct from the "will to know." Reciprocality in relationships with the other proved Beauvoir's critical theme, both personally and theoretically. Given this connection, interest in Beauvoir's private life is not in itself problematic. It only becomes objectionable when it leads to a definitive *judgment* on her life without bringing her work into the equation. If we are to do justice to the individuality of an author, we should not only use his life to explain his work, but also his work to explain his life. After an examination of Beauvoir's work, I will in fact attempt an evaluation of her life from this perspective (see chapter 10). Here, however, I will limit myself to a critique on a judgment on Beauvoir's life that is implied in three fairly recent studies.

Heath (1989) and Moi (1990) are both written from a viewpoint that is paradigmatic in contemporary feminist literary theory, i.e., so-called feminist-psychoanalytic text analysis. This approach defines the pre-oedipal order as "feminine," and the entry into language (by the child) is equated with taking up a "male" position. At issue in this approach is the discovery of "feminine" traces in male language. Women have closer ties to the pre-oedipal order, and the structure of their sexual desire is supposed to have been determined by it: they desire a life in duality with an other. Jane Heath reads Beauvoir's texts from this perspective and concludes from traces in her work that Beauvoir never fully deserted the pre-oedipal order; her preoccupation with Sartre (Sartre and I are one) and her lesbian relationships are seen as indicators. Heath expands on this point of departure using three of Beauvoir's novels. She focuses solely on a lesbian love theme in *She Came to Stay*; the ménage à trois examined by this novel is seen only in the light of the relationship between the two women. The Xavière character represents a disturbing femininity that undermines all (self-) control. The female desire has to be eliminated: Françoise murders Xavière and thus reinserts herself into the phallic order.

Heath also reads *Les belles images* and *The Mandarins* through psychoanalytic spectacles. The former is seen as representing resistance of the feminine to the phallic order. The main character, Laurence, resists the role imposed on her (for example, she refuses to eat), and tries to go her own way. In this novel, Beauvoir is said to give voice to that which is outside language, i.e., the silence of the feminine. Through its main characters—Anne, Henri, and Paule—*The Mandarins* is said to revolve around resistance of the female to the male order, personified by Dubreuilh; we are supposed to find the dark side here, the price of life in the phallic order.

Heath's analyses are crystal clear and worth reading, and they certainly shed new light on Beauvoir's texts. Yet, they suffer from reductionism and personalism. When Beauvoir's work and life are characterized as symptoms of the feminine, they are reduced to her gender and sexual preference, and Beauvoir's own thinking can never be heard. She herself had made the theme of female identity the subject of systematic reflection, and also made it central to her work. If her texts are read exclusively using the literary-theoretical approach (which is concerned with the reinsertion of "the feminine" in male texts), then Beauvoir's own reflections and intentions disappear from sight, and this certainly does no justice to the polysemy of her writings.

In spite of her assurances that the aim was textual and not personal, Heath becomes personalistic when, based on her textual analysis, she concludes that Beauvoir as a woman ranged herself on the side of the masculine and was obliged to pay a high price for it. In fact, this labels Beauvoir a masculine woman, and we are back to one of the prevalent tags for the identity of intellectual women. It certainly does no justice to what Beauvoir herself thought, wrote, and said.

Moi (1990) approaches Beauvoir from the same point of departure. She also fails to avoid a certain personalism when, in her review of the novel *The Woman Destroyed*, she asks why Beauvoir wrote such a "gloomy story" about a woman who, as the title suggests, is destroyed by jealousy of her husband's mistresses. Moi asks us, in spite of Beauvoir's denials, isn't this her own story? Doesn't Beauvoir protest rather too much against such a supposition in her autobiography (see ASD: 142)? Is jealousy not *the* theme in her oeuvre? Is this not an indication that her texts actually escaped her control? Moi answers these questions affirmatively. Her approach to reading the texts leads her to conclude that Beauvoir's femininity, as it were, "breaks into" her masculine language, and that in the texts we find revealed Beauvoir's deepest soul-searchings, which she herself failed to realize or recognize.

Now, there is nothing against such interpretive methods, in themselves. Beauvoir herself believed an author was barely able to perceive the meaning of his own work. She endorsed the fact that the interpretation of others could shed new light on her work. The problem with the reading of both Heath and Moi is that the work as a whole is approached from the angle of Beauvoir's sexual desire. Her *ideas*, especially her condemnation of the relative identity imposed on women, cannot be brought to light in this fashion. Both *Les belles images* and *The Woman Destroyed* are expressions of this condemnation, and Beauvoir made a conscious choice for an indirect narrative technique that articulates the subjective suffering of the main characters in order to put across her ideas more pregnantly.

In conclusion, we can say that through their approach Heath and Moi reduce Beauvoir's work to her person or, to paraphrase Moi's own words, to what she is instead of what she thinks. When Foucault characterized the "will to know," he saw psychoanalysis as a prime example. And we can certainly ask ourselves whether this psychoanalytic approach isn't stereotyping Beauvoir and reducing her to what is known, i.e., the existing definitions of femininity and feminine identity. It would seem to me more useful to search for the innovative in Beauvoir's life and work.

Does Bair's biography (1990a) have the answers? Beauvoir had accused her previous biographers, Francis and Gontier (1985), of a botched job.[7] According to Beauvoir, neither of the Franco-American women had the capacity to grasp her life and work. The biographer/contemporary should be superior to the subject, and few attain those heights: "*On ne domine pas facilement une vie autre*" (*Le Matin*, 5 December 1985). So, expectations were great when Beauvoir began to work with Bair, Samuel Beckett's highly respected biographer. Bair spent almost ten years on her 700-page study. She accumulated an enormous amount of material; she not only had numerous conversations with Beauvoir between 1981 and 1986, but also interviewed contemporaries, friends, and intimates, and tracked down documents, historical works and newspapers. Bair's study forces admiration for its thoroughness in research, and for the way she refined a mass of material into a readable, cohesive whole.

She made numerous corrections to Beauvoir's own autobiography. It cannot be used as academic source material, she warns, because data and events, names and places are recorded incorrectly by Beauvoir or are incomplete. Bair also has new facts: she reports that Beauvoir wrote a number of journalistic articles under Sartre's name, and she conjures up a so-far unknown Beauvoir essay entitled *It's about Time* (1950), on the future of heterosexual love. She also includes the most recent sales figures on Beauvoir's books: it appears that between three and four million copies of *The Second Sex* were sold, making Beauvoir financially independent for the rest of her life.

Beauvoir emerges from Bair's account as a sharp, efficient woman, who nevertheless harbored a lifelong dream and chased an illusion: to be *the* woman in Sartre's life. In Bair's version, Sartre is an eternal adolescent who was humored and spoiled throughout his life by Beauvoir and countless other women. (Beauvoir pointed out the fact that Sartre thought he was terribly ugly: you couldn't refuse him anything or he would have been deeply unhappy, she explained [Bair, 1990a: 235].) Bair manages to portray Beauvoir as a grass widow: the long-suffering, dutiful wife who subordinates her own life and work to his need to have her by his side and for her services as secretary, manager, nurse, and buffer against the big, bad world.[8] Bair offers no explanation for the specific nature of Beauvoir's love for Sartre, but refers more than once to the fact that Beauvoir needed Sartre for her own peace of mind and certainties. Beauvoir's heartache at Sartre's continual affairs has been elevated to leitmotiv for her whole life. Her work is considered an ongoing homage to Sartre, and particularly to his magnum opus *Being and Nothingness*.

There is no room here for the development of Beauvoir's own thinking. This is apparent, for example, in the very limited attention Bair gives to Beauvoir's moral-philosophical essays written in the period 1944 to 1947, when her philosophical creativity reached a peak. Bair refers to Sartre's absence—he was spending a lot of time with his lover in the U.S.—and considers this period in Beauvoir's life as introspective, with the essays relegated to the status of self-examination. In essence, *The Second Sex* receives the same treatment. It is seen as self-analysis, and is considered as an attempt to further define Beauvoir's own place in Sartre's theory.

Whereas Bair claims Beauvoir continued to be self-fixated, the essays from the period 1944 to 1947 actually form a turning point in the narcissism of her early years. Beauvoir reflected on the world around her, wrote about political events, tried to develop an ethical and political theory, and formulated a number of theoretical points of departure that would be determinant for the rest of her life. Beauvoir herself pointed out to Bair the importance of these essays as the starting point of her own oeuvre (p. 269), but Bair sticks to her theory that Beauvoir's philosophy ended with Sartre's *Being and Nothingness* in 1943. For example, Bair devotes only one paragraph to *The Ethics of Ambiguity*, a work in which Beauvoir builds on the perception that man is forced to accept the fact he is dependent on others, and has to enter actively into ties with others.

Bair says her aim was to combine biography and intellectual history, and describe the life and work of Beauvoir as a coherent whole. This approach excludes sensational revelations or intimate details for the sake of intimate details. In this sense, it breaks radically with the "will to know" about Simone de Beauvoir. Bair describes the long relationship between Beauvoir and Le Bon, but leaves aside whether this was a lesbian relationship. Bair has no intention of sticking on labels, and does not expand. But she also links Beauvoir's work and life in a one-sided way: she merely explains Beauvoir's work through her life, instead of the other way around. Beauvoir not only attempted to reconcile existentialist philosophy with an ethics in which a positive relationship with the other is possible, she also tried to make her life an example of this concept. Through the form of her own life, Beauvoir wanted to prove that a reconciliation between love and individual freedom was possible. In the final chapter we will make up the balance of that attempt, but first let us look at the content of her philosophy.

3

THE SECOND SEX AND PHILOSOPHY

In her voluminous study, *Le deuxième sexe* (1949), Beauvoir explored the historic situation of women and concluded they have been prevented from taking active control of their own lives. Woman has been unfree throughout history; she was subjected to man who, partly with woman's consent, made her merely an extension of himself. Men and women have never shared an equal relationship, and it would be advantageous to all if this situation were to change.

The Second Sex evoked intense criticism. As soon as it appeared, it was dismissed as one-sided and tendentious. Beauvoir herself was labeled a man-hater, frigid, or nymphomaniacal, depending on the critic, and this negative response continued for years to come. Although in the late 1960s, part of the emerging women's movement embraced Beauvoir, other sections reviled her. *The Second Sex* had been superceded by the new, "real" feminism that advocated radical change for women, and Beauvoir's book was said to contain a *male* view of women. Moreover, it was labeled a careless or meaningless work, unsystematic in structure, and overtaken by the facts.

However, in spite of enormous sales figures, this book appears to be at the same time one of the most criticized *and* one of the least read

works in feminism. Feminists have it on their shelves because it simply
has to be there, but few have actually read it. This is why I will dwell
fairly extensively on the contents.

First, I want to go into the background to the philosophical concepts
used in *The Second Sex*. A global summary of the contents themselves
will follow, then I will discuss the work's genre and structure. Beauvoir
wrote it in a very short period of time[1] which, she said, was only possible
because the book followed a logical structure. "Of all my books," she
said, "this was the easiest to write, especially in the beginning. The material seemed to organize itself in a natural series of analytical frameworks" (Bair, 1990a: 371). We shall take a closer look here at its structure.

Today's feminist theoreticians tend to consider the book a superceded
sociological study. New research has brought to light a wealth of empirical facts about women's lives that would have been inconceivable in
Beauvoir's day. The research shows that the reality of those lives was
often far more variegated than Beauvoir's study suggests. For example,
cultural anthropologist Judith Okely has come up with counterexamples
for a number of Beauvoir's claims with regard to non-Western cultures.[2]
However, it could well be that *The Second Sex* should not be evaluated
on the correctness of single facts because the work has a different aim.
Before making a final judgment on its actual content (see chapter 10), we
will have to determine the work's structure and genre. The chapter ends
with an examination of the critique of contemporary feminists who
claim *The Second Sex* contains a male view of women. Beauvoir's so-
called rationalism is the main focus of the attack: she is said to reject
the body in favor of consciousness, and to perceive as negative the female body in particular. We will evaluate the criticism that she embraced
masculine thinking and, with *The Second Sex*, produced a "masculine"
book.

The philosophical concepts of The Second Sex

In *The Second Sex*, Beauvoir made extensive use of the philosophical
concepts of Sartre's main work *L'être et le néant* (1943; *Being and Nothingness*). Before examining Beauvoir's actual text, we will look at this
conceptual framework. In *Being and Nothingness*, Sartre distinguished
two kinds of being: being-in-itself (*être en-soi*) and being-for-itself (*être
pour-soi*); the first refers to the existence of material things, the second
to the existence of consciousness. Sartre's primary goal was to articulate
consciousness as opposed to the being of material things. He characterized consciousness as non-being. In itself, it is no-thing, or rather

nothing(ness) (*néant*), for consciousness is always aimed at something other than itself; it is always a consciousness *of* something. That is why Sartre said it is not what it is, and is what it is not.[3] In order to exist, consciousness is doomed to transcend itself and reach out for a thing (*en-soi*), or it ceases to be consciousness and coincides with the being of things. Being no-thing, consciousness disengages itself from the things of which it is conscious, or as Sartre has it, it "negates." As it always has to focus on something other than itself, consciousness has to be pure emptiness. As soon as there is any question of content, then there is already an *inauthentic* human way of being. The counterpart of the *pour-soi*'s total emptiness is the *en-soi*'s absolute fullness or opaqueness (*opacité*). It is this that has to be given meaning through the *pour-soi*. But as such, it is completely meaningless or "contingent," a state that evokes disgust in the main character, Roquentin, in Sartre's novel *Nausea* (1938).

Sartre thus distinguishes radically between the *pour-soi* and the *en-soi*, i.e., the world of beings. If these have an immanent existence, by definition the *pour-soi* transcends: it reaches out continually and never coincides with itself. The fact that human consciousness is no thing means that a human being is not a permanent essence, but continually creates itself through intentional activity. The existence of a human being thus precedes every essence. As a consequence, Sartre argued, the human being is fundamentally free. Freedom and non-being are the characteristics of human existence.

But the human being also has a desire to *be*. If he gives in to that desire, and constructs an "I" from which he can experience and determine himself, he declines into an *être-en-soi*. If he lives as such, he fails to live a true and authentic human existence, but lives inauthentically or in "bad faith." Moreover, his desire to *be* is not fulfilled this way. The status of non-being is experienced by consciousness as a lack of being (a *manque d'être*); it wants to be a being *as* consciousness. Sartre called this man's *désir d'être*. This fullness of being as consciousness could only be achieved through a being-for-others: only through the observation of an other would it be possible for the *pour-soi* to exist simultaneously as entity and as nothingness. After all, consciousness could only be observed and reflected as such in the eyes of an other, resulting in the desired status of being an *en-soi* as *pour-soi*.

However, the problem is that in view of its *néant* nature (its existence in the form of a negation of being), every consciousness can only observe the other as a being—in other words, as an object and not as a "nothingness," as an *en-soi* instead of a *pour-soi*. I try in vain to meet the other as consciousness. My look petrifies him into a thing in the world: "everything happens as if I wished to get hold of a man who runs away and leaves only his coat in my hands. It is the coat, it is the outer shell which I possess." Sartre called the other "a reality which is on principle beyond my reach" and "a sphere of existence from which I am on principle excluded" (see BN, 1943: 393). Thus, our consciousness is radically separated from that of others. Our fellow man is always an object; we can never meet him as subject.

One result is that the *"désir d'être"* can never be fulfilled. The other can only exist as a being in relation to my consciousness; for me he loses his subjectivity and can thus no longer affirm me as consciousness. Second, this means the self can only ever exist through a negation of the other. We have already seen that consciousness as such is selfless because it consists only of intentionality, i.e., a focus on something else. (If this were not the case, consciousness would be a finite entity and thus identical to the being of things.) This implies that an experience of selfness can only become apparent in a focus on another consciousness. But as we have seen, the focus is always a negation. The self can thus only become manifest as negation of the other; I am not the other. Schuetz coined a term for this notion — "internal negation" — which indicates the negation is not of an external, spacial nature, but is constituent to the existence of the self and the other (Schuetz, 1948: 187). Arntz (1960) summarizes as follows:

> This is not about "John is not Peter." This would mean John and Peter manifest themselves to a third party who then places a negation between both. Such a negation would be an external negation. Sartre is concerned with an internal negation in which I position myself as not the other in the same way as when I focus on an *en-soi*. (Arntz: 144)

Contact between myself and the other cannot come about based on a selfness of both, but it is as such the constitution of the other as other, and of the self as not the other. It is not the case that I am there first and subsequently try to make the other into an object, but rather that making the other into an object is the basis of my existence. According to Sartre, in this process the other now loses not only his subjectivity for me, but also for himself. Under my look, the other knows he is a being; he feels that I give him a "being." We know this when we examine feelings evoked when other people look at us. We feel as though we have acquired an exterior; in other words, we feel we have become objects. Now, there are two possibilities here: either we accept our being an object for the other and thus subjugate ourselves to him (in which case we are no longer a free subject), or we make the other the object, the Other. The contact between people can only take the form of a subject-object relationship, and is continually concerned with who is the subject and who is the object within that contact. Thus, conflict is the basis of human relations. Sartre's statement, *"l'enfer, c'est les Autres"* (Hc: 609), is well known, and we now understand *why* the other is hell for me: under the gaze of the other, I can stultify into an object if I do not succeed in making him the object.

The notion of enmity and conflict between consciousnesses, which Sartre propounded, concurs with Hegel's ideas, but deviates from them inasmuch as Hegel argues that in a specific phase of history, enmity can be overcome if everyone recognizes himself in universal humanity. This is impossible for Sartre because of the internal negation mechanism which, by definition, causes a Self-Other structure in human contact, and separates us from each other irrevocably.

In *The Second Sex*, Beauvoir "gendered" this Self-Other structure. She argued that women in history have been made the Other and that men have appropriated the position of Self, or subject. Men wanted recognition of themselves as consciousness—which is a problem because pure matter cannot provide it. Woman appeared eminently suited to the role, an entity that was both corporal and at the same time gifted with a kind of consciousness. This is how man made woman the Other. She was made into the one who, through her kinship with the corporal, allowed him to experience continually his superiority as transcending subject; who through her corporality offered him the opportunity of losing himself in "being," and thus occasionally relinquishing the painful status of subject; who had just enough consciousness to observe and reflect him as superior subject. Thus, the myth of femininity is no more than a projection and a product of man. The experiences and way of life imposed upon woman in the name of femininity serve only *man's* needs.

Woman has only developed in the position of Other allotted to her by man. She formed no threat as alternating freedom. In her turn, she could never exist as a free human being and affirm herself the way the slave is able to in the (Hegelian) master-slave relationship (see chapter 9). Although this position was imposed upon her—in her introduction, Beauvoir speaks of an "oppression"—she often resigned herself to it through her (human) tendency to bad faith. "Half victims, half accomplices, just like everyone else" is the quotation Beauvoir used to introduce the second book of *Le deuxième sexe*,[4] and she borrowed it from Sartre. In history, woman never raised herself up as subject, turning man into the Other; her position was that of the absolute Other.

It will now be clear that, in *The Second Sex*, Beauvoir developed the norm that insists women must/can become subjects. Women should have the chance to realize their *pour-soi* potential so that men and women can be equal human beings in relation to each other. *The Second Sex* is a passionate call to women to shake off the status of the Other and to accept as equal human beings the freedom of existence *whenever they have the chance to do so.*

The text

The Second Sex runs to about a thousand pages and is divided into two "books," each composed of a number of sections which are, in their turn, organized into chapters. The first book, entitled *Facts and Myths*, comprises an introduction and sections on "Destiny," "History," and "Myths." The second book, *Woman's Life Today*, contains the sections "The Formative Years," "Situation," "Justifications," and "Towards Liberation." The compact introduction, which could actually stand alone as a pamphlet, covers some twenty pages and explains the theoretical framework in a nutshell. Here, Beauvoir advanced the theory of the Other applied in *The Second Sex*. Following Hegel's philosophy, she said, we discover in human consciousness a fundamental enmity toward every other consciousness. The subject constitutes itself in the Self-Other opposition. It positions itself as the subject, the essential, opposite the Other as inessential, as the object. The Self-Other structure is found at all levels and places in human life, Beauvoir argued, and it is therefore not surprising that we also find it at the gender level. Man has appropriated the role of Self and made woman the absolute Other: thus, woman has been made into an "*être relatif*," i.e., into a being that only exists in relation to man, and that is definitively subjugated to his sovereignty.

In the first section, "Destiny" (about seventy pages), Beauvoir argued that biological, psychoanalytical, and Marxist approaches all fall short as explanation for the historic supremacy of the male sex. Biology does not even explain the existence of two sexes (reproduction could be organized just as well in an alternative manner), let alone the hierarchy between the two. Biological facts are always embedded in social and cultural contexts and in themselves have no significance. It is culture ("second nature") that determines whether muscle power has an important role to play and whether pregnancy is an impeding factor for women. The merit of psychoanalysis lies in the fact that it has understood everything centers on human allocation of significance to the body. But it also fails to explain male dominance: "For Freud himself admits that the prestige of the penis is explained by the sovereignty of the father, and, as we have seen, he confesses that he is ignorant regarding the origin of male supremacy" (TSS: I, 81). Nor do economic factors explain why it is the woman and not the man who has become the slave.

In the following section, "History" (around a hundred pages), Beauvoir revealed the true facts behind the oppression of woman. Because woman has the greater physical reproductive function, a division of roles emerged: men appropriated the production sphere, i.e., the active conquest of nature, often risking their lives in the process; women remained limited to the reproductive sphere and the home, or rather to the repetition of life. The human race happens to allocate a different value to both roles. As human beings differ from animals in their ability to transcend life—a difference whose keenest expression is a human's conscious risk of life which makes clear he does not coincide with it—action is valued more highly than the mere repetition of life. This is how man was able to appropriate the role of subject and place woman in the position of the Other.

Beauvoir further described history as a succession of deeds of male supremacy over women. Even when a woman occupied a position of power, she occupied it only with male permission. So she always remained imprisoned in the immanent sphere, in spite of apparent indications to the contrary. Beauvoir examined the history of the family, law, and private property, whose emergence meant the definitive dethroning of woman: man denies her every right to her own possessions. Then it is the turn of literate women: their marginal role, the resistance they evoked, their attempts to live by their pens. Beauvoir also treated the history of women's industrial labor, contraceptive practices, and the women's suffrage movement. Finally, Beauvoir described the then-contemporary position of women and concluded it was still not equal to that of men.

In her third section, "Myths" (close to 160 pages), she provided an inventory of the representations of woman and femininity that man has created. To fulfill her function as the absolute Other, woman had to be invested with special traits. A whole range of apparently contradictory characteristics were attributed to woman, such as idol and handmaiden, healer and witch, madonna and whore. This contradiction is caused by the fact that, as the Other, she represents everything man is not. Everything man desires and fears, loves and hates, is projected onto woman. If she exemplifies evil because she forms the negation of the masculine, she also embodies good, because she is essential to man's existence.

As absolute Other, woman especially represents the corporal and nature. Thus, all ambivalent feelings evoked in man by nature have been projected onto woman: his fear of death, his need for life. For example, we find this reflected in the disgust for menstruation as "unclean," evil power, and in the importance of virginity (nature that has to be conquered); the exaltation of female beauty and the distaste for old and ugly women; the idolization of the mother alongside the hate (the mother-in-law and stepmother myths). Subsequently, Beauvoir explored the exceptional way these myths are presented in authors such as Montherlant, D. H. Lawrence, Claudel, Breton, and Stendhal—woman only emerges as a full human being in the work of the last writer. The myth of the real woman and the Eternal Feminine also plays an important role in everyday life. If the myth is contradicted by the behavior of flesh-and-blood women, then the accusing finger is pointed not at the myth, but at the women concerned: their behavior is considered unfeminine.

The myth of woman continues to live in men's hearts, but it could disappear one day: "the more women assert themselves as human beings, the more the marvellous quality of the Other will die out in them" (TSS I: 174). Undoubtedly, this will also be advantageous for men. What could be more wonderful than relating to a real human being, a person, rather than to an abstract cliché? The absolute nature of the position of woman as Other presupposes that she also has to be an Other to herself: the "real woman" was also the absolute Other subjectively. What did this subjective world look like? This is the question Beauvoir asks as she takes us into the second book of *The Second Sex*.

In this second book, *Woman's Life Today*, which opens with the famous line, "*On ne nait pas femme, on le devient*" (One is not born, but rather becomes, a woman), Beauvoir sketched the subjective world of woman from earliest youth to old age.

The first section, "The Formative Years" (consisting of around 150 pages), examines the raising of girls that imposes on them the identity of the absolute Other. All children attempt to combat the first separation from the mother by courting her approval. Seduction, seeking admiration, and seeking approbation—all are strategies used by both boys and girls in their first three to four years. Subsequently, a distinction is made in the raising of male and female children: boys are taught to avoid this behavior, whereas it is reinforced in girls. The boy is encouraged to realize himself in concrete projects. The girl is continually reinforced in tendencies to make herself into an object. There is a fundamental contrast between girls' autonomous existence and the role that is demanded from them, while for boys these matters are extensions of each other. As the girl does not focus her expressive abilities on the world, she becomes internalized: a whole inner world develops whereby romantic dreams and fantasies take on paramount importance. She becomes alienated from her body, acquires a narcissistic attitude and an inner insecurity. But a girl is also often more developed physically than a boy, and is more receptive to impressions, such as natural beauty. (In the world of flora and fauna she is a human creature, while in society she has to "relinquish" herself.)

Finally, at around fifteen years of age, she gives in to reality: she assumes her subordination and focuses on achieving marriage. The capture of a husband becomes an increasingly urgent task. It is therefore difficult for a girl to focus her interest totally on education, sports, learning a trade. Her attempts to realize her individual autonomy are only half supported by her environment. The girl is often afraid that if she puts too much energy into this or that enterprise, she will fail in her destiny as a woman.

Nor is she allowed to assert herself actively in a sexual way; she has to remain chaste. The man is the one who *takes*; the woman *gives* herself. Well used to her role as object, the woman only discovers her autonomy in pleasure after some time—if at all. She has to fight for it and overcome her passivity in order to achieve a relationship based on mutuality. This mutuality is possible if each partner both desires the other's body and recognizes the other's freedom, something that requires mutual generosity of body and soul. Only then can both—in their own way—know a reciprocal pleasure. The dimension of otherness may continue to exist, but it loses its hostile character.

The woman can also make a lesbian choice. The biological explanation that a lesbian has a disturbed hormonal balance, and the psychoanalytical approach to homosexuality as an incomplete development are inadequate. "The chief misunderstanding underlying this line of interpretation is that it is natural for the female human being to make herself a feminine woman," whereas such a woman is in fact an artificial product made by society "as formerly eunuchs were made" (TSS II: 428). The lesbian woman has found a way to avoid subordination to the fetters of femininity. She can establish herself as active subject and reject the role of the Other, or she can assume this role, but she can then find herself again by seeking her equivalent.

The second section, "Situation" (in the region of two hundred pages), opens with a treatise on traditional marriage. Socially speaking, the man is perceived as an autonomous and complete individual. His existence is justified by the work he does in the community's service. He can choose marriage or remain single—the choice is his. To him, marriage is a way of life, not a destiny. In contrast, the unmarried state reduces woman to the status of pariah. Marriage is her only source of income and the only social justification of her existence. In marriage, the woman becomes the man's *other half*, with the man as legal and economic head of the family. Marriage and love are difficult to reconcile because love can never be an obligation: "marriage is obscene in principle in so far as it transforms into rights and duties those mutual relations which should be founded on a spontaneous urge" (TSS II: 463). Eroticism is a movement toward the other; herein lies its essential nature. But spouses lose the function of other for each other: they become one self. No exchange is possible any longer, no gift, no conquest. Traditional marriage locks up woman in immanence. Her reward consists of her having avoided the feeling of loneliness. "Man is but mildly interested in his immediate surroundings because he can find self-expression in projects" (TSS II: 468–69). In contrast, a woman's home is the center of her universe.

Her household work is not an activity that wrests her from immanence. It is a Sisyphean task, an eternal fight against evil: dust, dirt, stains. It is a sad fate to be constantly focused on the repression of evil instead of on a *positive* goal. The housewife often becomes furious, fanatical, vengeful, or nervous. She only appreciates her husband's activities if they fit in with the framework she has built. Husband and children are always wanting to exceed the boundaries of the home. The woman tries to prevent them doing so: she is dependent on them; they justify her existence. However respected she may be, she remains subordinate, a second-rate figure, a parasite.

Marriage for the woman is a final destination, not a stop on the way; there is no other future for her. The limitations of her situation soon become clear to her. She transforms her disappointment into a maniacal need for her husband's proximity. Often older, he also has the advantage of professional training. As worker and citizen, his thinking is aimed at activity. He has developed a feeling for facts and a critical sense and thus usually acquires the role of mentor and guide. He likes to feel superior and so exaggerates woman's inabilities. Even if the woman recognizes male prestige, her husband's gloss soon fades. Sometimes, she will accept her subordination, but she also often rebels openly, attempts in her turn to tyrannize him, and to humiliate his manhood. But she still wants to "hold onto" her man—her social and moral security, her own home, the status of married woman, and a more or less successful surrogate for love and happiness are all at stake. Sophie Tolstoy, Belle van Zuylen, Madame Proudhon—there are countless examples of fiery and lively women who were suffocated by marriage. It is true that marriage also restricts the man, but it almost always destroys the woman. The traditional form of marriage is changing. The woman today has occupations outside the home and often has a profession that earns her money. But as long as the man remains economically responsible for the couple, equality is no more than an illusion. As long as he alone realizes himself in work or actions, and marriage for his spouse remains the primary "career," then their situation will continue unequal. The birth of a child usually obliges a woman to give up her job or education; it remains very difficult to combine motherhood with work.

For about a century, motherhood has been a choice and not a biological fate. But contraception is still difficult to obtain in many countries.
Abortion tends to evoke a sanctimonious attitude. In France, it is widely
practiced but remains a crime. Society, which is so active on behalf of the
fetus, ceases to be interested in the child once it is born. Mental and
physical abuse of children occurs on a massive scale but is punished
lightly. Those for and those against abortion agree that attempts at elimination have failed completely. An illegal abortion is often life-threatening
for a woman with no money. But it is also a trauma for the better-off
woman who can at least afford better treatment; even if she wants the
abortion, she still experiences it as a sacrifice of her womanhood.

Pregnancy and motherhood are experienced in very different ways,
depending on how they come about—in resistance, acceptance, satisfaction, or enthusiasm. Pregnancy for a woman is both an enrichment and
a mutilation. The embryo is both part of her and a parasite that exploits
her. The subject-object opposition is abolished in the future mother. She
forms a duality with the child. But ultimately it proves an illusion. The
mother does not control her future child—it proves a separate being.
This explains the contradictory fantasies and notions of a pregnant
woman. Even if she is happy with the child, her body can still resist, e.g.,
through excessive nausea. Pregnancy and labor are tolerated most easily
by women who do not allow themselves to become absorbed by their
bodies.

When the child is born, the mother's reaction is determined by a
whole range of socioeconomic and emotional factors. She seeks in the
child what men are continually seeking in women: an other who is simultaneously nature and consciousness, who is prey and doppelgänger. The
great danger to children in our culture is that the mother, to whom they
are entrusted completely, is almost always a frustrated woman. Through
her children she attempts to compensate for her frustrations: she kneads
the children into a model or makes herself their slave. The children develop feelings of guilt that often last a lifetime. The majority of women
tend to impose their own lot onto their daughters. It is a criminal para-
dox to refuse women all kinds of opportunities for self-realization and
then entrust to them the most delicate and serious task there is: the forming of a human being.

The marital relationship, housekeeping, and motherhood form a
whole in which all the factors are mutually influential. But real harmony
is still hard to achieve because the various functions allocated to women
are difficult to conform. Women's magazines give advice on how to reconcile sexual attractiveness with motherhood and thrift. The woman is
caught up in contradictions, and attempts to compensate through a "so-

cial life." The wife "shows off" herself, her home, her children, and her husband. Visits and parties thus often become a chore rather than a pleasure. Friendships between women have a totally different character than relationships between men. Women search for affirmation from each other. Their relationships are not built on individuality, but on sameness, which introduces an element of hostility. Because a woman's husband has lost his prestige in her eyes, she often gives other men the roles of guide and mentor (e.g., priests or doctors) and of lover.

But adultery, friendships, and social intercourse in married life are no more than diversions. They are illusionary escapes: none enables the woman to take control of her own destiny. The existence of the "fallen" woman makes possible the exaltation of the "respectable" woman. The prostitute is a scapegoat and is treated as a pariah. Basic prostitution is a tough profession in which the woman is oppressed both sexually and economically. Hetaerae, courtesans, Hollywood movie stars—all have a certain independence. Yet, when it comes down to it, they are all still dependent on the man. They lose their means of earning a living when he no longer finds them desirable.

The menopause is often a relief for working women, but it is a radical transformation for women who have focused totally on their femininity. They often experience a personal crisis, feel misunderstood, rekindle feelings of regret and sorrow. They sometimes attempt to salvage something of their failed lives in a sudden surge of energy. They fall in love with one young man after another, seek salvation in God or religious sects, spiritism, prophets, and charlatans. If the woman comes to terms with her aging, then her situation changes. She now becomes a sexless creature: an elderly woman. Released from her obligations, she finally discovers her freedom but often no longer knows what to do with it.

Woman's situation often leads her to a fanatic belief in the heroes and laws of the male world. The man knows that he can construct other institutions, another morality, and other laws. Women, on the other hand, are far more energetic than men when it comes to tackling misery and misfortune. There is a whole area of human experience that the man purposely chooses to ignore because he cannot *think* it. This is why women believe men know nothing of life, and for this reason they reject male logic.

In the section "Justifications" (in the region of fifty pages), Beauvoir looks at a trio of attitudes used by women in their attempt to turn their prison into a glorious heaven: the narcissistic, the infatuated, and the mystical. The narcissist tries to be *en-soi-pour-soi*. She devotes herself to herself in an attempt at independence. But she cannot maintain the illusion. No real relationship can exist between an individual and his double, because that double does not exist. The narcissistic woman suffers a radical defeat, which often ends in loneliness and paranoia. The woman who surrenders completely to love and makes her loved one her whole life also attempts to transcend her situation by accepting it absolutely. Self-effacement and "serving" her lover in all ways are supposed to make her happy. But the man she worships like a god is not a god, and that is where the trouble starts. This love religion often ends in catastrophy: the man leaves the woman who has imprisoned him in this way. The mystical woman offers herself to God in total surrender. This is not straightforward "sexual sublimation." Like the woman who idolizes her lover, the mystical woman seeks a sovereign glance full of attention and love for her, i.e., the apotheosis of her narcissism. A mystical glow, love, and narcissism can be integrated in an active and independent life. But as such, these attempts at individual salvation are doomed to failure; in human society, freedom is only achieved through acting positively.

In the fourth and final section, "Towards Liberation," (also comprising around fifty pages), Beauvoir states that having the right to vote and a profession is not sufficient to liberate women. The world still carries the stamp men have placed upon it. Privileged women who have found economic and social independence through a profession still do not feel at home in their new situation. A woman who deviates from current norms devalues herself sexually and as a result also socially because society has integrated sexual values. The woman knows she will always be judged on her appearance. She feels obliged to maintain a fairly complicated elegance. But she encounters real problems in sexual areas. Sometimes she compensates for her active existence with a masochistic love affair. She has to behave passively on the sexual market and be a so-called object. Fortunately, there are increasingly more men who are beginning to accept her equality. But motherhood remains difficult to combine with a profession and career.

The independent woman is also still torn between the interests of her job and her sexual vocation. It takes a lot of effort to find her balance, and she dares not aim too high in her work. Very few women in art and literature have had the boldness needed to create major works. As long as women have to struggle to become free human beings, there will be few creative women; until now women's abilities have been suppressed and have been lost to humanity.

Today, the new woman is still nowhere—not in Russia, not in France or America. But humanity is a historic becoming: the free woman is on the brink of being born. Men and women all win if woman can realize her full human potential. There will then be a mutuality that will allow the human couple to find its true form.

The Second Sex's *genre*

The Second Sex has often been weighed against scientific norms and found wanting. According to cultural anthropologist Margaret Mead, "theoretically, the book violates every canon of science and disinterested scholarship in its partisan selectivity" (Mead, 1953: 31). Bair quotes historian Mary Beard's dismissal of the book as "utter nonsense" and "folly" (Bair, 1990a: 392). Anne Whitmarsh also labeled *The Second Sex* bad science. Beauvoir is said to have attempted to carry out a sociological analysis, but only succeeded in piling up numerous literary examples (Whitmarsh, 1981: 149). This criticism assumes Beauvoir's pretensions were of a scientific nature. But is that really true?

Methodological remarks in *The Second Sex* are rare. In the introduction, Beauvoir stated her intention was to leave behind all earlier debates on the position of woman and to start all over again. She believed that, as a woman, she knew the world of women intimately and could therefore elucidate the problem. She went on to say, "But it is doubtless impossible to approach any human problem with a mind free from bias" (TSS I: 28). Beauvoir then raised the question of her own "ethical background" and stated that her position is based on existentialist principles. Subsequently, she discussed the specificity of woman's situation, i.e., her position as the Other, a position which, in Beauvoir's view, cannot be explained through either psychological, physiological, or economic factors alone, as scientific disciplines attempt to do. Instead we should investigate the *total* situation of woman: "We shall study woman in an existential perspective with due regard to her total situation" (TSS I: 83). This approach can be traced back to an affinity with a phenomenological perspective in philosophical anthropology, which approaches humans as situated beings. Beauvoir shares this approach, which is influenced by Heidegger and others, with Merleau-Ponty, Lévinas, and Sartre. The point of departure of the phenomenological perspective is that humans are always involved in the world, and so can only be understood within the total, very complex context of that world. However, this also implies that humans are seen as beings who continually give meaning to their situation. Thus, humans are objective subjectivity and subjective objectivity. According to this approach, the person should be understood within his or her situation; therefore, this situation itself has to be charted in an unbiased manner.

The point of departure here is that reality can be perceived directly if we are open to what the phenomena themselves tell us. Feelings, intuitive understanding, but also critical researches—all are ingredients of this basic approach. This epistemology derives from the thinking of philosopher Edmund Husserl. His aim was the refutation of Descartes' dualistic epistemology, which had introduced a strict distinction between thinking and being, and thus also between knowing subject and known object. Husserl only accepted the world of the phenomenon (*phainomenon* = "that which shows itself"). He argued that objects only exist as objects for a subject. He thus abolished the subject-object dichotomy. Husserl believed that phenomena could be described accurately and without bias, thus revealing their truth. For Husserl, explanatory, scientific theories were of secondary importance; according to him, *Aufklärung* (elucidation) rather than *Erklärung* (explanation) was required. Scientific approaches alone were inadequate, and as such had denied man access to phenomena and hidden reality from view. Philosophical phenomenology reinterprets the sciences by integrating them into a phenomenological total view.

Beauvoir narrated how Sartre turned pale with emotion when he first came across these ideas. "Aron pointed to his glass: 'You see, my dear fellow, if you are a phenomenologist, you can talk about this cocktail and make philosophy out of it.' " That was exactly what Sartre had had in mind for years: "to describe objects just as he saw and touched them and extract philosophy from the process" (PoL: 135). On the way home from the cafe, Sartre immediately bought Lévinas's book on Husserl, paging through it as he walked to see if Husserl had already formulated his ideas. Beauvoir concluded her account with the observation that, fortunately, this was not the case on a number of essential points (see PoL: 136).

In 1933, Sartre left for Berlin to make a serious study of both Husserl's and Heidegger's work. In that same period, Beauvoir immersed herself in the works of these German philosophers because, she said, she wanted to be able to follow the way Sartre's thinking evolved. Therefore, it is not surprising that from then on we also find traces of this philosophy in her work and that her thinking showed a clear affinity with phenomenology. Looking back on her discussions with Sartre during this period, Beauvoir recalled, "There was a phrase which we borrowed from phenomenology and much abused during these arguments: 'self-evident truth.' Emotions and all other 'psychological entities' had only a probable existence; whereas the *Erlebnis* (experience) contained its own self-evident truth (*sa propre évidence*)" (PoL: 258).

In her review of Merleau-Ponty's *Phénoménologie de la perception* (1945), Beauvoir expressed explicit approval of the *"élucidation phénoménologique"* method. She called the abolition of the subject-object dichotomy one of phenomenology's greatest achievements: "it is impossible to define an object by cutting it from the subject through and for which it is object; and the subject manifests itself only through the object with which it is involved" (TM, 1945: 363). Thus, our own judgments again acquire the relevance they are due. Through education and morality, the child unlearns the ability to take itself seriously as a presence in the world. Phenomenology restores the importance of subjectivity by denying a distinction between objectivity and subjectivity. It gives back to the adult the childlike audacity that allows him to say, "I am here," and to take seriously again his own judgments; an audacity that has to be recaptured from the sciences. The sciences present us with a universe full of "petrified" objects and teach us to perceive ourselves as subject to universal and anonymous laws.

Thus, Beauvoir also criticized scientific explanations of the world and wanted a return to direct observation of the world. Initially, she considered philosophy by definition superior to the sciences.

> The thing that attracted me about philosophy was that it went straight to essentials. I had never liked fiddling detail; I perceived the general significance of things rather than their singularities, and I preferred understanding to seeing; I had always wanted to know everything; philosophy would allow me to appease this desire, for it aimed at total reality; philosophy went right to the heart of truth and revealed to me, instead of an illusory whirlwind of facts or empirical laws, an order, a reason, a necessity in everything. The sciences, literature, and all the other disciplines seemed to me to be very poor relations of philosophy. (MDD: 158)

However, in *The Second Sex* her approach is more refined; she certainly applied scientific theory here. For example, she incorporated theories of Lévi-Strauss. In a footnote, she thanked him for allowing her to see the proofs of his *The Elementary Structures of Kinship* (see *Le deuxième sexe* I: 16–17). Lévi-Strauss's thesis on exogamy is the point of departure for Beauvoir's chapter on history. She also made use of Lacanian psychoanalysis when she referred to the mirror stage in the earliest development of the child as basis for her own socialization theory (see TSS II: 297). In general, in *The Second Sex* she applied the perceptions of sciences, such as biology, psychoanalysis, and historical materialism, but criticized them when they pretend to offer the whole explanation for the historically suppressed position of woman.

In her review of Lévi-Strauss's *The Structures*, Beauvoir stated that his theories can be placed in a broader philosophical framework—something Lévi-Strauss himself never ventured to do: "Lévi-Strauss never allowed himself to enter the domain of philosophy. He adhered strictly to scientific objectivity, but his thinking is clearly linked to the grand humanist tradition" (TM, 1949: 949).

So there is a question of division of tasks between the sciences and philosophy; philosophy places the results of the sciences in a broader framework. Beauvoir's view in *The Second Sex* is in line with Husserl's on this point. Her point of departure is also the necessity of a broad, direct approach, as opposed to the reductionism of the sciences.

Based on the foregoing, the structure of *The Second Sex* now becomes comprehensible. In this work, Beauvoir wanted to chart the whole situation of woman. She believed she knew that situation thoroughly, and in the introduction she stated that women are best suited to illuminating the situation of women: "we know the feminine world more intimately than do the men because we have our roots in it, we grasp more immediately than do men what it means to a human being to be feminine" (TSS I: 27). We should now see this against the backdrop of phenomenological epistemology, in which the immediate experience is decisive. It also gives us insight into how Beauvoir could claim she was beginning "all over again"; the phenomena could be observed and described directly. We also understand now that, in contrast to the sciences, she wanted to examine the *total* experience and circumstances, i.e., situation, of woman, this being the reason why *The Second Sex* became such a lengthy work, exploring such a broad set of aspects of women's lives.

As now becomes clear, far from being a clumsy eclectic work, *The Second Sex* is structured systematically as a philosophical phenomenological enterprise. Beauvoir was criticized by Whitmarsh for merely "piling up examples," but this is totally in line with the methodology of philosophical phenomenology; in this approach examples are not used as empirical evidence but rather as a means to show something, to pass on a specific insight. The Dutch phenomenologist Theo de Boer argues, "It is important that in a philosophical argument examples are chosen with the aim of transferring the spark of insight to the reader. Thus, the philosophical argument does not have the form of a deductive proof or an empiric theory" (de Boer, 1989: 181). My conclusion is that *The Second Sex* cannot be weighed against scientific norms alone but should be evaluated on its own merits, that is, as a philosophical work. When we come to examine the actual importance of *The Second Sex*, we will take its philosophical character into consideration. It may well be that some of the facts have been superceded, but this does not apply to the philosophical proposition of the work as such. We will come back to this point in chapter 10.

The Second Sex *in translation*

We have now seen that *The Second Sex*'s structure and conceptual framework rank it within the philosophical genre. In the original French text,

Beauvoir made free use of philosophical concepts. This shows she perceived the work as philosophical and intended it to be included in this
tradition, a tradition that by definition was critical of common-sensical
ordinary language and used its own jargonese. But *Le deuxième sexe* is
rarely read in the French. Interest in Beauvoir is almost nonexistent in
France (with the exception of Michèle Le Doeuff),[5] and Anglo-Saxon
readers are unlikely to use the French version.[6]

This makes it all the more regrettable that, in English (and Dutch)
translations, the philosophical concepts have either been suppressed completely or even wrongly translated, detracting greatly from the work's
philosophical vigor. Simons (1983) has shown this for the English translation—she discovered that translator Parshley translated *pour-soi* (for-
itself) as the opposite, i.e., as "in-itself." "*La réalité humaine*" becomes
"the real nature of man," a term that also means the contrary of what
Beauvoir intended, as she herself told Simons: "It is a serious mistake to
speak of 'human nature' instead of 'human reality' (*Dasein*-KV), which
is a Heideggerian term. I was infused with Heidegger's philosophy and
when I speak about human reality, that is, about man's presence in the
world, I'm not speaking about human nature, it's completely different"
(Simons, 1989: 20). The translation "nature of man" is incorrect, she
goes on to explain, "since the base of existentialism is precisely that there
is no human nature, and thus no 'feminine nature' " (Simons, 1989: 18).[7]

Masculine thinking?

The systematic philosophical nature of *The Second Sex* tends to go un-
recognized—partly through the translations in which it is read. If *The
Second Sex* is examined from a philosophical standpoint at all, usually
only the Sartrean notions it contains are considered. Because Beauvoir
applied these concepts, she is accused of unleashing male thinking on
(the subject of) woman. Male values are said to dominate in her work
because she is believed to place consciousness above the body, thinking
above feeling, activity over passivity, and transcendence above nature
(see e.g., Greene, 1980: 205; Leighton, 1975: 213; Moi, 1994: 153; Seigfried, 1984: 441). Margaret Walters believes Beauvoir's own life and her
view of human history comprise a devaluation of the feminine. In her
attempts to escape stereotyping, Beauvoir has lost something (see Walters, 1977: 377, 359). Mary Evans suggests Beauvoir took her own pro-
longed student existence as a measure: the values in *The Second Sex* are
those of a childless, hard-working bachelor (see Evans, 1985: 56–57, xi).
With *The Second Sex*, Beauvoir is said to have joined the ranks of our
culture's long tradition of mysogyny (see Lilar, 1970: 9 et passim).[8] All

these critics place the blame on Sartre's conceptual framework. Beauvoir's use of the Sartrean distinction between transcendence and immanence, and her adoption of his hierarchical relationship between both, are said to reproduce the Western rationalistic image of humanity and thus, through the underevaluation of the body, embrace a masculine thinking.

Now, in my view, this kind of strict gender-labeling of a certain philosophic thinking forms a problem in itself. The label is grafted onto socially prevalent definitions of masculinity and femininity: masculinity as consciousness and rationalism, femininity as body and nature. When, based on this, Sartre's philosophy is labeled masculine, the stereotypes that are so liberally available in our culture are only reproduced, and what still has to be proven is in fact presupposed. Besides this problem, the criticism of the book's content is also off the mark. As will become clear in the following chapters, Beauvoir did not simply copy Sartre's thinking. Her own ethical theory represents a wholly Beauvoirian version of existential philosophy's body of ideas, in which connection with fellow human beings, bodily contact, and emotion have a major place and, in contrast to Sartre's thinking, transcendence does not occupy the foreground.

However, Beauvoir's thinking was not deemed masculine on the above-mentioned general bases alone. Another, more specific reasoning was put forward by Genevieve Lloyd: Sartre's conceptual framework was said to be characterized by a rejection of the female body; in this sense then, *The Second Sex* was also believed to have a masculine content. According to Lloyd (1984), transcendence in Sartre signifies nothing less than an abhorrence of the *female* body. Thus, the masculine perspective was said to have made a definitive mark on the concept. We will examine this criticism more closely here. Is Sartre's existential philosophical framework sexist, and in *The Second Sex* does Beauvoir adopt and apply it to the subject of woman in an identical manner? Let us first look more closely at Sartre's reasoning in *Being and Nothingness*.

The first woman we meet in this work is the so-called "frigid woman." She serves to illustrate Sartre's argument that the unconscious does not exist. According to his argument, the frigid woman consciously ignores the pleasure that she, as her husband testifies (?!), actually experiences in the sexual act.[9] The frigid woman is presented to us as an example of bad faith: by assuming the attitude of frigidity, she falls back on a fixed identity and thus places herself on the side of the *en-soi*. The second woman we meet is similarly reproached. She has "accepted" a man's invitation to go out with him. So she knows what the man is after, but elects to ignore this for the time being, thus postponing her decision on whether or not to accept his advances. Sartre apparently hates this: according to him, the woman is shirking her responsibilities. In both cases, he cites woman as an illustration of bad faith, implying that she can, in principle, act as free subject, but, in practice, functions as object. So although woman potentially has a consciousness, in *Being and Nothingness* we see her continually in the role of an *être-en-soi*.

In the final section, which discusses the sexes explicitly, it becomes clear this is no coincidence.[10] Sartre talks here of the threat to the *pour-soi* from the "slimy," which is said to be a "moist and feminine sucking," a "sickly-sweet, feminine revenge." All "holes" threaten the *pour-soi*. These are an *"appel d'être"*; they seduce the subject into becoming flesh and thus fill the hole. And Sartre continues,

> The obscenity of the feminine sex is that of everything which "gapes open." . . . In herself woman appeals to a strange flesh which is to transform her into a fullness of being by penetration and dissolution. Conversely woman senses her condition as an appeal precisely because she is "in the form of a hole." . . . Beyond any doubt her sex is a mouth and a voracious mouth which devours the penis. (BN: 609, 614)

How should we think about these sexist passages in *Being and Nothingness*? Do they mean Sartre's conceptual framework is essentially infected by masculine thinking, as Lloyd argues, and does *The Second Sex* suffer from the same malady? Kaufmann McCall (1979) and Le Doeuff (1979) also addressed this question. Both distinguish gender-specific and gender-neutral sections in Sartre's work, and subsequently conclude Beauvoir took on board the latter only. Dorothy Kaufmann McCall introduces a distinction between Sartre's philosophical and "personal" contributions:

> When Sartre evokes the feminine in *Being and Nothingness*, his language bears more resemblance to the language of his obsessions in the novels than it does to the language of his philosophical discourse. . . . Sartre's descriptions of "the slimy" and "holes" in *Being and Nothingness* do not derive logically from his analysis of the *en-soi* and the *pour-soi*. They are not inherent in either his ontology or in existentialist thought in general; they are rooted in Sartre's particular sensibility. Obsessed with his horror of the vital in all its manifestations, Sartre the writer takes over from Sartre the philosopher, using words as magical means to impose those obsessions on his reader. (Kaufmann McCall, 1979: 214)

So Kaufmann McCall distinguishes the philosopher Sartre and the writer Sartre as the objective and subjective Sartre respectively. However, she forgets this distinction is one of philosophy's continually recurrent problems—what basis can we use for such a distinction? Kaufmann McCall builds her argument on a premise that in fact forms a problem in itself.

Sartre's sexual metaphors are probably not so much projections of his personal *Ängste*, but, according to Michèle Le Doeuff (1979: 52), more an indispensable part of his metaphysics of authenticity. Her view is that the sexual metaphors are not a coincidental appendage, but an essential tailpiece for Sartre's theoretic system. Woman fulfills the role of unceasingly drawing the *pour-soi* into the *en-soi*, so that the *pour-soi* is forced continually to transcend anew. According to Le Doeuff, Sartre needs woman to complete the circle and lend his theory the status of philosophical system.

Now, in my view, this is not the case. The fact that transcendence has to be striven for again and again is explained by Sartre through the constant tendency to bad faith present in every human being, which emerges from his *désir d'être*. The task of transcendence is completed only on death. So Sartre does not need woman to let transcendence start again and again. Moreover, by considering the sexual metaphors as a tailpiece, Le Doeuff herself introduces a distinction between those metaphors and the so-called real theory. Hazel Barnes also makes a distinction between Sartre's "objectionable images" and his theoretical system: these images only cast a shadow over his work and do not form its substance (see Barnes, 1990: 346).

The distinction between imagery and theory, however, is in itself problematic, as I suggested above. Wouldn't this be an ideal way to explain away the less agreeable elements in any philosophical work, by characterizing them as literary or metaphorical nonessentials that do not belong to the actual core of the body of philosophical ideas? The sexual metaphors in Sartre's theory articulate the characteristics of transcendence and immanence in gender-specific terms. So no other conclusion would appear justified than that Sartre's conceptual framework in *Being and Nothingness* includes a masculine thinking. If, to him, transcendence, consciousness, *pour-soi*, and being human are equivalents, then by making transcendence and the female body opposites, the female body is brought into line with immanence, nature, matter, *en-soi*. It would seem then that transcendence is the preserve of people with a male body, and woman emerges as the opposite of transcendence and consciousness.

The question now is in which form Sartre's conceptual framework appears in *The Second Sex*. Is it applied in its original form, and does Beauvoir also see the female body as the enemy par excellence of transcendence? We have already seen that *The Second Sex*'s central proposition is that man has made woman the Other. Beauvoir argues that an existentialist point of departure can make clear how this happened.

The female, to a greater extent than the male, is the prey of the species; and the human race has always sought to escape its specific destiny. The support of life became for man an activity and a project through the invention of the tool; but in maternity woman remained closely bound to her body, like an animal. It is because humanity calls itself in question in the matter of living—that is to say, values the reasons for living above mere life—that, confronting woman, man assumes mastery. (TSS I: 97)

How should we take this? Does Beauvoir also consider women's anatomy as their destiny? Can their subordinate position in history be traced back to their body? There are passages in *The Second Sex* that would suggest this. In the chapter on history, Beauvoir states literally that the historic position of women as Other originates in their anatomy. In this sense, she talks about the biological advantage of men. We can also find passages in which she speaks very negatively about female bodily functions, including those describing menstruation, pregnancy, and labor as extremely painful and disagreeable experiences for women (see e.g., TSS I: 61–62; II: 512–13).

In addition, however, in *The Second Sex* we also find an emphasis on the fact that the body is not a thing, but an always "experienced" reality. Beauvoir states explicitly, "it is not the body-object described by biologists that actually exists, but the body as lived in by the subject" (TSS I: 69), and "It is not merely as a body, but rather as a body subject to taboos, to laws, that the subject is conscious of himself and attains fulfilment—it is with reference to certain values that he evaluates himself. And, once again, it is not upon physiology that values can be based; rather, the facts of biology take on values that the existent bestows upon them" (pp. 68–69). So according to Beauvoir, the body always has a signifying component. Referring to the insights of Heidegger, Sartre, and Merleau-Ponty, she states that the body is not a thing, but a "situation" (see p. 66). By doing so, she approaches the body explicitly from the phenomenological perspective discussed above: the perception of the human being as objective subjectivity and subjective objectivity. For her, one can never be a mere body; there is always a dimension of meaning.[11] Thus, in *The Second Sex* reductionist biological perceptions of woman are subject to permanent criticism.

Here follow a number of Beauvoir's own comments on this subject:

[Woman is only a female] to the extent that she feels herself as such. (p. 69)

Woman is determined not by her hormones or by mysterious instincts, but by the manner in which her body and her relation to the world are modified through the action of others than herself. (II: 734)

. . . if body and sexuality are concrete expressions of existence, it is with reference to this that their significance can be discovered. (I: 77)

It is not nature that defines woman; it is she who defines herself by dealing with nature on her own account in her emotional life. (p. 69)

Experience, understanding, meaning, feeling—for Beauvoir the body is always linked to the human experience of it. It is never a separate entity, and woman's historic role as the Other can, therefore, never be determined by pure biology. The biological facts

are insufficient for setting up a hierarchy of the sexes; they fail to explain why woman is the other; they do not condemn her to remain in this subordinate role for ever. (p. 65)

Thus we must view the facts of biology in the light of an ontological, economic, social, and psychological context. (p. 69)

As we have seen, the two essential traits that characterize woman, biologically speaking, are the following: her grasp upon the world is less extended than man's, and she is more closely enslaved to the species. But these facts take on quite different values according to the economic and social context. In human history grasp upon the world has never been defined by the naked body. (p. 84)

As for the burdens of maternity, they assume widely varying importance according to the customs of the country: they are crushing if the woman is obliged to undergo frequent pregnancies and if she is compelled to nurse and raise the children without assistance; but if she procreates voluntarily and if society comes to her aid during pregnancy, and is concerned with child welfare, the burdens of maternity are light and can be easily offset by suitable adjustments in working conditions. (pp. 84–85).

If we examine more closely Beauvoir's own explanation for woman's historical position as the Other, then we find she indicates a combination of factors. Human beings find transcendence important; woman, through her greater role in procreation, is more subject to biology. That is why men have been able to appropriate transcendence and postulate woman as its opposite. So the oppression of women is a historical contingent result of a number of factors. Men have grasped women's biology to relegate women to a specific role—the Other. In history, the biology of woman has been assimilated into a process of specific cultural meaning, and as such has caused the development of the asymmetrical relationship between the sexes. Thus, biology certainly has its place in the explanation of woman's oppression, but it is not a unique place, because stating that biology has been used is not the same as stating it is an ultimate cause. Beauvoir's historic explanatory model perceives biology as a factor, but it is not infected by biologism.

There is no essence in woman, or in her body, that by definition places her on the side of *en-soi*; in principle, woman can also realize herself as subject, as self. Beauvoir claims woman has become the absolute Other through a historic contingent process, but states this is in no way an inevitable consequence of bodily functions. Woman has been the historic (contingent) Other but in no way the inevitable (necessary) Other. Through the central role of this thesis of woman as historic Other in *The Second Sex*, it is clear that whenever Beauvoir talks about the female body, she has the situated body in mind, i.e., the body embedded in and shaped by sociocultural practices and meanings. Beauvoir stated literally, "the situation does not depend on the body; the reverse is true" (II: 706). The phenomenological-anthropological approach of *The Second Sex*, i.e., the approach of woman as a situated human being, made it impossible for Beauvoir to share Sartre's rejection of the female body as such. In *The Second Sex*, Beauvoir removed the female body from Sartre's dualistic ontology and ranked it at a sociocultural level. Thus, Beauvoir has disaggregated Sartre's series of equivalents—nature/female body/immanence/*en-soi*, breaking down his antagonism between the female body and transcendence.

In her introduction to *The Second Sex*, she quoted the following passage from "Mister"—the intended irony is missing from the English translation—Lévinas's *Le Temps et l'Autre*: "Otherness reaches its full flowering in the feminine, a term of the same rank as consciousness but of opposite meaning" (TSS I: 16, note 1). She continued as follows: "I suppose that Lévinas does not forget that woman, too, is aware of her own consciousness, or ego. But it is striking that he deliberately takes a man's point of view, disregarding the reciprocity of subject and object. . . . Thus his description, which is intended to be objective, is in fact an assertion of masculine privilege" (ibid).

What Beauvoir actually did here was to reformulate Sartre's theory in a nutshell. Sartre had also defined the traits of transcendence in gender-specific terms (a transcendence of the female body). He also implied woman was diametrically opposed to transcendence. In *The Second Sex*, Beauvoir eliminated this gender-specific connotation by introducing her thesis of woman as historic Other. In doing so, she transformed the very core of Sartre's conceptual framework. *The Second Sex* opposes the traditional situation of woman, not the female body. Beauvoir's negative evaluation of female bodily functions is targeted against the experience of motherhood, labor, and pregnancy, which is inherent to a specific objective situation where women have no active control over their own bodies and lives. My conclusion is that criticisms of Beauvoir that claim she is in opposition to the female body as such ignore the main thesis in *The Second Sex*, which we can characterize as the thesis of woman as the historic Other.

Beauvoir opposed a specific cultural embedding and organization of the female body, which made it impossible for women to develop and experience themselves and their bodies as active subjects. If women could live as active subjects, also in their reproductive role, they would also experience pregnancy, labor, and motherhood actively, and real love between mothers and children and between men and women would then be possible. Beauvoir herself noted, "It was said that I refused to grant any value to the maternal instinct and to love. This was not so. I simply asked that women should experience them truthfully and freely, whereas they often use them as excuses and take refuge in them, only to find themselves imprisoned in that refuge when those emotions have dried up in their hearts" (FoC: 201).

In the following chapters we will see how Beauvoir conceived love while simultaneously retaining Sartre's concept of the Self-Other structure in human contact. It will appear that she also transformed this aspect of his theory to the very core, and that *The Second Sex* comprises a theoretic framework of Beauvoir's own.

4

A PLACE FOR LOVE

In *The Second Sex* Beauvoir argued that real love can only exist in free-dom. "For it [love] to be genuine, authentic, it must first of all be free" (TSS II: 491). However, in this book she also made use of Sartre's ideas on human freedom and especially of his concept of human relations.

Can love be reconciled with these ideas? For Sartre, conflict is the basis of our relationships with others, and all contact with fellow human beings is, in fact, impossible because of the Self-Other structure of human relationships. We will see how Beauvoir amended one important point in Sartre's theory, creating a place for intersubjectivity within the framework of existentialist philosophy and making love possible. But we will also see that in doing so she retained the sting of Sartre's thinking. Let us first take an in-depth look at both Beauvoir's and Sartre's notions of sexual love. Beauvoir's amendments to Sartre's theory are most clearly manifest on this point. They show convincingly how an intersubjective contact with other people can exist, whereas this was impossible for Sartre.

Beauvoir's thinking on sexual love

The work in which Beauvoir expresses her notions on sexual love most clearly is her treatise *Faut-il brûler Sade?* (1952; *Must We Burn De Sade?*

[1953]). Here, love emerges as a fusion: "The state of emotional intoxication allows one to grasp existence in one's self and in the other, as both subjectivity and passivity. The two partners merge in this ambiguous unity; each one is freed of his own presence and achieves immediate communication with the other" (MBS: 33). In this essay on the life and work of the Marquis de Sade, Beauvoir stressed we can truly meet the other in sexual love. She pities Sade for his emotional isolation and for his inability to experience emotional intoxication. His sexual preferences are a compensation for this lack. They are generated by an autism "which prevented him from ever forgetting himself or being aware of the reality of the other person" (p. 33).

But Sade also had his merits. He had the courage to show sexuality as egoism, tyranny, and cruelty. He demonstrated that the interests of people are irreconcilable, and he focused attention on a dimension of human relations which those in control are all too eager to suppress: i.e., the dimension of the master-slave relationship. These revelations are of inestimable importance because, if we are ever to overcome the separation of individuals, we will first have to recognize it. Sade's greatest contribution is that he forces us to "reexamine thoroughly the basic problem which haunts our age in different forms: the true relation between man and man" (p. 89).

Beauvoir clearly had in mind here "forms" of existentialism and Jean-Paul Sartre's in particular. Wasn't it Sartre who had argued the fundamental separation of individuals, who had stated, "Hell, that is the Other." In a later review of her essay, Beauvoir even characterized Sade's problem in literal existential philosophical terms: Sade posed the problem of the other in its most extreme terms and, through all his excesses, revealed the core of the dramatic confrontation between man as transcending being and man as object (see FoC: 255). It seems to me justified then to read Beauvoir's essay on Sade as a piece dealing with a problem in existential philosophy. Let us look more closely at the text from this perspective.

As is clear from the above quotation, Beauvoir attributed a special status to sexual love: it is a liberation from one's own presence and realizes an immediate contact with the other. This contact comes about because both partners undergo a metamorphosis into flesh (*chair*) through emotional intoxication, and experience themselves and the other simultaneously as subjectivity and as passivity. Beauvoir spoke here in terms of "the subject's psycho-physiological unity" (MBS: 33). Body and consciousness become a unity when consciousness is absorbed into the body. A fusion can then take place through physical love which comprises an immediate contact (*une communication immédiate*) with the other: "an understanding of the other person as consciousness through the flesh" (*une appréhension de l'autre comme conscience à travers la chair*) (p. 34; FbS: 35). So, this is not only a contact with the other's body, but most definitely also a contact with the other's consciousness. For Beauvoir, becoming "flesh" through emotion is a unification of body and consciousness. She continues, "Normally, it is as a result of the vertigo of the other made flesh that one is spellbound within his own flesh. If the subject remains confined within the solitude of his consciousness, he escapes this agitation and can rejoin the other only by conscious performance" (MBS: 34).

For Beauvoir, Sade was prototypical of the subject who remains confined. He was cursed with a total emotional isolation (*un isolisme affectif radical*). In his stories, sensuality never once emerges as self-forgetfulness, swooning, or abandon (p. 43). He seeks a substitute for anxiety in the infliction of suffering or pain. His cruelty enables him "to apprehend through the other person the consciousness-flesh unity and to project it into himself" (p. 43). That is why the contortions and moans of his victim are necessary. These are proof of the fact that this is a human being (i.e., a consciousness) and not an object. But, "If one fails, in the course of an actual experience, to grasp the ambiguous unity of existence, one will never succeed in reconstructing it intellectually. A spectacle, by definition, can never coincide with either the inwardness of consciousness or the opacity of the flesh. Still less can it reconcile them" (p. 46).

This is why each representation evokes another, and why stories occupy such an important place in Sade's writings. There is no risk of disappointment in the imaginary world. Sade's eroticism only achieves fulfillment there. However, his erotic scenes have strong limitations. They are stripped of every human and social dimension. Sade's heroes are no more than abstract figures. So eroticism loses its exceptional nature; it is no longer a revelation, a unique experience. It is clear Beauvoir was not exactly a fan of sadomasochistic rituals. She was interested primarily in the immediate contact that can be achieved through sexual love with the other; there lies the dramatic and fascinating nature of love.

The idea of love as a fusion recurs throughout Beauvoir's whole oeuvre. It also appears in *The Second Sex* (which was published three years earlier than the Sade essay), although obliquely and more implicitly.[1] She criticized the institution of marriage here as fatal for the fusion experience. But the main thrust of her argument in *The Second Sex* is that romantic ideals of love, in which fusion predominates, are insufficient; true love for another person requires generosity, and fusion also requires that generosity, a point that will become clear later.

Beauvoir also showed physical love as fusion in "It's about Time" (1950), the article discovered by her biographer, Bair. The incarnation, i.e., the becoming flesh, of consciousness and freedom is said to be an overwhelming and wonderful experience for both men and women.[2] Her essay *Brigitte Bardot and the Lolita Syndrome* (1959) again emphasizes this emotional dimension of physical love. It is to actress Bardot and director Vadim's credit that in their films they portray eroticism as an independent dimension, and show an active female sexuality. However, their movies are too analytical. The main characters remain anonymous beings, and viewers are thus denied any emotion. So sexual love is stripped of its humanity. As in *Must We Burn De Sade?* Beauvoir again argued that sexuality is a reduced experience if emotion is not part of the process. She preferred a sexuality that involves the whole person, and talked of love (*amour*) as distinct from *éroticisme*.[3]

She clearly pursued this thinking throughout her work; in her late study on *Old Age* (1970), we again find physical love emerging as a positive feeling of fusion:

> in the turmoil and desire of sexual activity the consciousness and the body become as one in order to reach the other as a body and in such a way as to enthral and possess him; there is a twofold reciprocal embodiment. . . . If it takes on the character of a struggle then it begets hostility: more often it implies a "togetherness" that encourages tender affection. In a couple whose love does away with the distance between the "I" and the other, even failure is overcome. (OA: 355)

Now that we have established meeting the other in physical love is a constant theme in Beauvoir's work, let us turn to Sartre's concepts of love and compare both perceptions.

Must we burn Sartre?

In the previous chapter, we saw how in *Being and Nothingness* Sartre developed the notion that the other can only be an object for me. According to Sartre, concrete relationships with the other are therefore very problematic. If we can never meet another person as subject, then even our attempts to do so through physical love are futile. Physical love is a striving to achieve immediate contact with someone else through reciprocal incarnation. But this striving is doomed to failure. If I try to seduce the other into incarnation, then I myself am not incarnate, but am present as consciousness. Through my look, the other thus becomes a thing in the world, and his subjectivity escapes me. So I attempt in vain to meet the other as freedom.

In sadism the failure of sexual love is indulged: the only aim of consciousness is to make the other into flesh while itself remaining present as pure consciousness. Beauvoir saw sexual love and sadism as opposites, but Sartre perceived them as extensions of each other. There is also a second reason why Sartre considered love impossible. Man wants to justify his existence and has a *"désir d'être"* (a desire to be rather than to transcend—see chapter 3). So man also has a desire to become an essential object for the other. As every person is motivated by this masochistic desire, love is by definition characterized by conflict and not by reciprocality. Only sadomasochistic relations are possible here. At no time in *Being and Nothingness* is love expressed in any other form; it is never presented in a positive sense. The difference between this concept and Beauvoir's notion of love as fusion is unmistakable. If we now try to reduce this difference to its core, then in my view we will find a real difference in attitude to emotion.

Sartre explored his concept of emotion in *Esquisse d'une théorie des émotions* (1939; *The Emotions*). However, if we are to understand his theory on emotion, we must go back to *La transcendance de l'ego*, published three years earlier. In this treatise, Sartre aimed his barbs at psychologists and so-called idealistic philosophers (Brunschvicg and Husserl) who assume the existence of an I or an inner self as a separate ontological dimension. In contrast, he claims consciousness is empty and, unlike the idealists' representation, is not a vessel full of content. After all, the *pour-soi* is pure intentional focus on something outside itself. When the *pour-soi* thinks about itself, its thinking is still focused on something and therefore (on) something other than itself. Something other in this case is an I, which thus acquires the status of an object or thing. The I is therefore different from the *pour-soi*, which is a continually escapist activity, or rather has to be if it does not want to stultify into an object and thus lapse into bad faith. Sartre's theory on emotion was an extension of his crusade against the inner self. As consciousness has no content (see chapter 3), he argued, how can we perceive emotions as experiences in consciousness? In his work *The Emotions*, he was at pains to show us that emotions also represent the intentional relationship of consciousness to the world.

This concerns then a relationship in which consciousness lapses at the time when it no longer can or wants to see something "face to face." At that moment, it resorts to a magical fundamental attitude; it creates a magical world in which objects have fixed qualities. Instead of recognizing that I myself attribute qualities to the world, I pretend the objects have fixed characteristics. Thus, I see something as being frightening, and I deny that it is I, myself, who attribute a specific significance to it. So, I no longer see the world as changeable through an active intervention on my part. Emotion is the sudden relapse of the consciousness into this magical fundamental attitude.

Sartre appeared to deviate somewhat from his concept of emotion as giving meaning to the world when he introduced a distinction between emotions that we ourselves bring about and those that happen to us. In the case of emotions that happen to us, a magical world *reveals itself* to us. For example, we see a grinning face at a window, which frightens us. But consciousness also has an active role here, he added immediately. We eliminate, for example, the fact that the window first has to be broken and that a certain distance has to be covered before the grinning face can actually threaten us. We are afraid because we switch off everything that can arrest the magical and that can reduce the event to its real proportions.

The experience of emotions is, therefore, always an active—but reprehensible—choice because consciousness makes a foray into the world of the magical instead of remaining in the world of tools. Consciousness thus declines into an attitude of bad faith. What is in fact an active deed of consciousness (and as such is an act of negation) is experienced as an overwhelming passive experience. Emotion is a form of self-deceit (see also Murdoch, 1953: 66).

It is now time to compare Beauvoir's concept of emotion with Sartre's. In Beauvoir's essay on Sade, the inability to experience emotion represents an impotence, while emotion itself is seen as a positive psychophysiological experience through which contact with others occurs. Emotion emerges as a convergence of body and consciousness, this in contrast to pure consciousness and the separation between people. There is no question here of Sartre's concept of emotion as bad faith and self-deceit. Beauvoir herself said she and Sartre disagreed about emotion from the start. On their differing reactions to seeing a beautiful landscape, she wrote,

> I felt elevated by this spectacle, and reproached Sartre for his indifference to it. He talked about the forest and the river far more eloquently than I did, yet they did not make him feel anything. He defended himself against this charge by asking what the real definition of feeling was. He had no taste, he said, for all those disordered physical reactions—violent palpitations of the heart, trembling, or giddiness—which paralyse verbal communication. (PoL: 39)

Not only had Sartre no emotional sense, he was also contemptuous of it. Emotion was not authentic, because it was not lucid. "If you gave way to tears or nerves or seasickness, he said, you were simply being weak. I, on the other hand, claimed that stomach and tear ducts, indeed the head itself, were all subject to irresistible forces on occasion" (p. 129). Beauvoir called her feelings an "experience of fulfilment" (FoC: 671). For her, they were a "direct contact with the world" (p. 661), and "nothing else but the presence which is attentive to the world and to itself" (EA: 42). The world reveals itself to us only "through rejection, desire, hate and love" (p. 78).

Admittedly, she developed no separate *theory* on emotion, but her thinking on its place and status were clearly different from Sartre's. Emotion always represents the unity of body and consciousness. Nowhere in her work do we find emotion as a conscious act in the Sartrean sense. In Sartre, consciousness also has to be understood as a negation of the body—he described the *en-soi* in (female) physical terms as that which the *pour-soi* has to negate (see chapter 3). Thus, for him, emotion is in fact also a negation of the body. The consequence here is that incarnation based on emotionality, in the form of a convergence of body and consciousness, is by definition self-deceit to Sartre. Real contact with fellow beings in the emotional sphere is unthinkable for him; the internal negation mechanism between human beings also embraces the sphere of emotion.

Sartre's existential philosophy has often been labeled a solipsism (see e.g., Murdoch, 1953: 66; Merleau-Ponty, 1955: passim). Sartre himself thought this unjustified. He referred to the fact that the *pour-soi* has knowledge of the existence of the other as subject because it knows the experience of becoming an object under the look of the other (see chapter 3); I know other subjects exist so there can be no question of an ontological solipsism. However, the perception of the other *as* subjectivity was impossible for Sartre. My subjectivity stops where that of the other begins, and vice versa. I can never meet the other as subjectivity even though I know he exists. Schuetz coined the term "practical solipsism" (1948: 199) to characterize this impossibility in Sartre's theory. In my view, this is an extremely apt characterization of Sartre's existential philosophy. Given his all-embracing—it even includes emotion—concept of internal negation, it is absolutely impossible to imagine how we could ever meet the other; we are doomed to spend our lives in total individuality.

Beauvoir does not follow Sartre's theory of emotion and thus breaks with the practical solipsism of his theory.[4] Through emotion, we can certainly meet the other as the other. In my view, we can interpret *Must We Burn De Sade?* as her—indirect—response to Sartre's thinking. In this essay, she places her concept of love as emotion against Sade's representation of physical love. Both Sartre and Sade saw love as an impossibility and emphasized the conflict, the enmity, and the separation between people. Beauvoir deplored Sade's inability to forget himself as a consciousness and introduced emotion as the ability to capture the duality of life in an actual experience, and thus to achieve contact with the other. It would appear we can replace Sade's name with Sartre's and that we can translate the proposition in her article as: *Faut-il brûler Sartre?*[5] The following sections will show how her own view embraces a complex and subtle answer to this question.

My tears decide who my neighbor is

We have seen how Beauvoir broke down the separation between people using the experience of emotion, and we find the same leitmotiv in her essays on ethics. Here, too, the emotional dimension emerges as the meeting place with fellow human beings. After a brief prologue, the essay *Pyrrhus et Cinéas*[6] opens as follows: "I knew a child who cried because the concierge's little son had died. His parents let him weep, but then became irritated: 'He wasn't your brother.' The child dried his tears" (PC: 241).

But if these parents are right, then we could deny any tie with our fellow human beings, and we could withdraw into total indifference (as does the main character in Camus' novel *L'Etranger* (1942; *The Outsider* [1946]). This type of attitude is inhuman. If I were only a thing in the world, there would indeed be nothing I could call my own. All social, organic, and economic relations would only be extraneous to me. Because there are no ties between things, their existence is "separation and loneliness" (pp. 242–43). But man is no thing; he is characterized by subjectivity, and that involves a movement toward the other. Man is a spontaneity that desires, loves, has a will, and acts (which Camus' Outsider actually denies). It is through this that the difference between myself and the other is resolved and "I can call the other mine." True, the little boy is not my brother. But if I cry for him, he is no longer a stranger. Who my neighbor is cannot be determined in advance: "my tears decide" (p. 245).

Here again, emotion resolves the difference between myself and the other. According to Beauvoir, man is a creature of flesh and blood, who knows pain and joy, desires and cares. He is a physical creature who exists in time and place, or in other words is situated, and as such is a *corps vécu*: a unity of body and consciousness. However, we can attempt to rise above our earthly nature, which continually causes turmoil. For example, we can adopt a detached attitude like that preached by the Stoics, or only be concerned with Humanity in the abstract and remain aloof from real life. But if we distance ourselves from our situation and only consider the world from a contemplative standpoint, everything becomes the same. We then know no desires, no preferences, no refusal, no joy. The view from the mountain is only a real joy if we have first climbed it; it is the long trek that makes resting a pleasure, or thirst that gives taste to a drink of water. It is not through absolute detachment and inertia that we experience the joy of existence, but through transforming our freedom into concrete actions. For Beauvoir, the situated person is a consciousness in physical, sensual, and emotional form. The "emotional life" of man refers directly to man-in-situation (see e.g., TSS I: 69).

As situated being we share our world with fellow human beings. They too live as a unity of body and consciousness, and our contact with them is thus intersubjective. There is a social community in which we are a human being among human beings. Moreover, everyone is dependent on that community. If man were alone in the world, then his actions would have no sense—they only have meaning in a *world* of meaning. Others are needed to recognize his actions as freedom, and thus give them meaning. The situated being is therefore a social creature who is dependent on a social community. In this sense, the emotional dimension, synonymous with the situated being that lives as unity of body and consciousness, again emerges in Beauvoir as the place of reciprocal contact between people.

Yet, in the same *Pyrrhus et Cinéas*, she also emphasized there is an irremovable separation between people. Each and every person is a subject for himself, and ultimately this experience can never be shared as such. This is because interhuman contact does not reach into the core of human freedom, the pure *pour-soi*: "insofar as he is freedom, the other is radically separated from me, and there can be no single relationship between me and that pure inner essence upon which, as Descartes has shown clearly, not even God can get a grip" (PC: 330).[7]

Apparently there is both a link between people, which arises from the nature of their situatedness, and a fundamental separation between them, which springs from their *pour-soi* character.

This ambiguous view of human beings also emerged in Beauvoir's review of the work of philosopher Maurice Merleau-Ponty. She is clearly sympathetic to his concept of man as unity of body and consciousness. But she still brings in Sartre's notion of man as *pour-soi*.

In her review of Merleau-Ponty's *Phénoménologie de la perception* (1945), Beauvoir only mentioned the difference with Sartre's concept in passing, and her discussion of Merleau-Ponty's view was primarily acquiescent. Merleau-Ponty argued rightly that the human body is no object.

It is in the world in a different way than a stone: it inhabits the world. Our body is our grasp on the world and the way we experience it. Conversely, our consciousness always expresses itself through our body; it is always *engorgée par le sensible* (TM, 1945: 367). For Merleau-Ponty, consciousness is thus no "nothingness" or "hole" (*néant, trou*) as it is in Sartre, but a "hollow, a fold" (*"un creux, un pli"*). Beauvoir saw Merleau-Ponty as concerned with the "real nature of the subject which, according to him, is never a pure *pour-soi*" (p. 366). Only the use of "according to him" is an indication of a certain reserve on her part. However, in a second article, entitled "Merleau-Ponty et le pseudo-sartrisme" (1955), she attacked his concepts overtly. During the first half of the 1950s, Sartre and Merleau-Ponty were at odds on communism; Merleau-Ponty was against, Sartre was for. Beauvoir felt the need to defend Sartre's thinking against Merleau-Ponty's attacks. In his *Les aventures de la dialectique* (1955), Merleau-Ponty had claimed Sartre's theory offered no place for real social history, and was therefore politically naive.[8] He thus labeled Sartre's theory pure subject philosophy. For Sartre, consciousness existed in isolation; it lent meaning to an *en-soi* that was, as such, meaningless; the relationship of the I to the other was limited to a look; everyone remained locked inside his own universe, and there was no social dimension.

Wrong!, Beauvoir stated. Merleau-Ponty's representations of Sartre's pseudo-Sartism theories were nothing more than pseudo-Sartrism. First, Sartre seldom used the word "subject"—Merleau-Ponty used it without distinction for consciousness, ego, man. Secondly, Sartre's theory on consciousness was no subject philosophy—only the I is a subject, and consciousness does not consist of an I. Moreover, Sartre always stressed that the *pour-soi* was totally dependent for its content on the *en-soi*, and that it expressed itself in the world. Beauvoir's conclusion was that "the reconciliation between Sartre's ontology and phenomenology generates problems," but that his ontology and phenomenology are inextricably linked to each other (MPps: 271).[9] Merleau-Ponty's pseudo-Sartrism failed to recognize that, to Sartre, man is also a unity of consciousness and body; and it failed to do so even though, throughout his oeuvre, Sartre placed more and more emphasis on the incarnation of consciousness (see p. 271).[10]

Beauvoir admitted here implicitly that incarnation was not central to Sartre's early work. But she also claimed that the phenomenological and ontological poles in Sartre's thinking were inextricably linked, although reconciliation of the two was not easy. We have seen that Sartre's existentialist philosophy cannot be reconciled with incarnation (because of the comprehensiveness of consciousness, with its internal negation mechanism) and lacks a place for intersubjective contact with fellow human beings. Sartre did not pursue a theoretic reconciliation, and such a reconciliation is actually impossible in his thinking.

Beauvoir seems to have been defending her own pseudo-Sartrism against Merleau-Ponty when she argued that such a reconciliation *is* possible: she was defending a Sartrism that is, in fact, a Beauvoirism.[11] But how then did Beauvoir herself reconcile the unity of body and consciousness and ties with fellow human beings with man's *pour-soi* nature and the fundamental separation between human beings? According to Sonia Kruks, she simply placed these aspects alongside each other and can therefore be accused of eclecticism; Beauvoir swung back and forth between Sartre's and Merleau-Ponty's views of man (see Kruks, 1990: 99).[12] But is Beauvoir really ambiguous on this point, or did she adhere to a systematic theory on man in which he appears as an ambiguous creature? For an answer to this question we should look at the collection entitled *Pour une morale de l'ambiguïté* (1947; *The Ethics of Ambiguity* [1948]).

Ethics

If the emphasis in *Pyrrhus et Cinéas* was on the fact that people are situated beings, the central theme in *The Ethics of Ambiguity* is that man is an ontologically free being but has to *assume* his situatedness. Living as a situated being emerges here as an ethical choice based on our ontological freedom. In *Pyrrhus et Cinéas*, Beauvoir stated that man cannot turn away from the world indifferently, but should develop himself in involvement with the world. In the first part of *The Ethics of Ambiguity*, Beauvoir underpinned this idea theoretically. She introduced a distinction between "being free" and "willing oneself free" (*se vouloir libre*, also *vouloir vivre*), between "ontological" or "original" freedom on the one hand, and "moral" freedom on the other. "What meaning can there be in the words to will oneself free, since at the beginning we are free?" (EA: 24)

The answer is that ontological freedom in itself says nothing about what we do with it. For example, man can lose his freedom through cowardice, frivolity, or laziness. But if he "wills himself free," he will consciously assume his ontological freedom in a positive recognition of the negative (the nothingness). Man's original freedom is a pure spontaneity, and as such is no more than a "vain living palpitation" (p. 25). But, "To will oneself free is to effect the transition from nature to morality by establishing a genuine freedom on the original upsurge of our existence" (PMA: 35). When man identifies positively with his *néant* nature (or rather his *manque d'être*: his lack, his defect), he "coincides exactly with himself" (EA: 13).

In this connection, Beauvoir refers to Hegel's dialectic: "In Hegelian terms it might be said that we have here a negation of the negation by which the positive is re-established. Man makes himself a lack, but he can deny the lack as lack and affirm himself as a positive existence. He then assumes the failure" (p. 13). Yet, Hegel's dialectic model does not suffice, she added immediately. In Hegel, the *aufgehoben* terms are only present as abstract moments, "whereas we consider that existence still remains a negativity in the positive affirmation of itself" (p. 13). Instead of an *Aufhebung*, "conversion" is at issue here. She elucidated:

> There are thus two ways of surpassing the given: it is something quite different from taking a trip or escaping from prison. In these two cases the given is present in its surpassing; but in one case it is present insofar as it is accepted, in the other insofar as rejected, and that makes a radical difference. Hegel has confused these two movements with the ambiguous term "*aufheben*"; and the whole structure of an optimism which denies failure and death rests on this ambiguity. (p. 84)

Thus, on the one hand, Beauvoir used Hegel's idea that the negation of a negation restores positiveness, and on the other hand, she rejects his progressive concept. By willing ourself free, we do not live merely as a lack, but this becomes a positive experience (we live our lack to the full). But the negativity as such does not disappear. Hegel considered incorrectly that the negativity which our life as individual comprises is a phase that can be overcome; man can recognize himself in humanity and thus rise above his individuality.[13] In contrast, Beauvoir argued that the individual exists at all times, and as a result, negativity, the human lack, continues to exist, as does man's desire to escape from it. His *désir d'être* will drive man eternally to the subjection of his fellow human beings (trying to fulfill his desire to be an *en-soi* as *pour-soi*; see chapter 3). That is why "the plane of hell, of struggle, will never be eliminated; freedom will never be given" (p. 119). Man will continually attempt to neutralize his lack by fleeing his freedom.

The only real solution (which must be won time and again from man's *désir d'être*) is a moral conversion; when man recognizes his ontological freedom and identifies positively with an existence as free being, he no longer wants to *be*, he wants to be *free*. The *désir d'être* is replaced by the *se vouloir libre*. Negativity, and the ensuing "failure is not surpassed but assumed" (p. 13). Because his *néant* nature means man is always dependent on the *en-soi* to achieve himself, "willing oneself free" therefore encompasses the acceptance that he is dependent on the world around him; he takes on his situatedness and enters into concrete ties with the world.

We can now conclude that through the configuration of conversion, Beauvoir combines the negativity of man and his positive existence as human being in the world. Conversion brings together both the continuing presence of ontological freedom, and the active entering into of ties with other people. The moral attitude means man recognizes his *pour-soi* nature as basis, but situates himself actively from that basis. Thus, man rises from ontological freedom to the level of life as situated being. But this is no definitive elevation. Given the ever-present *néant* nature of man, this moral conversion has to take place continually. The bad faith mechanism

> permits stopping at any moment whatsoever. One may hesitate to make oneself a lack of being, one may withdraw before existence, or one may falsely assert oneself as being, or assert oneself as nothingness. One may realize his freedom only as an abstract independence, or, on the contrary, reject with despair the distance which separates us from being. All errors are possible since man is a negativity, and they are motivated by the anguish he feels in the face of his freedom. (p. 34)

Thus, "willing oneself free" demands a continual effort from man, an effort of a moral kind.

But why should we call this a moral attitude? If we will ourselves free and become actively involved with the world and people around us, we can equally become involved in "evil affairs," i.e., in values and projects that are usually considered bad and immoral. Beauvoir also raised this question, "We have just described only the subjective and formal aspect of this freedom. But we also ought to ask ourselves whether one can will oneself free in any matter, whatsoever it may be" (p. 26). But this is impossible because "willing oneself free" also means we want freedom as such; we take up a position against every form of oppression of freedom, both our own and that of others. Willing oneself free thus entails a positive involvement with other people that is not passive in nature; we do not adopt a noncommittal attitude to others, but oblige ourselves to become concerned with their fate and welfare. This is why Beauvoir saw "willing oneself free" as a moral attitude.

Beauvoir called her ethics "an ethics of ambiguity." We have seen that man's condition is ambiguous because his ontological freedom remains the basis for his life as active, situated person. As people always "remain radically separated" (see p. 105), this means we can never speak for another, and abstract morality, i.e., so-called "idealistic moral theories" (p. 22), are incorrect. In *Pyrrhus et Cinéas*, Beauvoir already expressed her disapproval of the "universal moral theories" of Kant and Hegel (see

PC: 363).[14] In this type of ethics, the individual is obliged to give himself up in favor of the common good. But this denies the irreducible value of man, i.e., his individual freedom. The interests of the concrete individual in no way coincide with the so-called common good. The terms "useful to Man" and "useful to this man" are by no means analogous because "universal, absolute man exists nowhere" (EA: 112). Beauvoir stated, "it is true that each is bound to all; but that is precisely the ambiguity of his condition: in his surpassing toward others, each one exists absolutely as for himself; each is interested in the liberation of all, but as a separate existence engaged in his own projects" (p. 112).

Looking back on her younger years, Beauvoir said neither she nor Sartre wanted anything to do "with what is known academically as 'moral values.' . . . Duty and virtue are concepts implying the subjection of the individual to laws outside himself. We denied such vain notions, and countered them with a living truth: wisdom" (PoL: 43). In both *Pyrrhus et Cinéas* and *The Ethics of Ambiguity*, Beauvoir remained faithful to this attitude. In *Pyrrhus et Cinéas* we read, "without me, there are no ready-made values imposed on my decisions according to a hierarchical pattern" (PC: 333). In *The Ethics of Ambiguity*, Beauvoir introduced a different kind of ethics *in opposition to* abstract moral theory. The concrete, ambiguous existence of the concrete individual is the place where ethics makes its entrance. This is the reason why universal moral laws do not exist and why only man himself can evaluate and determine his own actions. The ethical person cannot believe in external absolute values, such as a God. The person who wills himself free recognizes that he himself creates his values. He recognizes that moral rules based on abstractions such as humanity or universal reason do not exist, and that ethics are always situational or rather contextual in nature. We should not "serve an abstract ethics" (EA: 136). Abstract moral principles are empty formulas: "the dilettant who pretends to care for everything actually loves nothing" (PC: 345). If I reject my situatedness, then values disappear: "The infinite multiplication of ties which bind me to the world is a way of denying my ties here and now, on this specific place in the world; I then no longer have a mother country, or friends, or parents . . . there is no more desire, no fear, no unhappiness, no joy. Nothing belongs to me anymore" (p. 264). And "no human individual can establish a genuine relationship with the infinite, be it labelled God or Humanity" (PoL: 548).

A place for love

If we initially discovered ambiguous statements on human existence in Beauvoir's work in the sense that separation and engagement are placed alongside each other as two human characteristics, we now see that she conceived this human existence itself as ambiguous by nature. Man is both positiveness *and* negativity, a positive unity of body and consciousness *and pour-soi*, i.e., a negating consciousness. We questioned earlier whether Beauvoir could be accused of eclecticism in this sense, or whether she had a theory of her own. Our conclusion must be that she had her own theory. Man's *pour-soi* nature and his situatedness are not merely set alongside each other, but are placed by Beauvoir in a very specific—hierarchical—order.

The incarnate, i.e., situated, human being appears as a higher phase, above the pure *pour-soi* being. The *pour-soi* forms, as it were, the background against which and from which man rises to the surface of a situated existence, in which he is a unity of body and consciousness. If the emphasis in Sartre's existentialist philosophy lay on the fact that man is a *pour-soi* and has to achieve himself as absolute freedom, Beauvoir considered life as situated being as the decisive characteristic and the actual task of man.[15] She expressed her rejection of those who refuse to accept their situatedness more than once. In *The Second Sex*, for example, she criticized the writer Montherlant for his refusal to accept his human condition. He locked himself up in a so-called sovereign subjectivity and refused to identify himself as a *liberté engagé dans le monde à travers une chair* (LDS I: 312). In her essay on Sade, she stated she could not concur with "the solution he offers" (MBS: 87).

Sade's merit lay in his raising the question of a fundamental separation between people, but this has to be broken down, according to Beauvoir. She saw the pure *pour-soi* way of life, or rather pure negativity and individuality, as morally reprehensible. We can now make up the balance of Beauvoir's perception of love. We have already seen that love was made possible by means of emotion, which brings about an incarnation in which man becomes a psychophysiological unity. This is how he is able to meet the other as other subjectivity—a meeting that was impossible for Sartre. We can conclude that to Beauvoir the experience of emotion is a moral attitude. "What is called vitality, sensitivity, and intelligence are not ready-made qualities, but a way of casting oneself into the world and of disclosing being" (EA: 41).

Thus, love emerges as a moral attitude in which man takes on his ontological freedom. Given this backdrop, Beauvoir's point of departure in *The Second Sex* of the possibility of real love becomes understandable. Love is generosity of body and consciousness ("*générosité de corps et âme*"; LDS II: 168). It is a victory over the human tendency to bad faith: through his desire to be, man has a tendency to use his fellow beings as mirror and extension of himself. But if he assumes his *néant* nature, his lack and his situatedness, he can meet the other. If we accept ourselves and the other as separate and free human individuals, and do not use the other to make up our lack, then love, tenderness, and sensuality are possible: "the dimension, the relation of the other still exists; but the fact is that alterity has no longer a hostile implication" (TSS II: 422). The Self-Other structure of human contact remains present (after all, our *pour-soi* is always the basis of our existence), and has to be broken down time and again. Thus, real love is a moral attitude which has to be substantiated continually.

Beauvoir also raised the possibility of love and solidarity in existentialism as a a moral attitude in her article *L'existentialisme et la sagesse des nations* (1948). It is said that existentialism is a cheerless and pessimistic philosophy. But aren't prevalent opinions, such as those expressed in popular proverbs, extremely cheerless? Notions such as we shouldn't stick our necks out too far, that everyone should look after his own backyard, that you have to make your own happiness, that we cannot expect too much from others, that happiness does not exist and love and friendship are an illusion? Existentialism argues that man himself can shape his relationship to the other. Love, friendship, and fellowship are not given in advance, but have to be won continually. That is the real reason why existentialism arouses perturbation: not because it despairs of man, but because it asks of him a continual effort.

We can now answer the question on whether Beauvoir's thinking implies Sartre's theory should be burnt at the stake. This turns out not to be the case. We have already seen that Beauvoir broke through Sartre's practical solipsism. We can now conclude that she also retained it in part. In my view, it is useful here to introduce a distinction between an "emotional" and a so-called "intellectual" practical solipsism.[16] We can then state that Beauvoir eliminated Sartre's emotional solipsism, but not his intellectual practical solipsism, i.e., his point of departure that consciousnesses in pure form cannot meet each other. Beauvoir spoke emphatically of a conversion and not of an *Aufhebung* of ontological freedom to indicate that ontological freedom, or the *pour-soi* nature of man, continues to exist. It is not our *pour-soi* which is seen by the other, but our existence-in-the-world, as situated person. "*Il ne s'agit pas, comme le croit Hegel, de faire reconnaître en nous, la pure forme abstraite de moi*" (PC: 339). Thus, people cannot meet each other without the incarnated dimension, i.e., on a pure intellectual level. This intellectual practical solipsism brought Beauvoir to the proposition that no universality can be attributed to one's own value judgments and that a generalized moral theory has no right of existence. After all, we cannot speak for another on a purely intellectual level. At the conclusion of *Must We Burn De*

Sade? she stated we cannot elevate our opinions to universal law because "every person is imprisoned in his own skin and cannot become the mediator between separate persons from whom he himself is separated" (MBS: 86).

Intellectual practical solipsism, i.e., the fact that I can never know the subjectivity of the other as such, implies I cannot speak in his name or for him. But this intellectual solipsism in Beauvoir does not go hand in hand with an emotional solipsism, as is the case in Sartre. An intellectual solipsism and living ties with fellow beings are very reconcilable in Beauvoir. The fact that I cannot know the other on an intellectual level does not mean I cannot meet him in the physical-emotional dimension. There is an intersubjective contact at this level, which is the location of the moral dimension.

In this way Beauvoir has solved the dilemma of Sartre's theory, i.e., the impossibility of an intersubjective and genuinely moral relationship with fellow beings, without eliminating the sting of Sartre's practical solipsism. With the concept of "willing oneself free," she introduced a specific place for the moral dimension, and thus for a specific type of ethics. By willing himself free, man accepts the fact he is dependent on the existence of the people around him, and he practices a moral relationship with them. At the same time, he endorses his ever-present *pour-soi* nature and the fact that he creates his own values, while accepting that a generalized theory of morals is impossible by definition. As early as 1941, Beauvoir formulated the impossibility of *"prendre dans son action un point de vue moral sur autrui (du point de vue d'autrui)"* (JG: 367). Her ethics continued to be coupled to this fundamental rejection of a generally applicable morality.

Thus, she was shocked when shown the text of a series of conversations an older Sartre had with the Maoist Benny Lévy, alias Victor, and that were published against her will in *Le nouvel observateur* (in 1980). In these conversations, Sartre rejected out of hand his former point of departure on the fundamental separation between people, and called his ideas tendentious. He now proposed a morality based on "brotherhood between all people." He called this morality the ultimate goal of a revolution and even talked about a messianism (see Bair, 1990a: 579 ff; AFS: 119 ff). Beauvoir heard here the phrases of the Maoist Lévy and considered the whole project as a betrayal of the original Sartre: "This vague, yielding philosophy that Victor attributed to him did not suit Sartre at all" (AFS: 119). She was especially eager to see that the sting from Sartre's thinking was preserved—the notion we called intellectual practical solipsism, and which by definition is contrary to messianic messages such as Maoism.

Commentaries

Simone de Beauvoir's contribution to ethics has gone almost unremarked in philosophical circles. The odd study, such as Anderson (1979), reports the importance of Beauvoir's work in the field of ethics, but still considers her Sartre's exegete: *her* work is said to form the proof that *his* theory comprises an ethics. In feminist theory Beauvoir's own philosophical ethics has yet to be explored. The ambiguity of Beauvoir's ethics is neglected here. In their interpretation of her ethical theory, feminist theorists either neglect her emphasis on the ties between people,[17] or her preservation of Sartre's intellectual practical solipsism. This oversight leads Singer (1985) to state unequivocally that *The Ethics of Ambiguity* comprises an ethics of care. The work is interpreted from the perspective Gilligan applies in her study *In a Different Voice* (1985). She presupposes a specific morality of women in which the subject is fundamentally oriented toward the other, this in contrast to the morality of men in which the subject is totally sovereign. It is a fact that Beauvoir placed great emphasis on ties with fellow beings, and that this is a very different approach from Sartre's stress on the sovereign individual. But she also held firm to an individualism and to the Sartrean perception that we can never speak for another. Her ethics is therefore far from Gilligan's morality of caring.

Hansen (1979) also eliminates the Sartrean sting from Beauvoir's thinking. She bases this on Beauvoir's concept of "situation" in *Pyrrhus et Cinéas*, which represents man as unity of subjectivity and objectivity. According to Hansen, this means that by definition there is an intersubjective meeting between people. She thus reduces Beauvoir's theoretical insights because she identifies human existence totally as positiveness, and eliminates the *pour-soi* nature that is ever-present in the background, and that, as we have seen, makes man also negativity for Beauvoir.

In contrast, Simons (1987) has an eye for Beauvoir's ambiguous view of humanity. She also picks up on the fact that Beauvoir herself called her ethics ambiguous. But she makes no connection between the continuing presence of negativity in man conceived by Beauvoir and her *type* of ethics, i.e., the fact that to her it is diametrically opposed to a universal abstract morality. Like Singer, Simons considers Beauvoir's ethics an example of a so-called morality of caring (referring to Gilligan, 1985). However, Beauvoir's ethics cannot be reduced to this type of positive morality.

Kruks (1990) also misses Beauvoir's own theory on the fundamental ambiguity of the human condition. *The Second Sex* is said to be hopelessly inconsistent because of Beauvoir's theoretical contradictions, i.e., embracing the thinking of both Sartre and Merleau-Ponty. Beauvoir could only have escaped these if she had relinquished Sartre's concepts (see Kruks, 1990: 99 ff). Kruks does not see Beauvoir's specific reconciliation of Sartre and Merleau-Ponty.

Finally, Bair (1990a) also fails to recognize Beauvoir's own philosophizing. For Bair, Beauvoir is a complete Sartre epigone as regards philosophy. *Pyrrhus et Cinéas* is said to reflect no more than Sartre's concept of freedom (see Bair, 1990a: 270), whereas we have seen that this essay lays the basis for Beauvoir's own existentialist ethics. The fact that Beauvoir defended Sartre's original ideas against Benny Lévy is for Bair no more than a sign of Beauvoir's glorification of the early Sartre (see p. 579 ff). The essay on Sade is said to have justifiably aroused the anger of feminist critics. It is seen as inconsistent and contradictory, a hotchpotch of existential philosophy, trendy psychoanalysis, and an ill-considered view of pornography (see p. 662). Beauvoir stressed to Bair that her collection *Privilèges*, in which the Sade essay occupies an important place, can be considered as an introduction to her philosophy (see p. 662). And indeed this essay appears characteristic of her view on the ambiguity of human existence, i.e., for her idea that love can break down the separation between people although it remains present in the background.

To conclude, it should be noted that Beauvoir herself claimed her ideas only did justice to Sartre's actual intentions. In *The Ethics of Ambiguity* she argues that "in *Being and Nothingness* Sartre has insisted above all on the abortive aspect of the human adventure" (EA: 11) and that he had described primarily an attitude of bad faith (see p. 52). Sartre was said to have implied that the original attitude of consciousness is bad faith, but that this can be replaced by an attitude of good faith in which we can achieve a positive reciprocal relationship with the other. Arntz (1960) and Jeanson (1947) also attempt to show that, in principle, *Being and Nothingness* offers space for a bond with fellow beings, and therefore for morality.

Arntz, whose dissertation *Love in Sartre's Ontology* (1960) occupies a lonely height in the Dutch reception of Sartre's work, refers to a trio of very brief formulations in *Being and Nothingness*, in which Sartre points out the necessity of ethics.[18] *Being and Nothingness* is said to describe only an attitude of bad faith, which man assumes spontaneously through his *désir d'être*, and to imply a moral appeal to relinquish this attitude in order to adopt a positive one toward the other via a purifying reflection. Moreover, a moral point of view is required to make speaking of "bad" faith possible; thus *Being and Nothingness* in its totality is said to imply an ethics. In his *Le problème moral et la pensée de Sartre* (1947), Jeanson reasons in a similar fashion. Sartre's ontology is said to describe the natural attitude of man only, and to contain a call for the relinquishment of this attitude through purifying reflection. The same applies to love, which is "a hard won reconquest against all the temptations of false tenderness. The first maxim of morality could be: 'Beware of tenderness' " (Jeanson, 1980: 173).

But it is questionable whether Sartre's own emphasis on the necessity of an ethics is adequate proof of its presence in his existential philosophy. Even the posthumously published *Cahiers pour une morale* (1983) do not get us any further. The *Cahiers* reflect Sartre's failed attempts to reconcile his growing Marxism with the ontology of *Being and Nothingness*. In these unsystematic notes (Kraüs [1989] calls them a *"monologue intérieur"*), made in 1947, Sartre himself said *Being and Nothingness* only describes the bad faith attitude that has to be transformed into a moral attitude through purifying reflection. But, as others have remarked (Hunyadi, 1985; Kraüs, 1989; Kruks, 1986; Struyker Boudier, 1987), his text exhibits all the traces of a struggle to reconcile this notion with his original ontology. When the freedom of one means the death of the freedom of another, how can there be any question of a reconciliation of freedoms, or rather of a coexistence with fellow beings?

Sartre himself considered the whole *Cahiers* project a failure and put it aside in order to concentrate on something else.[19] The solution both Arntz and Jeanson put forward, arguing for the presence of an ethics in Sartre's existential philosophy, is totally inadequate because the possibility of contact with fellow beings is not supported. Both authors treat only the moral task of focusing on the other in good faith by means of purifying reflection. But in itself, this does not appear to solve the isolation of Sartre's *pour-soi*. After all, purifying reflection implies the transcending presence of consciousness and can only impede contact with the other. For the ability to enter into direct contact with the other, reflection and good faith do not seem to be by any means the most useful tools. They are inadequate for salvaging the moral dimension in Sartre because they do not imply we *can* enter into effective ties with our environment. The well-intentioned attempts of Jeanson and Arntz only take us further from home. They cannot contribute to the solution of what can apply as the real dilemma in Sartre's theory—the impossibility of contact with our fellow man.

We have seen that Beauvoir did more to "salvage" the moral dimension for existential philosophy. She broke down Sartre's creed on internal negation on the point of emotion. In her work, emotion appears as a psychophysiological positive, rather than as a negating act of consciousness, and only then are a meeting with fellow beings and the bonding of the individual to his environment possible. The elimination of Sartre's emotional practical solipsism can thus be considered as Beauvoir's most important amendment to his theory. She has managed to retain the sting from Sartre's existential philosophy and to achieve a reconciliation between that existentialist barb and a moral perspective. *Faut-il brûler Sartre?* Beauvoir's answer proves very subtle.

5

FORMS OF ETHICS

Freedom for all

In the previous chapter we saw how Beauvoir reconciled existential philosophy with love: her conception of emotion as positive psychophysiological experience broke down Sartre's practical solipsism and made
possible the existence of intersubjective relationships, thereby creating
space for love, solidarity, and friendship, which proved to be a moral attitude; not only did her ideas have space for morality, but the moral dimension emerged as their central theme.

In this chapter we will examine how Beauvoir treated the moral dimension in the different phases of her work.

First, we will look at the form the moral dimension assumes in *The
Ethics of Ambiguity*, a collection of essays that appeared in 1947. In this
work, the normative dimension proved subject to boundaries through a
specific delineation of the intersubjective space (the *pour-soi* continued to
work in the background); there was no place for abstract morality. By
definition, ethics proved to be linked to the situated existence of the real
person, i.e., the emotional dimension of human existence. Beauvoir
clearly rejected the Kantian type of ethics, which knows absolute moral

laws. Yet, on closer inspection, her ideas show certain similarities to Kant's. During a conversation with her biographer, Bair, Beauvoir said Kant was her inspiration in this period, then added that she was only influenced by his style of argument, and not by his ethics as such (see Bair, 1990a: 271).

Let us look at the extent of that influence. Beauvoir called "willing oneself free" explicitly a moral act of will (EA: 25), and spoke in this sense of man's "good will," a term that refers directly to Kant's moral theory. When man wills himself free, he wills himself moral, and he does what, based on his freedom, he is *obliged* to do (p. 159). Like Kant, Beauvoir believed we have to subordinate the original spontaneity of our intentions and motives to a moral will. But that will is not only dictated by duty, as in Kant, but also by self-interest.

As our actions only have meaning when they are given meaning by other, i.e., free, people, striving after the freedom of others is in our own interest. Man can only find a justification of his own existence through the free existence of others: "he needs such a justification; there is no escaping it" (p. 72). It is this, and not "an abstract law," that leads existential morality to condemn conflict and tyranny, and to strive after the freedom of others. Their freedom is to our advantage, and that is why we concern ourselves with them. Beauvoir then questioned whether ethics is at issue here: "It may perhaps be said that it is for *himself* that [man] is moral, and that such an attitude is egotistical. But there is no ethics against which this charge, which immediately destroys itself, can not be leveled; for how can I worry about what does not concern me? I concern others and they concern me. There we have an irreducible truth" (p. 72). According to Beauvoir all morality can be traced back to self-interest; however, this does not mean we do not have a moral will.

But why does she raise the necessity of freedom of *all* others? Wouldn't it be enough if all the people in our immediate surroundings were free? Anderson (1979) argues Beauvoir fails to show this. Kruks (1990) believes Stone (1987) has provided a satisfactory answer: in principle, we can become involved in some way with everyone, and that is why the freedom of all is essential (see Kruks, 1990: 199). Stone attempts to prove Beauvoir's reasoning as logical necessity: our freedom is interdependent by definition, and we cannot be free if others are not, because interdependence is so far-reaching that the unfreedom of every other person is disadvantageous to ourselves. The examples he puts forward here speak for themselves: the worker who agrees with imperialistic wars maintains the possibility of moving capital to low-wage countries and thus undermines his own position on the labor market; the man who leaves all the household chores to his working wife disadvantages himself, because he maintains a system of superexploitation of women whereby their position on the labor market is weakened and the wages they can contribute to the household budget remain low (see Stone, 1987: 131). However, Stone only examines people's economic interests, and does not produce convincing arguments against the notion that other interests can play a role in concurring with oppressive structures. In my view, the *necessity* of freedom for all cannot be theoretically underpinned; we should see it purely as the stipulative rule in Beauvoir's ethics.

The universal principle of pursuing freedom for all is the point to which Beauvoir referred when she said she was influenced by Kant's *style of reasoning*. Kant formulated a so-called categorical imperative: that which we desire for ourselves should also be desired for others. Beauvoir applied this universal rule to the moral principle of having to will ourselves free; she argued that we strive after freedom not only for ourselves but also for others when we endorse freedom as such. Beauvoir simply *advanced* the desire for freedom for all as the central moral principle. She herself talked of a "moral exigence" (EA: 87). It is this universal principle that makes her theory of "willing oneself free" into an ethics. It functions as a demarcating moral code; it determines what is good and bad, what is moral and immoral. If "willing ourselves free" is to be a moral attitude, then placing ourselves in the service of freedom for all people is the general principle to which we must keep. She stated explicitly that we can only enter into specific ties of friendship and solidarity, but if these are to be of a moral nature, they must not "contradict the will for universal solidarity" (p. 144).

Another important point in Beauvoir's ethical writings of the mid-1940s is her linking of man's ontological freedom (his *pour-soi* nature) with his *social* situation.

> There are beings whose life slips by in an infantile world because, having been kept in a state of servitude and ignorance, they have no means of breaking the ceiling which is stretched over their heads. . . . This is the case, for example, of slaves who have not raised themselves to the consciousness of their slavery. . . . This is also the situation of women in many civilizations; they can only submit to the laws, the gods, the customs, and the truths created by the males. (p. 37)

> Ignorance and error are facts as inescapable as prison walls. The negro slave of the eighteenth century, the Mohammedan woman enclosed in a harem have no instrument, be it in thought or by astonishment or anger, which permits them to attack the civilization which oppresses them. Their behaviour is defined and can be judged only within this given situation. (p. 38)

Man's social situation can thus impede his ability to exercise his ontological freedom; a certain level of social freedom is a precondition here.

Beauvoir noted she and Sartre disagreed on this point. He believed
man was always free and could rise above his circumstances, whatever
they may be. In their discussions, she grudgingly admitted Sartre was
right (see PoL: 433), but held to her own view in her theoretical treatises.
This view was already present in *Pyrrhus et Cinéas* (1944), and we can
therefore conclude she was aware from the very beginning of the limitations social conditions could impose on individual freedom. In contrast,
in his 1946 lecture *L' existentialisme est un humanisme*, Sartre argued
that man can never attribute his failures to circumstance. In later work,
i.e., in *Questions de Méthode* among others, Sartre focused extensively
on the social and historical context in which an individual exercises his
freedom and creates himself.[1] He then articulated existential psychoanalysis as the complement to the Marxist method.

However, in her early philosophical essays, Beauvoir had already emphasized the influence of social circumstances on the life of individuals.
She did so without any explicit reference to Marxism, but ranked the
influence of social factors on the individual's freedom under the term
"situation." In *The Ethics of Ambiguity*, she elaborates her idea of the
necessity of social freedom into the proposition that we have to liberate
(ontological) freedom; we have to take a stand and action against every
form of oppression of our fellow human beings. The moral code of her
ethics reaches into the political arena; we have to take a stand against
injustice and oppression. Beauvoir not only made her ethics into a political one, but through her connection of ontological and social freedom,
she also gave her moral subject a social base. The subject who assumes a
moral attitude is socially situated and is not left floating in a vacuum as
in Kant. People are not automatically in a position to will themselves
free. The social circumstances have to be such that they are also *able* to
assume this attitude. We can now see that Beauvoir's perception of human existence has, in fact, three levels.

First, there is the situatedness of man as given: every person is embedded in time and place, and as such every person lives as "subjective
objectivity." But his situation can mean he is unable to experience actively and realize the *pour-soi* element he carries within. Thus, his situatedness is an absolute given, over which he can exercise no power. Man
must have a certain social freedom if he is to realize himself as *pour-soi*[2]
(the second level). Only then can he take on his freedom and actively
situate himself or, in other words, search out positive ties with others (the
third level). Access to the *pour-soi* is a precondition here: this is the background against and from which man can will himself free and actively

situate himself in a way that contributes to the freedom of others. This three-level configuration is the core of Beauvoir's own theory of human existence, a theory that comprises an ethics in a broad sense. Social freedom is an essential precondition for the realization of ontological freedom, which in its turn forms the precondition for moral freedom.[3]

In the light of Beauvoir's own theory, we can now comprehend what is at issue in *The Second Sex*. Beauvoir described reality from the point of view that woman must have the chance to experience the *pour-soi* element of her human existence. Her *pour-soi* dimension must not be suppressed because it forms the basis of her potential development into a moral subject. Beauvoir wants woman to become a moral subject who can relate in freedom to (the freedom of) others. Only in this way is an equal relationship possible between the sexes; only in this way can real love between partners, parents, and children exist. "[T]he same is true of affection as of physical love: for it to be genuine, authentic, it must first of all be free" (TSS II: 491).

Moralism

So far, we have seen how Beauvoir introduced a demarcating moral code in her book *The Ethics of Ambiguity* through the rule on the pursuit of freedom for all. But otherwise she placed every emphasis on the subjective construction of "willing oneself free." In the first and second parts of this work, Beauvoir stressed continually that, unless it is open to universal solidarity, this attitude to life is empty of content and has to be filled in by each individual. Yet, remarkably, in the third section she switches to a treatment of a "positive aspect of morality" (EA: 73). Let us examine how she goes about it.

Beauvoir stated that, although there are no fixed values or laws, certain procedural rules can help the individual person make decisions. One of these rules is that we should only respect freedom if it serves freedom, and not when it flees itself, distances itself from itself, or impedes the freedom of others. Thus, oppressing the oppressor is justified, even when it is coupled to violence and claims innocent victims. Beauvoir then brought in the dilemmas confronting the resistance movement against Nazism: should acts of resistance be committed if innocent hostages are subsequently shot in reprisal? Each war demands terrible sacrifices, but this truth is so abhorrent that it is camouflaged all too often. If, for example, one's point of departure is the essential development of history (she was referring here to Hegelianism and the Marxist communism of her day), the individual is totally subjugated to the community and moral problems emerge as technical problems only: "if the unrolling of history is fatal, there is no longer any place for the anguish of choice, or for regret, or for outrage; revolt can no longer surge up in any heart" (p. 109). But if the individual is unimportant, how can state and society have any value?

> In order for this world to have any importance, in order for our undertaking to have a meaning and to be worthy of sacrifices, we must affirm the concrete and particular thickness of this world and the individual reality of our projects and ourselves. . . . if the individual is set up as a unique and irreducible value, the word sacrifice regains all its meaning. (pp. 106–7).

Politics should always be focused on concern for the individual. In violent political actions, people are sacrificed to save others, and thus ends and means become contradictory. However, we still should not exclude altogether actions of this kind. But then well-considered, fully deliberated decisions have to be made, and the action should not be justified either dogmatically or ideologically. Politics should be an open process of considerations. We should never allow ourselves to be led by blind faith in specific ideals. We can only act according to the "rule" that we "sacrifice the people of today for those of tomorrow," because "only the future can carry on the present and keep it alive by going beyond it" (PMA: 166).

But then we should realize this future's nature is as finite and ambiguous as that of the present; a completion of history and a reconciliation between people will never take place. This also means our choices aimed at the future remain open choices. So, according to Beauvoir, we see that "Ethics does not furnish recipes any more than do science and art. One can merely propose methods" (p. 134). This method consists of a case-by-case deliberation on "what genuine human interest fills the abstract form which one proposes as the action's end," and subsequently attempts to find a balance between ends and means (p. 145).

Beauvoir summarized her method as consisting "in each case, of confronting values realized with the values aimed at, and the meaning of the act with its content" (p. 152). Thus, for example, we cannot make generalized judgments on Stalinist policies in the Soviet Union, but we have to unravel continually the relationship between ends and means, which opponents and supporters of the Soviet Union all too often failed to do. "Against the death of Bukharin one counters with Stalingrad; but one would have to know to what effective extent the Moscow trials increased the chances of the Russian victory" (pp. 146–47). Although Beauvoir noted that a calm, mathematical calculation is impossible (see p. 148), she still believed her method could, in principle, provide solutions. However, she had become caught up here in an odd contradiction. She brought in the Kantian type of moral theory she had rejected wholeheartedly in the same *Ethics of Ambiguity*; the notion that the concrete ethical choice is subject to universal moral rules. So where did this strange contradiction come from?

In my view, her article "Idéalisme moral et réalisme politique," written in 1945, offers clarification. In this article she took the Kantian type of moral theory explicitly to task. In its contemporary version, it tells people to "subject their behaviour to universal, timeless imperatives [and] to attune their actions to the great ideals which are etched into an intelligible heaven: Justice, Law and Truth" (Imrp: 37). However, such a generalized morality is sterile. It consists of no more than a collection of abstract prescriptions and offers no positive help whatsoever in making concrete decisions of the kind that have to be made, for example, at political levels.

> It is impossible—Kant has often been accused of it—to distill an exact application from the fundamental principle's universal form. The notion of Justice, the notion of Law do not map out the future world. Just as universal laws on gravity cannot suggest to an inventor plans for a flying machine, but can only indicate the preconditions for the possibility of such a machine, universal and abstract moral prescriptions can only limit the areas of action of politicians without helping them to find solutions for specific problems. (p. 38)

Not surprisingly, Beauvoir added, many politically aware people reject such a morality and proclaim themselves "realists." In antiquity, Creon and Antigone symbolized two different worlds: the temporary, earthly world and the eternal, divine world. However, today it would appear as though the conflict between them had assumed the form of two mutually exclusive attitudes in the same, earthly world; there is a continually widening rift between morality and politics. The decline of political thought into a so-called political realism, and of ethics into an absolute morality—a game that is the preserve of a very few experts—has to be broken down. Politics and ethics are, in fact, an inextricably interlinked whole.

Countless moral choices are inherent in every political action. The so-called objective aims pursued are already very specific answers to the question of how man and the world should look. Placing oneself in the political arena means making human history, means making man. Thus, politics should not become entrenched in "objective" rationales of ends-versus-means, but should realize that political aims also embrace choices. It should relinquish the certainties of a so-called objective realism.

In its turn, ethics should be concerned with the concrete actions of man and be related to the practical problems confronting him. The moralist should descend from his throne and abandon his purity. Beauvoir concluded her article with a plea for a so-called "realistic morality" (p. 55). Thus, she wanted to introduce an ethics in opposition to Kant's moral theory, which would be related to the reality of every day, and so formulated in *The Ethics of Ambiguity* positive rules for making political decisions. At the conclusion of this work, she stated literally that politics and morality should come together (EA: 131 ff.). Her notion of the possibility of a so-called realistic morality was clearly influenced by the political situation of her day. After World War II, Beauvoir became convinced that intellectuals should not remain aloof from politics or leave it to technocrats. Her attempts to reconcile politics and morality should be seen against the backdrop of the optimistic climate of the immediate postwar years, when there was a universal belief in the victory of Good, and a clear distinction between Good and Evil. This is how the formulation of unequivocal rules for Good politics appeared possible.

Using her method, Beauvoir attempted to answer the question on whether war criminals deserved the death penalty in her article "Oeil pour oeil" (1946). People want to "hit the criminal in the heart of his criminal activities" (OO: 81), but this cannot be achieved because of a lack of synchronicity in deed and legal process, through the distance between criminal and the person standing trial. Although in this thinking every legal punishment based on revenge appears doomed to failure, it does not mean we have to renounce such punishment altogether. There are cases in which the evil is an absolute evil. It should be punished in the name of the human values in which we believe, as an expression of those moral values.

Here, Beauvoir is applying her method of well-considered ends and means. But her argument hangs in a complete vacuum.[4] In retrospect, she believed her "method" for a so-called realistic morality "quite as hollow as the Kantian maxims." She was "in error when I thought I could define a morality independent of a social context" (FoC: 76). And she spoke disparagingly of "the 'moral period' of my literary career, which lasted for several years" (PoL: 547).[5]

If, in *The Ethics of Ambiguity*, Beauvoir made it seem as though all emphasis in her ethics lay on the open, well-considered decisions of the individual who "wills himself free," and represented her method only as a tool in this ethics, in retrospect she concluded she was actually advancing abstract moral formulas. In fact, positive moral codes (prescriptive rules) were introduced, such as the rule that when faced with unavoidable choices, we, the people of today, should sacrifice ourselves for those of the future. In the years after World War II, Beauvoir gradually lost her belief in the victory of Good over Evil. The attempt to establish a new social order by the former restistance groups who had once worked closely together had floundered hopelessly in dissension. Beauvoir felt "what was then called 'the failure of the Resistance' as a personal defeat; the triumphant return of bourgeois domination" (FoC: 275).

Disillusioned by this state of affairs, she reviewed her optimistic notions on the existence of an objective method that could distinguish Good and Evil: "The triumph of Good over Evil ceased to be a matter of tacit assumption; it even seemed gravely threatened" (p. 274). For the rest of her life she would resist the idea that such an absolute distinction existed. She was irritated by the Manichaeism of her friend Claude Lanzmann: "He had to be able to see his adversaries as the representatives of absolute Evil; the army of Good had to be without defect if it was to restore lost Paradise" (p. 295).

The foregoing means we cannot limit ourselves to *The Ethics of Ambiguity* in our search for the form Beauvoir's ethics assume. But where *should* we look for the continuation of her thinking on ethics? In my view, her article "Littérature et métaphysique" ("Literature and Metaphysics"), written in 1946, forms the key to answering this question: we should turn to her (ideas on) literature.

Literature and philosophy

In "Literature and Metaphysics," Beauvoir defended the existence of the so-called philosophical novel. This does not mean the novel *à thèse*, she stated, because literature should show the ambiguity of life and should not attempt to prove propositions or teach lessons.[6] However, philosophy and literature can go together in a different way. Beauvoir began her argument on a personal note: "I read a lot when I was 18. . . . When I had explored the universe with Spinoza and Kant, I wondered: 'how can people be so futile as to write novels?' But when I finished Julien Sorel or Tess d'Urberville, it seemed to me senseless to waste time constructing systems. Where did the truth lie? On earth or in eternity?" (LM: 89–90).

This is not about an or/or, she continued. As human existence has two dimensions, one universal and one bounded by time and place, it is the task of philosophy, which aims to articulate the truth of the human condition, to express *both*. Pure philosophy attempts to trace the essence of universal human existence and to represent it in abstract theoretical language. But this does not make explicit the level of the subjective—the singular and dramatic aspect of human existence. Only the literary genre has the means to achieve this. Only literature can reflect human experience in all its richness. It *shows* both the singular and the event. If it wants to give expression to the subjective dimension of the human condition, philosophy will have to link up with the literary genre. In this sense, Beauvoir talked of the "philosophical novel," or of the "*roman métaphysique*," and the "*théâtre d'idées.*"

The philosophical novel occupies the middle ground between pure philosophy and pure literature. Pure philosophy provides an intellectual reconstruction of human experience. In contrast, the novelist claims to show this experience "in its original form" (p. 91). But is the philosophical novel then not a contradiction in terms? Good literature is characterized by the author's lack of ready-made scheme; he or she is carried away by the intrigue and, with the reader, embarks upon a voyage of discovery whose end result is not determined in advance. Both writer and reader have to be willing to join the adventure. Well, if by definition philosophy consists of system building alone, then the philosophical novel is indeed an impossibility. But metaphysics also has a subjective form: all people have "metaphysical experiences" in which they experience themselves as such within the totality of the world. Such metaphysical experiences are, for example, fear, defiance, the pursuit of power, fear of death, flight, craving the absolute. According to the precepts of good literature, this dimension can be expressed in the form of a spiritual adventure. The writer should be capable of describing these experiences in their actual, concrete form, without reducing them to dry formulas (see p. 104 ff.). Unlike the psychological novel, the metaphysical novel should not only go deep into the behavior of man *tout court*, but should also show human experiences in their metaphysical dimension; it should show a kind of authenticity or essence of subjective experience.

Beauvoir argued that existentialism has a place for the singular and temporal expression offered by literature because it wants to articulate the essence of both the human condition in general and its subjective nature. "If read and written honestly, a metaphysical novel provides a revelation of existence which has no equivalent in any other form of expression" (p. 106). For Beauvoir, philosophical literature was an essential part of philosophy. In this genre, the subjective truth, i.e., the truth of concrete experiences of people in concrete situations, can be explored without molding them into abstract schemes or formulations.

In my view, "Literature and Metaphysics" should be considered as a program for the further development of her work because it reveals her preoccupation with philosophical literature. The first novel she wrote after this article was *Les Mandarins* (1954; *The Mandarins*), and we should approach it as philosophy of the subjective dimension, in which the essence of human experience in its individual and temporary form is articulated. Now, because Beauvoir also saw the subjective dimension as the location of ethics (the so-called situated dimension of human existence—see chapter 4), I would like to look at whether *The Mandarins* comprises a continuation of her thinking on ethics. We will examine this novel closely here.[7]

But caution is needed. In "Literature and Metaphysics," Beauvoir stressed more than once that intellectual reconstruction can destroy the meaning of a novel. A good novel cannot be translated into abstract terms. If this were the case, then one might as well write a treatise. Nor can the philosophical novel be reduced to formulas. For this reason, our search for ethics in *The Mandarins* will be somewhat roundabout; to avoid intellectual reductionism as much as possible, the approach will be illustrative rather than analytical, with short summaries punctuated by long quotations.

The Mandarins

According to Beauvoir, *The Mandarins* ranked with *The Second Sex* and her autobiography as her most important work (see chapter 1). It took four years of hard work to complete, but it would bring her instant fame and recognition: *The Mandarins* was awarded the Prix Goncourt, and Beauvoir was propelled out of Sartre's shadow. The novel sketches the lives of a group of left-wing intellectuals in Paris (similar to the group to which she herself belonged). The action takes place in the early years after World War II and follows the development of a number of characters during that period. Two first-person narrators, the writer Henri Perron and the psychiatrist Anne Dubreuilh, tell the story in alternating chapters.

In the first chapters, both attempt to pick up the threads of their prewar lives. Both grasp at old certainties from that earlier time, but these are gradually undermined. Anne's mainstay in life was her marriage to writer and political commentator Robert Dubreuilh. For Henri it was the once-underground newspaper, *L'Espoir*, of which he is still editor-in-chief. However, on a trip to America Anne starts an affair and has to make a decision about her marriage, while Henri has to decide on the paper's future course. Their choices take the form of an open moral deliberation. Both are aware "Good" does not exist; every well-intentioned choice also brings an evil with it. Anne decides to remain with her husband, but by doing so damages her relationship with her American lover who finally ends the affair. Grief-stricken, she contemplates suicide, but ultimately allows her sense of responsibility to friends and family to prevail. Henri's decision results in his forced resignation from the paper.

He chooses to immerse himself completely in writing, but is ultimately caught up in politics once again, and finally remains faithful to his political engagement.

The Mandarins is constructed around a number of moral dilemmas confronting the main characters, which is a first indication of the validity of our assumption that Beauvoir pursued her thinking on ethics in this work. Fallaize (1980) also points out *The Mandarins* is concerned to a major extent with moral choices,[8] in the sense of, how should I act? Ethical decisions are central to the story. Let us first examine in detail those Henri has to make.[9] Henri's loss of *L'Espoir* is brought about by a conflict with his friend Robert Dubreuilh. Dubreuilh had worked on Henri and persuaded him to affiliate the paper to the political party, the SRL, that Dubreuilh had founded. The SRL's aim was to offer a so-called third alternative to capitalism and communism, i.e., an alternative to the United States and the Soviet Union. Any loss of readers would be compensated by a well-intentioned financier. Dubreuilh assures Henri his editorial freedom is guaranteed, but it soon appears the financier wants to exert his own influence and steer the paper toward the right. In the meantime, Henri and Dubreuilh have received irrefutable evidence of the existence of mass concentration camps in the Soviet Union. Should they publish? Dubreuilh refuses. In the prevalent political climate, publication would mean a definitive shift of *L'Espoir* and the SRL to the right. The financier demands publication. Henri has to make a decision that means he risks losing either his paper or his friendship with Dubreuilh.

> There were camps in which fifteen million workers were being reduced to a subhuman state, but thanks to those camps Nazism had been defeated and a great country was being built, a country which held out the only hope for a thousand million subhumans slowly dying of hunger in China and India, the only hope for millions of workers enslaved to inhuman conditions, our only hope. . . . "Is that why I'm taking refuge in doubt?" he asked himself. "Am I rejecting the evidence out of cowardice because the air wouldn't be breathable if there were no longer a corner of the earth towards which mankind could turn with a little confidence? Or, on the other hand," he thought, "maybe I'm cheating by complacently accepting those horrifying pictures. Unable to rally to Communism, it would be a relief to hate it resolutely. If only you could be completely for, or completely against! But to be against, you've got to have other hopes to offer mankind. And it's only too evident that revolution will come about through the Soviet Union, or there'll be no revolution. And yet, if Russia has merely substituted one system of oppression for another, if she's established slavery, how can one have the least friendship for her? . . . Perhaps evil is everywhere," Henri said to himself. He remembered that night in a shelter in the Cévennes Mountains when he had

voluptuously drowsed off in innocent delight. But if evil were every-
where, innocence didn't exist. Whatever he did, he'd be wrong: wrong if
he printed a garbled truth; wrong if he hid the truth, even though it was
garbled. He went down to the walk alongside the river. If evil is every-
where, there's no way out, neither for humanity nor for oneself. Would
he have come around to thinking that? He sat down and in a daze
watched the water flowing by. (M: 400–401)

There is a brief respite, but Henri Perron is ultimately faced with the decision.

He didn't want the Communists to see him as an enemy, and, more important, he would have liked to hide from himself the fact that in Russia,
too, something was rotten. But all that was nothing but cowardice. He
got up and walked down the stairs. "A Communist would have the right
to choose silence," he thought. "His positions have been stated, and even
when he lies, he's not, in a way, deceiving anyone. But I, who profess to
independence, if I use my credit to stifle the truth, I'm a swindler. I'm not
a Communist precisely because I want to be free to say what the Communists don't want to say and can't say." (p. 493)

Henri makes a decision. "The article appeared the next morning. . . .
That evening, a messenger brought Dubreuilh's letter. The Committee of
the SRL had expelled Perron and Samazelle; the movement no longer had
any connection with *L'Espoir*" (pp. 500–501).

The paper is embraced by the right. The communists malign Henri.
Moreover, he becomes entangled in blackmail. The young actress with
whom he is having an affair turns out to have been the mistress of a German officer during the war. Henri decides to prevent this affair's becoming public knowledge, whatever the cost. He is forced to perjure himself,
and through Henri's failure to tell the truth, a former Gestapo informer
is freed. The affair leaks out in a small circle, and leads to the loss of
support of Henri's few remaining loyal coworkers at *L'Espoir*. The other
editors want to shift allegiance to the right. Henri is against this move
and is forced to resign. In the meantime, Dubreuilh's political party has
also folded. The concept of a third alternative has failed.

We have seen how Henri's choice emerged from his personal identity
and professional conduct. A communist could have remained silent. "But
I, who profess to independence [in my work[10]], if I use my credit to stifle
the truth, I'm a swindler" (p. 493). Earlier in the story Henri had also
referred to his specific identity and professional ethos:

"I admit that under certain conditions telling the truth can be a luxury.
That may well be the case in Russia," he said, smiling. "But in France,
today, I don't recognize anyone's right to suppress the truth. Maybe it

isn't so simple for a politician, but I'm not on the side of those who are doing the manoeuvring; I'm with the ones they are trying to manoeuvre. They count on me to keep them informed of what's happening as well as I can, and if I remain silent or if I lie I'd be betraying them." (p. 170).

And when, at the end of the book, he decides to allow politics back into his life instead of devoting himself to writing in the Italian countryside, this again forms a reinforcement of his chosen identity and life's work as a politically committed writer. The certainty of always doing the right thing has vanished, the hope of achieving good in the form of the Soviet Union has been dashed, and his notion of becoming a writer in the service of world peace has proved unfeasible. But this does not mean political action has disappeared from Henri's agenda. In Italy,

> as in Paris, the whole earth would be present around him, with its miseries, its crimes, its injustices. He could spend the rest of his life fleeing and he would never find a refuge. He would read the papers, he would listen to the radio, he would receive letters. All he could gain would be that he could say to himself, "There's nothing I can do." Suddenly, something exploded inside his chest. No. The solitude that was suffocating him that evening, that mute impotence, that wasn't what he wanted. No. He would never consent to say to himself for the rest of his life, "Everything is happening without me." Nadine had seen through him: not for a moment had he really chosen that exile. He suddenly realised that for days he had been suffering the thought with dread. (p. 755).

The loss of the socialist ideal, and also the disappearance of political certainties, does not mean political action has become superfluous. Henri concludes that it is not enough to say that history is sad in every way: "It is essential that it be more or less sad" (p. 734). He chooses based on the fundamental moral choices inherent to his existence and remains true to them. The choice of the other main character, the psychiatrist Anne, not to take her own life but to assume her responsibilities to her fellow human beings, both now and in the future, is also consistent with her identity and professional ethics: her fundamental choice as psychiatrist is to try to make other people's lives more bearable and to alleviate their suffering.

Dubreuilh also remains true to his (professional) identity. His doubts increase as the story progresses, but he continues faithful to his fundamental life-project of politically committed writer, even though his own analysis is that the role of the intellectual in the political force field is played out. He sets up a new weekly magazine, and again involves Henri. When the two have been reconciled, Henri admits his perjury to Dubreuilh:

"I'm certain Josette would have done away with herself. Could I let her die?" he asked vehemently.

"No," Dubreuilh said. He seemed perplexed. "You must have had a difficult moment!"

"I made up my mind almost immediately," Henri said. He shrugged his shoulders. "I don't say I'm proud of what I did."

"Do you know what it proves, this story?" Dubreuilh said with sudden animation. "That personal morality just doesn't exist. Another one of those things we used to believe in and which have no meaning."

"You think so?" Henri said. He very definitely didn't care for the kind of consolation Dubreuilh was dispensing today. "True, I found myself trapped," he went on. "At that particular moment, I no longer had any choice. But nothing would have happened if I hadn't had that affair with Josette. I suppose that's where the fault lies." (pp. 645–46).

Dubreuilh replies, saying a proper life in an improper society is an impossibility.

"No personal salvation possible."

Henri looked at Dubreuilh uncertainly. "Then what's left to us?"

"Not very much I'm afraid," Dubreuilh replied.

There was a silence. Henri didn't feel satisfied with that generalised indulgence. "What I'd like to know is what you would have done in my place," he said.

"I can't tell you, because I wasn't in your place," Dubreuilh replied. "You'd have to tell me everything in detail," he added.

"I'll tell you everything," Henri said. (p. 646).

Henri does not share Dubreuilh's conclusion that a personal ethics is meaningless. Both men finally decide to explore the specificity of Henri's concrete moral dilemma in order to form an opinion.

Thus, the notion of a "personal ethics" in the form of a personal identity that is shaped by a specific life-project emerges from *The Mandarins*. Beauvoir even introduces a separate term for this type of project. One of the young people in Henri's circle, Lambert, for whom Henri has an exemplary function, urges him to write novels that can provide a leitmotiv for personal actions: "First of all, we need an ethics, an art of living[11] (*art de vivre*)" (p. 180). And later Lambert says, "You have a sense of what is real. You ought to teach us how to live for the moment."

Henri protests:

"Formulating an ethics, an art of living, doesn't exactly enter into my plans."

His eyes shining, Lambert looked up at Henri. "Oh, I stated that badly. I wasn't thinking of a theoretical treatise. But there are things that you consider important, there are values you believe in." (p. 182).

Henri finally decides he has to start writing again to encourage Lambert and others to see the world through his eyes.

Beauvoir introduced the concept "art of living" here as an equivalent to ethics. Our hypothesis that in *The Mandarins* she pursues her thinking on ethics is thus confirmed. Not only are moral decisions the central theme in the novel, we also see the emergence of a specific type of ethics. The concept "art of living" expresses in compact form how moral decisions are made; it not only articulates the fact that ethics takes on the form of a concrete, individual approach to life, but also represents the attitude that moral decisions come about in a continual creative process without the application of general methods, moral laws, or rules. The ethos in *The Mandarins* is completely open: the moral code has been pushed into the background. The only trace of a moral code here is the socialist conviction of all the main characters, which for them implies they strive after social freedom for everyone. The moral principle of freedom from oppression for all is no longer present in the form of positive rules for political action—Henri and Dubreuilh have no rules whatsoever to guide their political decision making. The principle of striving for everyone's freedom is there, but only in the background, as demarcating moral code.

At the end of *The Ethics of Ambiguity*, Beauvoir characterized "willing oneself free" as a *"mouvement constructif"* (i.e., man does not exist without action) and as a *"mouvement négatif"* (i.e., rejecting oppression of both the self and the other) (PMA: 226). But it is only in her later work that Beauvoir really drew the consequences of this idea. The moralistic form that the principle of "willing oneself free" still had in *The Ethics of Ambiguity*—that of absolute positive moral rules—is missing entirely: in her later oeuvre, the universal moral principle only acquired form as a *negative* moral code stating that we have to reject every oppression of freedom. Solidarity and responsibility remained absolute values for her (PoL: 547), and she continued to emphasize that existentialism is not a nihilistic philosophy (see FoC: 75).

In her introduction to *The Second Sex*, Beauvoir stated that in writing the book she applied existentialist ethics (TSS I: 28–29). And apart from *The Second Sex*, later writings, such as lectures on feminism, the article "La pensée de droite, aujourd'hui" and the study *Old Age* criticize sociopolitical processes and structures that impede the freedom of people. What we have here is an absolute political stance. Beauvoir said she was Manichaeistic in a political sense and did not scruple to adopt an absolute position (see Jeanson, 1966: 276). But this universal moral principle is only found in the form of "negative" reasoning: freedom (including women's) may not be limited or denied.

In elaborating her ethics, Beauvoir ultimately drew the consequences of her ethics of ambiguity: she abandoned every notion of a positive general morality. The universal side of her ethics is only found in the form of a negative moral code, which states that no person may be oppressed. After her moralistic period, Beauvoir's ethics breaks down into a positive art of living and a negative moral code. In the following chapter we will round out the contours of her thinking on ethics as art of living.

Commentaries

In conclusion, it should be noted that the literary philosophical genre of *The Mandarins* is usually ignored. Beauvoir herself said her literary work was inspired by the direct narrative techniques of modern American writers, such as Dos Passos, Faulkner, and Hemingway. She found especially appealing Hemingway's style, which in tone and rhythm remained close to spoken language (see PoL: 345).[12] In *The Mandarins* she also wanted to stay close to normal idiom; she wasn't interested in a "good style" and, she admitted, was more concerned with the effectiveness of her dialogues than with pure literary content (see FoC: 284). This can now be understood against the backdrop of her attitudes on philosophical literature, which always has other aims than pure literature.

Those critics who accuse her of an indifferent literary style tend to miss the point.[13] Beauvoir was not about literature as such. Nathalie Sarraute condemned *The Mandarins* for its traditionalism, but Beauvoir was not interested in the "*nouveau roman*" style. Writers of such literature turn away from the world and lock themselves up in a "maniacal and untruthful subjectivism" (FoC: 284). Beauvoir stated emphatically that *The Mandarins* was no novel à *thèse* because it suggested no solutions. The book's aim was to show truth in all its ambiguity and contradictions (see FoC: 197, 282). Selle (1980) does not distinguish between the thesis novel and the metaphysical novel, and so concludes incorrectly that Beauvoir used the metaphysical novel in an attempt to illustrate preconceived philosophical ideas. Beauvoir was said to have departed from this approach to literature only *after The Mandarins*, which was seen as containing an all-knowing narrator. Selle thus ranks this book with earlier novels. In my view, she misses the point of the work, which can be summarized as: ethical decisions are open by definition.

Fallaize (1980) shows that the narrative structure of *The Mandarins* is characterized by the fact that the external narrator is almost completely absorbed by the main characters' perspective, so his power is greatly reduced: "With a few exceptions . . . the narrator does not offer opinions or information outside the character's knowledge or competence" (p. 225). Beauvoir herself said the double narrative structure (two main characters who narrate events, turn and turn about) served to bring out the ambiguity of truth (see FoC: 276–77). Fallaize disagrees because Anne's and Henri's opinions on people and events are such extensions of each other that they express the same truths. She adds that this is hardly surprising as Beauvoir admitted both characters were semiautobiographical. The sole function of the double narrative structure was to replace an external narrator: the objective story would emerge through the illumination of one main character through the eyes of the other, and vice versa. Thus, *The Mandarins* could not avoid didacticism (Fallaize, 1980: 230).

In my view Fallaize's notion that the ambiguity of truths would only emerge if the perspectives of the two main characters were different is incorrect. Beauvoir stated that the points of view of the Anne and Henri characters are not symmetrical, but sometimes confirm, refine, or contradict each other (see FoC: 277). In this way, the truths of each character are questioned. The double narrative structure of *The Mandarins* is aimed not so much at showing the contradictions between two different sets of truths, but more at the ambiguity of truths as such. Fallaize's suggestion that this structure replaces an omnipotent narrator and turns *The Mandarins* into a novel *à thèse*, seems unjustified. Beauvoir rejected the idea that her book comprised a message: "I showed some people, at grips with doubts and hopes, groping in the dark to find their way; I cannot think I proved anything" (FoC: 283).

The Mandarins is also often considered a key novel. People see, and not without cause, in the characters of Anne, Henri, and Dubreuilh, traces of Beauvoir herself, of writer Albert Camus, and of Sartre, respectively. Ernst van Altena, who did an excellent job of translating the book into Dutch, believes that, through her portrayal of Henri as a man of too few principles, Beauvoir was taking revenge on Camus (van Altena, 1983: 720).[14] Beauvoir rejected the idea of the book as a key novel. "The extent and the manner of the fiction's dependence upon real life is of small importance; the fiction is built only by pulverizing all these sources and then allowing a new existence to be reborn from them" (FoC: 280). Her objection is aimed at the reduction of *The Mandarins* to no more than a key novel. In fact, it should be seen as a philosophical novel and evaluated accordingly.

6

ETHICS AS ART OF LIVING

In the previous chapter we found that, following Beauvoir's so-called moralistic period, her ethics could be divided into a negative moral code and an ethos in the form of an art of living. In this chapter I would like to concentrate on her art-of-living concept and further specify its characteristics.

As early as *The Ethics of Ambiguity*, Beauvoir's ethics was an attitude to life ("willing oneself free") that had to be created by the individual, but so-called methodical rules as tools were still in evidence. We saw how Beauvoir later rejected the idea of methodical rules and in her further work, especially *The Mandarins*, ethics took on the form of a fully open ethos (with the moral code continuing to work in the background). Thus, she drew the consequences of her argument in *The Ethics of Ambiguity*—that a positive ethics is always ambiguous. When making an inventory of Beauvoir's thinking on ethics after her moralistic period, we can therefore use as a guideline her expatiation in *The Ethics of Ambiguity*, while leaving aside the moralistic form the ethical attitude to life was still given there in the form of so-called methodical rules.

If we want to specify Beauvoir's art-of-living ethics, we will have to discover *on behalf of what* it works, what its *substance* is, what its *means* are, and what its immanent *aim* is. Thus, we are asking, why, what, how, and to what end (for this approach, see chapter 1). In compiling this inventory, we will use a comparison with related concepts in Sartre's work. Once this approach has given us an extensive definition of Beauvoir's so-called art-of-living ethics, we can then compare her thinking again with Sartre's existentialism so that the individuality of her philosophy will be supported clearly.

Why?

If we first attempt to chart on behalf of what the art-of-living ethics operates, then we find Beauvoir's philosophy of human freedom, which she developed in the early 1940s, plays a prominent role. Like Sartre, Beauvoir believed man has no essence, but creates himself. Through his *néant* nature—his ontological freedom (see chapter 3)—man is no thing with ready-made characteristics. His freedom means he has to create himself. But, unlike Sartre, Beauvoir concentrated from the very beginning on the social dimension of human existence and emphasized the fact that man has to shape his freedom by entering into ties with other people. We have already seen how she introduced the notion of "willing oneself free," analogous to Kant's concept of "good will." If we "will ourselves free," then we accept that we are "nothing" and only exist in relation to the world around us and the people in that world. In other words, we practice our original freedom by transforming it into a concrete engagement, chosen by ourselves.

After her moralistic period, Beauvoir's thinking on ethics built on this perception from her earlier work. She retained the idea that, because of his freedom, man has to create himself through moral commitment. However, he no longer does this through applying a universal moral method, but through designing for himself a coherent, practical way of life, thus creating an identity for himself. In *The Mandarins*, Henri wonders who he really is. That had been unnecessary in the past because his life was still in front of him.

> But now, he had to admit to himself that he was a mature man: young people treated him as an elder, adults as one of them, and some even treated him with respect. Mature, bounded, finite, himself and no one else, nothing but himself. But who was he? In a way, his books would ultimately decide; but on the other hand, he had to know the truth about himself in order to write them. (M: 185)

Henri makes it his aim to discover who he is. However, he is not concerned here with discovering a given, existing identity. We have seen that in Beauvoir man is ambiguous. Even in the situated, emotional dimension, where man is a unity of body and consciousness, there is still no question of a coherent identity. After all, we can be overwhelmed by conflicting emotions. Beauvoir considers man an open collection of heterogenous elements. His life is "pulverized by events, scattered, broken" (FoC: 287). However, it is man's task to bring together that abundance of elements into a unity. Man has to *capture* a coherent identity for himself by continually tackling his own life. His existence has to be "won constantly" (EA: 129).

In two lectures, "Que peut la littérature?" (1965) and "Mon expérience d'écrivain" (1966), Beauvoir emphasized that human life is fragmented, or "detotalized": we are never the total of our experiences. The one emotion will always escape us as we experience another. Nor is memory capable of forging the diversity of all moments into a unity. Only literature can succeed in reconciling the irreconcilability of all our experiences. Literature is able to pursue two themes simultaneously just as a symphony develops various themes at the same time. In *The Prime of Life*, Beauvoir stated in so many words that man can save his own existence through literature (FA: 83). Literature is the means by which we can appropriate an identity of our own based on our myriad experiences.

Henri concludes that he needs writing in order to feel really alive (M: 184). We now understand why: writing is self-creation. However, this does not concern the creation of a psychological entity. Henri realizes that "the truth of one's life is outside oneself, in events, in other people, in things; to talk about oneself, one must talk about everything else" (p. 341). Beauvoir never lost her disgust for the 'inner-self'. The I is a construction in writing.

Her concept of the necessity of a conscious construction of one's own identity out of a heterogenous collection of elements is diametrically opposed to Satre's thinking. In essence, his theory requires us to *remain free from* an identity: consciousness has to remain empty because otherwise we would become a thing, and our human existence would be inauthentic. It is true Sartre also saw man as a being who creates himself, and he stated that every human life is characterized by a *"projet fondamental"*.[1] But this fundamental project can only be reconstructed in retrospect from a person's actions. For Sartre, self-creation should not be striven after on a conscious level. It cannot form a conscious way of living, because then we would live as though there is an I that guides our actions and to which our experiences manifest themselves. This would be an attitude of "bad faith." To be authentic, we must not live as though we are an identity: a collection of fixed conscious contents.[2]

Time and again, Sartre emphasized we have to renew ourselves at any given moment, and we have to be able to give our lives a totally different course. In an interview entitled "Self-portrait in My Seventieth Year," he called himself an anarchist but without wanting to refer to the anarchistic movement. The interviewer observed, "After May 1968, you said to me: 'If people re-read all my books, they will see that, all things considered, I have not changed and that I have always remained an anarchist. . . . ' " And Sartre endorsed this remark: "This is undoubtedly true. . . . Yet I have changed in the sense that when I wrote *Nausea* I was an anarchist without knowing it. . . . Later I discovered my anarchistic bent through philosophy" (*Le nouvel observateur*, 1975).

Sartre's biographer Annie Cohen-Solal shows he in fact practiced his principle of continual renewal in his own life. In the years before his death, he retracted all his earlier opinions—much to Beauvoir's annoyance (see chapter 4). According to Cohen-Solal, he was secretly thrilled at the consternation his new tack caused in the Sartrean "family," and especially in Beauvoir (see Cohen-Solal, 1987: 545 passim).[3] So, we can ascertain Sartre was fundamentally anarchistic, both in his theoretical notions (the *pour-soi* nature of man means he has to escape an identity continually, and does not have to strive after continuity with the past) and in his way of life.

Compared to the anarchism or "nomadism" of Sartre, Beauvoir emerges as a "moralist": in her thinking, everything a person does should contribute to his own identity. She stated, "Renouncing all previous anger and desires and giving preference to the emotions of the moment means smashing human existence into worthless fragments, erasing the past" (OO: 88). Instead, "it is the task of everyone to realize his individual unity by involving his past in aims for the future" (pp. 87–88). Man should assume his responsibility for a specific collection of moral values by providing himself with a coherent identity. This does not imply a finalized or closed identity. A coherent identity remains open to the future (although, based on the past, this openness is limited—see ASD: 10). Reflecting on the past, we have to be conscious continually of who and what we are. Beauvoir stated she wrote her autobiography because she loved constructing herself so that she could continue to create herself from a firm base (see Jeanson, 1966: 289). Life for her was "an undertaking that had a clear direction" (ASD: 8).

In this light, Beauvoir's autobiographical work emerges as the core of her oeuvre. It forms the conscious construction of an individual identity and way of life. Sartre's autobiographical *Words* (1963) has a very different aim—to unmask systematically and demolish completely the young Poulou he once was. "I was . . . this monster they were forming out of their regrets" (W: 53). He systematically turned his thinking against himself (see FoC: 273); he "vitriolized his image" (Willems, 1972: 40). Conversely, Beauvoir's own autobiographical work reflects her attitudes to ethics as art of living.

Various authors have remarked that, in her autobiography, Beauvoir is extremely economical with the truth (see e.g., Bair 1990a: 668). But she was more than aware of this. She emphasized that autobiography ranked with literature and, in contrast to what people usually think, composition and inventiveness play a major role. Autobiography is also a creative process because it "made as many demands on my powers of imagination and reflection as it did on my memory" (FoC: 384). Although it concerns a *description* of a life, the author still makes a mark on the experiences in style, tone, and rhythm of the story. "The I that speaks stands at a distance from the I that has been experienced, just as each sentence stands at a distance from the experience out of which it arises" (ASD: 130; see also p. 133).

We can conclude here that she had a different aim in mind than a pure representation of facts; we should interpret her autobiography as a self-stylization and as an ethical self-creation rather than as a self-description. Beauvoir's American lover Nelson Algren formulated this concisely when he exclaimed, "Autobiography—shit! . . . Autofiction, that's what she wrote" (Bair, 1990a: 500). Beauvoir also stated that she wanted to create herself through her autobiographical work and noted, for example, how in later years, she would often reread it to remind herself who and what she was: "I often reread my memoirs to see what I thought about things, to remember what I felt, to relive relationships and recall places that were important to me" (Bair, 1990a: 594).

Using an extremely detailed description of her way of life, she attempted to create a coherent identity for herself. Her thinking on ethics as art of living was applied through elaborating on an individual art of living in her autobiography, and thus assuming specific moral values. Man who makes himself a unity and introduces order into his life is a recurrent theme in her autobiography. She described approvingly the attempts of her lover Claude Lanzmann to bring himself back into unity against the chaos of the world: "he wanted to be a Jew," and thus he consciously accepted the exclusion that had been forced upon him by others (FoC: 294). Beauvoir was interested in how people managed to reconcile conflicting identities (see p. 234). Of her own autobiography, she spoke of terms of a need for "totality" (p. 288). The conclusion to the question, for what reason? must be that Beauvoir's art-of-living ethics was aimed at providing oneself with a coherent identity based on freedom.

What and how?

Let us now look at what the ethical substance of Beauvoir's art of living is, and its means (the what and the how).

We have already seen that Henri in *The Mandarins* was not engaged in introspection. In trying to discover who he is, he is not concerned with revealing deep intentions or emotions, but with giving direction to his relations with the world. Henri concludes, "to talk about oneself, one must talk about everything else" (M: 341). This is precisely what Beauvoir was about in her autobiographical work. Her descriptions of all her actions and activities were minute and exhaustive.

The background here is her concept of man as a "nothingness" who has to relate to his environment in order to be something. Beauvoir stated, "we loathed the whole idea of a *vie intérieure*" (PoL: 245), and "Everything possessed an external situation and actuality: physical objects, statements of truth, emotions, meaning, even the self" (p. 187). Throughout her life, she remained loyal to this concept, which Sartre had elaborated in his phenomenological-psychological studies (see chapter 4). For her, man was what he did. She was strongly opposed to Freud's psychoanalytical theory because its point of departure is a deep truth of the self, which has to be brought to light through analysis. Beauvoir saw this as an invalid assumption of a fixed identity—invalid because in her view man had to be a constituting activity. In opposition to the idea of a deep, hidden self, she placed the emphasis on the superficial: man is his actions and his involvement with the world. Thus, the goal of her autobiographical work was not self-examination or self-analysis.[4] Her autobiography is not aimed at revealing an inner world beneath or behind her active life, but at charting and styling that active life. Thus, while talking about herself, she was able to speak of very different matters. This is possible "since, whether imaginary or real, what is called a character's richness is the interiorization of his or her environment" (FoC: 279, see also ASD: 40). When a young woman came to see her and asked advice, Beauvoir told her to think about other things than herself, and to read rather than talk (see FoC: 424).

The similarity between Beauvoir's autobiography and earlier letters and diaries emerges from the meticulous way she reported all her occupations. In the letters to Sartre, she described her day-to-day life in truly minute detail. The recent publication of these letters (at the same time as her war diary for the years 1939 to 1941) earned them the almost unanimous criticism that they were most remarkable for their triviality. We could ask ourselves whether Beauvoir ever intended these writings for publication, but another point should be noted here. From the very beginning, Beauvoir believed she was what she did. This is why she kept careful notes of what she did and followed a very strict schedule. She organized her days according to specific rituals and patterns. How you get out of bed and breakfast, where and with whom you spend the day, the way your time is used every day, the meals, the places you enter—Beauvoir made the most elementary day-to-day matters into a terrain for self-stylization. Her careful schedules were a way of creating and organizing herself, and that is why reporting on them was a very serious business.

A comparison with the moral attitude Foucault calls "care for the self" ("souci de soi"). and saw as typical of the second century A.D., can provide elucidation. For example, Foucault quoted the following letter from Marcus Aurelius: "We are well. I slept somewhat late owing to my slight cold, which seems now to have subsided. So from 5 A.M. till 9, I spent the time partly in reading some of Cato's *Agriculture*, partly in writing. . . . Then we went to luncheon. What do you think I ate? A wee bit of bread . . . " (Foucault, 1988 b: 28–29).

Foucault went on to point out the context of this letter. At first sight, the everyday description it contains appears trivial. But in the background is the notion—also shared by Marcus Aurelius—that this sort of detail is important because it represents who you are. Foucault showed that interest emerged in the administration of the self in the first and second centuries A.D. The self is more something to be stylized on the surface than to scrutinize in depth.[5] Care for the self is also linked to the technique of constant writing. Attention was paid to the subtleties of life, and experience of the self was intensified and increased through writing (see pp. 27–28).

Foucault also pointed out the emergence during the early Roman period of personal notebooks, called "*hypomnemata*"; a new technology that "was as disrupting as the introduction of the computer into private life today" (Foucault, 1983: 245). These notebooks were used to record profundities and insights, which formed guidelines for one's own actions. Letters and diaries act as touchstones and comparisons for the notebook: did I do what I planned? Thus, writing becomes a means of organizing the self.

Let us just look at the first missive from Beauvoir's *Letters to Sartre*: "I'm writing this in bed. Yesterday, I couldn't have managed it; . . . I had a very sore throat and even some temperature. . . . Today I'm fine . . . ; I've eaten two nice little boiled eggs and some bananas and I feel like reading Rabelais" (LS: 4). The similarity to Marcus Aurelius's trivial letter is striking. He also reports the state of his health, what he is reading, the food he has eaten. It would seem to me that what Foucault saw as typical of the first and second century A.D. is also a close characterization of the aim of Beauvoir's initial, self-directed writing activities. She organized and guided herself through her writing and used it as self-practice within the framework of a "*souci de soi*." And for Beauvoir too, the self is something to be stylized on the surface rather than examined in depth. This basic approach would later culminate in the writing of an autobiography whose aim was to be useful for *others*. But here too Beauvoir used the inventory technique in order to weigh and determine herself continually. Based on her thus created "history" and according to the task she had set herself within the framework of her art-of-living ethics, she designed an identity for herself as she went along. As regards the what and how of her art-of-living ethics, we can now conclude the what, the ethical substance, is the actions of man. It is not his intentions, feelings, or desires, but his concrete actions and behaviors that should be made the subject of moral activity. The question of how, the question of practices and techniques that man applies to stylize himself into a moral subject can now also be answered: these self-techniques consist of a careful control and guidance of daily actions through compartmentalizing, planning, and inventorying them.

To what end?

Finally, we come to the question of the immanent aim of art-of-living ethics. What kind of subject should we become? Let us first turn to *The Mandarins*. Looking back on a conversation with Lambert, Henri reconsiders his plans. "Helping people to think straight, to live better lives — was his heart really set on it, or was it only a humanitarian daydream?" (M: 185). He finally decides he must assume his responsibility to other people and try to do something real for them. Both Anne and Dubreuilh are also possessed by this ideal. However, they all see different ways of achieving this. The level of practical, political engagement is particularly disparate. But what they do have in common is the desire to relieve suffering in the world and to combat unhappiness — although they have no hope of a definitive result. The main characters in *The Mandarins* want to help improve the quality of life of others and to be committed to them. Henri continually carries on discussions with himself and with people around him on the utility and purpose of literature. By degrees literature emerges as a means of supporting others in their own lives. Lambert asked Henri to help young people by giving them a novel that would provide them with specific moral values.

This was also Beauvoir's purpose with her own literary work. She continually emphasized that her aim was to articulate her own experience so that it could be useful for others. And this applied not only to her autobiography, but also to her novels.[6] In a contribution to the *Que peut la littérature?* debate which took place in 1965, she argued that the purpose of literature was to provide concrete support to others in their lives. She specified her ideas as follows. The writer opens up his own world for us. There is always a question of a certain perception of the world because everyone lives in his own specific situation; everyone's life has its own unique flavor. But that situation is opened up to that of all others: we are not monads—we can communicate. Literature enables us to communicate the very things that separate us. It is the voice, the world of one person with whom I can identify while remaining simultaneously in my own universe. That is the miracle of literature. "Another truth becomes mine while continuing to be the other. I distance myself from my own 'I' in favor of the one who speaks; yet I still remain myself" (QL: 82).

As Proust has already pointed out, literature is intersubjectivity's privileged place. Words can form a counterbalance to the fundamental separateness of individuals. Everyone who writes has in some way suffered from that separation and wants to eliminate it. The act of writing is already a belief in communication and the fellowship of man. After all, one rarely writes in a state of absolute despair. Language reintegrates us into human society. Thus, literature emerges as the means whereby we can contribute to abolishing man's loneliness. In an interview with Sartre on her authorship, Beauvoir concluded she had succeeded in her aim of talking to people in such a way that they could identify with heroes and heroines from her novels and profit from what they said (Dayan and Ribowska, 1979: 76). Beauvoir believed literature had to give people real handholds to help them live their lives.

If we now go back to comparisons, then it seems obvious to examine Sartre's contribution to this same debate, *Que peut la littérature?* What is immediately striking is the very different angle he uses. Sartre did not want to identify with the writer, but with the reader. His argument placed the emphasis on the reception of literature, and stressed the active role the reader plays in establishing meaning. Literature's main aim is to present readers with a universe in which the characters determine their actions freely so that the reader himself—albeit only momentarily—can experience that freedom, something he will remember for the rest of his life (QL: 107–27).

We find a similar emphasis in Sartre's *Qu'est-ce que la littérature?* (1948). The writer appeals to the freedom in others and writes because he wants freedom. In Sartre's conception, the aim of so-called metaphysical literature is to show human freedom as such. However, for Beauvoir, this concept represented a literature that can show the *meaning people give to their lives.* She believed a writer had to give some indication of the way he fills in his own freedom, a belief that was alien to Sartre. For Sartre, literature's task was to light a spark of freedom in the reader. The following comparison illustrates clearly the difference in both perceptions.

In *Existentialism and Humanism* (1946),[7] Sartre said one of his students had come to him for advice. He refused to give it. His only reply was, you are free, make your own choice. Let us compare this to the following scene from *The Mandarins*. Lambert, whose father had collaborated during the war, comes to Henri for advice. Can he meet up with his father again? Henri's answer is, "Go and see him, do as you see fit, and don't worry about what anyone else has to say. . . . It's not cowardly to live as you feel" (M: 182).[8] Thus, the writer Henri *does* give an answer. In contrast to Sartre, Beauvoir believed we can and should help others with their lives. The aim of her art-of-living ethics is that we have to be a subject who offers others practical assistance in realizing their freedom.

Art-of-living ethics versus moral nihilism

Based on the foregoing, we can now formulate a rounded definition of Beauvoir's concept of ethics as art of living: in the name of our freedom, we must create ourselves as an individual identity, styling and developing our daily behavior in all its aspects, with the aim of contributing concretely to the quality of the life of others.

But doesn't Sartre have a similar concept of ethics? In chapter 4 we saw how a number of authors (Arntz, Jeanson, and Beauvoir herself) tried to pin on Sartre an ethics based on the argument that *Being and Nothingness* only described bad faith (i.e., this would mean a moral point of departure was inherent to this work). Others, such as Phyllis Morris (1975), differ in that they see the concept "*projet fondamental*" as the location of the ethical dimension in Sartre's work. But we have seen that Sartre used this term—and also a number of others, such as "*projet originel*" (EN: 648) or "*projet initial*" (p. 650) or simply "*projet*"—to indicate an individual's specific fundamental choice, a choice that can only be reconstructed in retrospect through a so-called existential psychoanalysis (see note 1). According to Sartre, man "chooses" by acting; although there is no question of a conscious choice, the action itself is a form of choice. In this way, so-called existential psychoanalysis can extract and reveal a person's fundamental choices, i.e., that which forms the hidden unity of his life, from the totality of his life. Sartre used this approach to analyze the lives of Baudelaire and Genet, among others.[9]

Morris, however, claims the fundamental project implies a continual choice for specific values, thereby making the person a moral agent. After all, Morris argues, the individual is morally liable and responsible if, in the form of self-creation, continuity and coherence are present in his actions and behaviors.

Now, it is a fact that Sartre himself also spoke in terms of ethics when he indicated individual self-creation in his book on the writer Jean Genet among others. This claim becomes problematic, however, as soon as we examine further *Saint Genet, Actor and Martyr* (1952).[10]

Sartre's extensive study comprises an existential psychoanalysis of Jean Genet, ward of court, thief, tramp, beggar, smuggler, pederast, pornographer, and ex-con, to give just a few of the epitaphs Genet earned in his time. Sartre describes Genet's life and work in positive terms as a victorious passage. Caught in the act of stealing, the child Genet also *wanted* to be a thief. This fundamental choice has to be seen as the highest expression of freedom: the child Genet wanted to create himself, he *willed* himself. Genet altered his original motives for stealing. He wanted to live his life in the service of Evil, generating as much abhorrence as possible in both himself and other people (see p. 67).

Genet also wrote with this intention in mind: "his work aims at being an evil action" (p. 547). In other words, "Genet wants to write good books with bad sentiments" (p. 558). He is not concerned with pure Art, but with the moral tenor of his books. They are "systematically conducted ethical experiments" (p. 559) in which ultimately the beauty of Evil triumphs. But, Sartre continues, by articulating and experiencing the extremes of his moral experiments with Evil in his writings, Genet actually *liberated* himself from Good and Evil, although he was not aware of this. In his work, both became linguistic events; they became constructions that only have meaning *within* the work. "When the work grows silent, when, dragged down by its own weight, it sinks to the depths of darkness, Good and Evil sink into the same nothingness. . . . The deeper meaning of Genet's moralism is finally disclosed: he has put the moral element into words in order to get rid of it" (p. 567).

Sartre considered Genet's project as an admirable act of self-creation. He also pointed out that Genet's choice could not be applicable universally. In fact, the opposite was the case: "it is from this refusal to universalize that their universality is due: the universal and the incommunicable experience which they offer to all as individuals is that of solitude" (p. 589). This is why Sartre claimed Genet's work was moral, but not moralizing (see p. 559).

So, we find Sartre discussing Genet's life as a moral project while at the same time arguing that Genet had placed himself beyond Good and Evil. But can we then still claim, as Morris did, that Sartre's concept of personal self-creation comprises an *ethics*? Morris herself raises the point that Sartre had no universal moral criteria that could act as boundaries for the *kind* of project that can be chosen. The self that can be chosen "may be what the moral philosopher or the ordinary person would consider bad, as in the case of Jean Genet's choice to be a thief" (Morris, 1975: 150). She then states Sartre had formulated such boundaries in a different work, *Existentialism and Humanism*. Thus, also according to Morris, the *"projet fondamental"* as such does not offer adequate grounds to support the notion of a moral dimension in Sartre's work. Absent is a positive relationship with the other, which is the primary criterion for an ethics.

In my view, Sartre's concept of a *"projet fondamental"* means no more and no less than that man is free and therefore always creates himself. Morris incorrectly interprets self-creation as an event that occurs at a given place and time in an individual's life, a real change in attitude. She claims Sartre prescribed such a fundamental choice. *Saint Genet* certainly could give rise to this interpretation, because Sartre praised Genet. But in *Being and Nothingness*, Sartre introduced the *"projet fondamental"* in connection with existential psychoanalysis. He discussed self-creation from the perspective of the biographer (citing Flaubert as a subject for biography; he later actually wrote it). It is the biographer's task to distill the specific self-creation from his subject's whole life, and it is not the case that his subject lived according to or strived after this self-creation, or was even aware of it.

Elsewhere, in the work Morris quotes, *Existentialism and Humanism*, we find the *"projet"* concept, also called the *"projet individuel,"* in a purely descriptive sense: self-creation there is the characteristic of man as such rather than a specific event in his life. Sartre said, "there is no difference between free being—being as self-committal (*'être comme projet'*), as existence choosing its essence" (EH: 47). Thus, the concept *"projet"* functions as synonym for being human, i.e., being free. According to Sartre, Genet's choice was beyond Good and Evil. Sartre's main aim was to make Genet visible as an individual who practiced an ultimate human freedom; Sartre's theoretical work at this time was focused on human freedom and not on the moral dimension.[11]

The play, *Lucifer and the Lord* (1951), also shows this clearly.[12] This piece for theater (that—it must be said—bears more than passing resemblance to a boy's adventure story) is set in an imaginary country fraught with popular uprisings. The rebellious city of Worms is under siege by General Goetz. Initially, Goetz is out to personify Evil and is planning to murder all the inhabitants in a punitive exercise. When a despairing priest convinces him the earth is already saturated with Evil, and it is impossible to do Good, Goetz feels challenged to prove the opposite. He spares the inhabitants of Worms and founds a "city of the Sun" based on collective ownership, where happiness, virtue, and love should triumph.

However, Goetz's resolve to achieve Good in the here and now produces the opposite effect. Peasants murder the city's inhabitants when they refuse to participate in the popular rebellion. Finally, Goetz realizes he is guilty of their deaths and concludes that men cannot avoid doing Evil. He emerges from his isolation and joins up with the rebels.

> Goetz: I need you. *[pause]* I want to be a man among men. . . . Men of today are born criminals. I must demand my share of their crimes if I desire my share of their love and their virtue. I wanted love in all its purity; ridiculous nonsense; to love a man is to hate the same enemy; therefore I will embrace your hatred. I wanted to do Good: foolishness: on this earth and at this time, Good and Evil are inseparable; I accept my share of Evil to inherit my share of Good. (LL: 172).

He is finally persuaded to take command of the rebellion when the leaders are about to give in. When one of them protests, Goetz replies:

> Come here! Nasti has nominated me captain and general. Will you obey my orders?
> The captain: I'd rather die.
> Goetz: Then, little brother, die! *[He stabs him.]* . . . A fine start. Nasti, I told you I would be hangman and butcher. . . . I shall remain alone with this empty sky above me, since I have no other way of being among men. There is this war to fight, and I will fight it. (pp. 175–76).

In Goetz's contemplation of an empty sky, Sartre symbolized the isolation of the absolutely free human being. Again we find it is primarily the freedom of the man Goetz that is set before us.

But did Sartre in fact formulate criteria elsewhere, which have to be met by the chosen project if it is to be considered moral? In contrast to other authors, who referred us to *Being and Nothingness*, Morris recommended Sartre's lecture *Existentialism and Humanism*. Here we also find the military leader as prototype for the free, i.e., responsible, individual. "When, for instance, a military leader takes upon himself the responsibility for an attack and sends a number of men to their death, he chooses to do it and at bottom he alone chooses" (EH: 32). And he experiences fear when he makes that choice, a fear that is inherent to the isolation of man who has to discover his own values and finds no holdfast, either inside or outside himself. Man is alone; he is "doomed to be free." Sartre pursued this line of thinking through the example already discussed above. He recounted how one of his students asked for advice during the war. Should he join the resistance or stay with his sick mother for whom he was the "only consolation" (p. 35)? According to Sartre, "I had but one reply to make. You are free, therefore choose—that is to say, invent" (p. 38).

But is such a decision then merely random? No, "rather let us say that the moral choice is comparable to the construction of a work of art" (p. 48). But that does not mean we are talking about aesthetics here. The only claim is that we find ourselves in a situation similar to that of creative artists:

> when we are discussing a canvas by Picasso, we understand very well that the composition became what it is at the time when he was painting it, and that his works are part and parcel of his entire life. It is the same upon the plane of morality. There is this in common between art and morality, that in both we have to do with creation and invention (p. 49).

The only general gauge we have in evaluating the self-creation is authenticity or veracity: "any man who takes refuge behind the excuse of his passions, or by inventing some deterministic doctrine, is a self-deceiver" (p. 51). This is a formal criterion—if an act is inauthentic, then total freedom is obscured; the act becomes mendacious and blame-worthy. "Here one cannot avoid pronouncing a judgment of truth" (p. 51). Those who act authentically also endorse the value of freedom as such, and thus the freedom of others, Sartre then argued. At first sight, he appears to be introducing a moral criterion, but it soon turns out to be a sidetrack in his argument that is not further elaborated. He merely went on to expand on untruth: "Thus, in the name of that will to freedom which is implied in freedom itself, I can form judgments upon those who seek to hide from themselves the wholly voluntary nature of their existence and its complete freedom" (p. 52). He then stated that man can choose at will. "The one thing that counts is to know whether the invention is made in the name of freedom" (p. 53).

Existentialism and Humanism can only frustrate our search for moral boundaries or criteria. The only proposition we find on the relationship with the other—and Sartre noted it two years after Beauvoir had already formulated it—is that we have to desire the freedom of all. But it remains no more than a formula that is not elaborated theoretically. Mary Warnock points out the fact that this universalizing proposition is Kantian in nature and as such is wholly irreconcilable with Sartre's own theory in *Being and Nothingness*, where he had argued at length that our relations with others were characterized by conflict and enmity (see Warnock, 1967: 39 ff). Warnock calls the ethics presented in *Existentialism and Humanism* an "aberration" (p. 47).

There is no question of an ethics in the proper sense in either of the existential phenomenologists, Heidegger and Sartre. They are looking for theoretical answers to the question of how to live. They attempt to specify human existence in the context of all being in order to define the actual task of man in life. Veracity or authenticity, life as free being, proves then to be the assignment of man, which has to be fulfilled because of his humanity. Thus, ethics become part of a metaphysical or ontological plan. But this kind of "metaphysical ethics" (see p. 53, 16) *is* no ethics, because ethics is a "theory of how people should live *together*" (p. 38). As Sartre's theory implies the freedom of one is irreconcilable with that of the other, ethics is by definition, lacking, according to Warnock.

However, I do not endorse her final conclusion that an existentialist ethics cannot exist at all. In my view, Warnock has failed to consider the contribution of Simone de Beauvoir. Beauvoir also assumed ethics is a theme in its own right. She introduced a clear distinction between ethics and ontology (or metaphysics), for example when she said of Sartre, "In *Being and Nothingness*, he's not looking for the moral, he's seeking a description of what existence is. . . . It's more an ontology than a morality" (in Simons, 1989: 18). She also emphasized that existentialism did not automatically imply an ethics—so she added one herself.[13] Beauvoir introduced an *autonomous* ethical perspective into existentialism and showed how this could be reconciled with that philosophy.

In the previous chapter we noted that Beauvoir had said Kant had inspired her. To biographer Bair she remarked that Sartre found her Kantian orientation irritating and was afraid it would influence her work.[14] It would appear Sartre's own work was also influenced by her Kantian orientation. Beauvoir's Kantianism in this period could explain Sartre's odd sidestep in *Existentialism and Humanism*. What remains an empty formula in Sartre is theoretically worked out and reconciled with the doctrine of existential philosophy in Beauvoir (see chapter 4). She grounded this ethics by making conceivable a positive relationship with the other in the situated dimension (with the dimension Other relegated to the background), and thus introduced the human fellowship that was impossible in Sartre.

Art of living instead of living as work of art

In my view, Sartre's notions on self-creation as they emerge in, for example, the study on Genet discussed above, cannot be called ethics, but rather aestheticism. Sartre appeared primarily interested in the splendor of the lonesome hero, for which the military leader continually faced with life-and-death decisions seemed the perfect symbol. Authenticity proved the individual's primary task. Rather than being concerned for others, he should continually examine whether his actions are genuine. The grandeur of the lonely hero is *exalted* here in an aesthetic sense.

This aestheticism also emerges from *Saint Genet*, in which Sartre characterized Genet's project as a quest for Beauty. Annie Cohen-Solal considers the Genet in this book as Sartre's double, although a successful double, "whose life as such is a work of art: an esthetic provocation, a sublimation" (1987: 342). In contrast, Lolle Nauta claims the aesthetics in Sartre were already rocky in *Saint Genet*. For Nauta, the aesthetic element is the romantic, aloof attitude aimed at keeping hands clean (see Nauta, 1966: 83). And this attitude is certainly absent from *Saint Genet* because the lonesome hero is no longer placed opposite Evil, but is in the middle somewhere. According to our definitions, however, *Saint Genet* is characterized by an aestheticism because the making absolute of grandeur, of the Beauty of (our) actions, is still playing tricks on Sartre.

In Sartre, aestheticism is slowly but surely exchanged for a passionate belief in politics as supplier of absolute criteria for actions. The play *Lucifer and the Lord* was already a harbinger of what was to come.[15] But as we have seen, in the main character, Goetz, there is a very specific mix of aestheticism and politics: although collective struggle ultimately offered a way out for the desperate hero, he was still doomed to function in lonely and splendid isolation as military commander.

In the end, Sartre would come to see politics as the only criterion for action. It would seem as though he simply solved the absence of an ethics in his theory in this way. In 1947, he joined the practical political organization, the *Rassemblement démocratique et révolutionnaire* (RDR), an organization whose aim was to build a Europe independent from both the United States and the Soviet Union. He began work on a synthesis of praxis and ethics in the form of *Cahiers pour une morale* (see chapter 4). When the RDR disintegrated not long afterward, Sartre concluded that society's historical material development had been decisive. The RDR was doomed to failure from the very start: people cannot *create* a movement. He dropped his *Cahiers* project because he became convinced that "the moral attitude appears when technical and social conditions render positive forms of conduct impossible. Ethics is a collection of idealistic tricks intended to enable us to live the life imposed on us by the poverty of our resources and the insufficiency of our techniques" (FoC: 210).

Thus, in Sartre ethics always loses out, first through ontology—all Sartrean roads lead to freedom—then through politics, which he would later consider the only useful way to build for the future. The absolute judgments that appeared impossible for individual actions proved possible for Sartre at a political level. Having a monopoly on truth does not appear to have been a problem here.[16] For instance, he allowed himself to be seduced into the most rabid political judgments and propositions—his anything-but-subtle pronouncements on the Soviet Union were certainly not welcomed.[17]

In contrast, a scepticism on the absoluteness of the political dimension emerges from Beauvoir's *The Mandarins*. Dubreuilh, whose views are similar to Sartre's during his Marxist period, claims the social level is determinant and concludes "personal morality just doesn't exist" (M: 645). Henri protests violently. He continues to believe there is a place for the moral dimension. For him, politics is also a moral project. "A morality necessarily includes a political attitude. . . . And vice versa" (LM: 134). *The Mandarins* expresses the notion that positive political construction cannot be based on objective truths and insights, but is an open moral choice within the framework of a personal art of living.

If we take stock of Sartre's thinking, it always appears to lack an ethical perspective. Only authenticity is of concern for individual people, and later only the supraindividual political perspective is decisive for action. In Simone de Beauvoir, ethics is the main theme, and this it remained. She herself stated that Sartre never got round to ethics.[18] We have seen that Sartre spoke in terms of ethics, e.g., in *Existentialism and Humanism*, when he suggested that a moral choice was comparable to a work of art. Despite this, and despite his claim that it was not morality itself that was aesthetic, but that the concept aesthetic only indicates the status of morality—its coming about is a permanent creative process—we can still conclude that his existential philosophy was characterized by an aesthetic rather than an ethical criterion for human action.

We also find Beauvoir comparing morality with art in *The Ethics of Ambiguity*: "not that we are likening action to a work of art or a scientific theory," she argued here, but the comparison is only interesting "because in any case human transcendence must cope with the same problem" (EA: 130). She pointed out a similarity between ethics and art, but at the same time in her ethics she discarded aesthetics emphatically, whereas Sartre discarded them through moving over to politics. Beauvoir stressed the creative moment of a moral decision—that is why she called her concept an *art* of living—but eliminated Sartre's exaltation of the Beauty of the lonesome hero's life. In *The Ethics of Ambiguity* she criticized the aesthetic attitude to life whose only perspective on the world is Beauty.

This represents her definitive departure from the attitudes she held before World War II. If her primary concern at that time was her private life, the war put an end to this "quasi-solipsism" and this "illusionary sovereignty": "I woke to find myself scattered over the four quarters of the globe, linked by every nerve in me to each and every other individual" (PoL: 369). From then on, she would no longer remain locked into her limited personal life. Nor did she want her autobiography to be qualified as work of art. "I did refuse to have the notion of a 'work of art' attached to my autobiography" (ASD: 129). "The term suggests a statue dying of boredom in some villa garden. . . . No; not a work of art" (FoC: 6). She dismissed explicitly those authors who made the beauty of their own lives the main focus, such as Oscar Wilde and Anaïs Nin (see ASD: 170, 165). We can conclude that Beauvoir distanced herself from an aesthetic attitude to life, i.e., a striving to transform one's own life into an autonomous work of art. But she never gave up her commitment to the art of living. For Beauvoir, art of living is ethics rather than aesthetics. We can thus talk of a nonaesthetic art of living.

All in all, it appears the notions "freedom" and "art-of-living ethics" are the most appropriate to typify the difference in the existentialist philosophies of Sartre and Beauvoir. This difference also emerges clearly when we compare their treatment of a *poète maudit*: Sartre's approach to Jean Genet's life written in 1952 and Beauvoir's essay on the Marquis de Sade produced in the same year. Each work is of a very different tenor. Sartre praised Genet for his choice of Evil, and talked of daring and courage; in contrast, Beauvoir wrote about Sade in terms of his failure, and saw his choice of Evil as wrong. Against this choice, she placed the option of solidarity among people (see MBS: 88).

7

SIMONE DE BEAUVOIR'S ART OF LIVING

Up until now, we have explored the *type* of ethics Beauvoir conceived and have concluded that in her work ethics exists as positive art of living against the backdrop of a negative moral code. Now, we will turn to the content of her own positive ethics, i.e., to the content of her *own* art of living. First, we will examine what she had in mind in shaping her own life. Then, based on a broader perspective, we will analyze what moved her and what the real issue was in her personal art of living.

What did Simone de Beauvoir want?

"*Was will das Weib?*" Freud asked in confusion at the end of his life. His theory had not provided him with a satisfactory answer to this pressing problem. And Beauvoir agreed Freud had failed to understand women: "*je le tiens pour absolument nul—sur le plan féminin, ainsi que tous les freudiens et freudiennes qui ont suivi!*" she exclaimed (Jeanson, 1966: 260). In *The Second Sex* she polemicized Freud's concepts of femininity and unfolded an alternative perspective. According to Freud, if a girl is to become a normal woman, she has to undergo a complicated sexual development. She has to relinquish her initially active, clitoral sexuality and her focus on the mother as love object. When she compares herself to a man and discovers her lack of the penis—the emergence of penis envy and the castration complex—she has to make up this lack by focusing on the father as love object. Her desire takes on the form of a desire for a superior being, and for a child as a compensation for penis deprivation. As a result, a normal woman's sexuality is by nature vaginal and passive. In Freud, femininity is characterized by passivity and masochism.[1]

Various contemporaries of Freud, such as Lou Salomé and Karen Horney, added amendments to this development scheme,[2] but remained within the boundaries of psychoanalytical theory because they continued to perceive unconsciousness and sexuality as central themes. In *The Second Sex*, Beauvoir did the exact opposite. She departed from the psychoanalytical angle, but took on board Freud's pattern of female development. Like Freud, she attributed an important role to the discovery and acceptance of the lack of the penis in the development of girls; she also concluded that in (sexual) love, the girl focuses on a sovereign being; and she also saw the baby as a woman's equivalent for the penis. In her discussion of Freudian psychoanalysis in *The Second Sex*, Beauvoir pointed out this resemblance:

> The reader will note a certain parallelism between this account and that of the psychoanalysts. (TSS I: 83)

> We . . . decline to accept the method of psychoanalysis, without rejecting *en bloc* the contributions of the science or denying the fertility of some of its insights. (p. 81)

> Thus it is that we shall agree on a certain number of facts. . . . But we accord them by no means the same significance as does the Freudian or the Adlerian. (p. 83)

Beauvoir's approach differed from Freud's because she analyzed *the situation of woman*, rather than woman herself. In earlier chapters we have seen that, for Beauvoir, the situated human being is a unity of body and consciousness. For this reason, woman to her is by definition a being who gives meaning to its existence. "For us woman is defined as a human being in quest of values in a world of values, a world of which it is indispensable to know the economic and social structure" (p. 83). As situated human being, embedded in time and place, woman is an objectivity permeated with subjectivity and a subjectivity imbued with objectivity. Thus, through the concept situation, the social structures within which man lives come immediately into focus for Beauvoir.

Her approach to people as situated beings means she rejected Freud's notions on the central role of sexual urges. Sexuality and eroticism are embedded in the entirety of a person's existence. They are the subject of rather than the motive for the choices people make in their lives. Freud's theory on a girl's sexual desire actually describes an existential *choice* made by the girl. The process he describes is in fact "a full abdication of the subject, consenting to become object in submission and adoration" (p. 315). The choice made by the girl should be placed in a social context. The overvaluation of the penis as a symbol for the masculine and the supremacy of the masculine in culture are factors that explain penis envy. The girl actually longs for the privileges the penis provides. "The place the father holds in the family, the universal predominance of males, her own education—everything confirms her in her belief in masculine superiority" (p. 74).

The girl is impressed with the notion that she is the absolute Other, and she is pressed in all possible ways into assuming that identity: "the delights of passivity are made to seem desirable to the young girl by parents, teachers, books and myths, women and men; she is taught to enjoy them from earliest childhood" (p. 325). Thus, social factors are decisive in the development of the girl; the passive attitude to life that is seen as typically feminine is not a fixed, essential trait in women, but the outcome of all kinds of historical processes.

In this way, criticizing Freud's absolutism, Beauvoir relativized the role of sexuality. By focusing on the influence of real social structures on the development of the girl, she historicized the discoveries of psychoanalysis. "Psychoanalysis can establish its truths only in the historical context," she stated explicitly (p. 80).[3] The girl's choice will change when culture becomes less phallic. But, as a result of specific social changes, women could already opt for a life as active subject. For the first time in history, contraception had become widely available, and women had increasing access to paid employment. Thus, they now had the opportunity to live their lives as subject and leave behind the role of absolute Other.

If, according to Freud, female development follows a fixed pattern, Beauvoir countered with the notion that women, like all people, have to create themselves through a personal project for life. As soon as social circumstances allow her to realize herself as *pour-soi*, a woman can "choose between the assertion of her transcendence and her alienation as object" or rather between "solutions of diverse values in the ethical scale" (p. 82). She has to assume her freedom (i.e., to will herself free) and thus develop into a moral subject (see chapters 4 and 5).

If we now examine Beauvoir's autobiography in this light, it becomes clear she wanted her life to illustrate this proposition, i.e., that girls in her day could already choose a subject position. She retroactively allocated subject status to her girlhood self. In *Memoirs of a Dutiful Daughter* she continually described herself in terms of an active, choosing subject. The accuracy with which she followed her notions from *The Second Sex* is apparent from the following example. In *The Second Sex*, Beauvoir had stated possessing a penis was certainly an advantage. A child has a natural inclination to project itself into an object, as a kind of escape from itself. For a boy, the penis means this inclination can be expressed in a less alienating form than for a girl. The boy can embody his alter ego in the penis, while it remains part of *himself*. In contrast, a girl has a doll pushed into her arms. This symbolizes her whole body and is, moreover, a passive thing. As a result, a girl is encouraged to alienate *her whole persona* and to consider it an inert given. While the boy attempts to rediscover himself as autonomous subject in the penis, the girl fusses with her doll and dresses it up in a way she herself dreams of being fussed over and dressed up. But the doll can also have another function—as an adequate replacement for the doppelgänger, that "natural plaything," which is the penis (see I: 81–82; II: 306). In *Memoirs of a Dutiful Daughter*, Beauvoir recalled the special relationship both she and her sister had with their dolls: "they could speak and reason, they lived at the same rate, and in the same rhythm as ourselves, growing older by twenty-four hours every day: they were our doubles" (MDD: 56). With the concept "doppelgänger," she expressed the fact that both she and her sister remained present as subjects and did not alienate themselves in their dolls.

We see how carefully Beauvoir worked out her attempt to provide the young Simone with a subject position. She also described masochistic games in which, assuming the role of tortured saint, innocent spouse of Bluebeard, or remorseful sinner, she threw herself at the feet of a sovereign lord and master: "when I begged for pardon, I experienced sensual delight. But," she added immediately, "whenever I abandoned myself to these delicious downfalls, I never for one moment forgot that it was just a game. In reality I refused to submit to anybody: I was, and I would always remain, my own master" (p. 59).

Through a complicated rationale she also explained that her lover Sartre, whom she considered superior to herself, should not be seen as a replacement for her father. The reason for her desire for a superior man was different:

> If in the absolute sense a man, who was a member of the privileged species and already had a flying start over me, did not count more than I did, I was forced to the conclusion that in a relative sense he counted less: in

order to be able to acknowledge him as my equal, he would have to prove himself superior in every way. (p. 145)

In this way, she excluded herself from the feminine type of love that wants to surrender submissively to a sovereign subject—*she* wanted companionship and equality and that is why she longed for a superior man. Moreover, she added, she wanted to receive, not give, and her social life with a future partner had to create opportunities for her to take on the world. Here again, we find Beauvoir carefully excluding herself from the female position of absolute Other. In subsequent autobiographical works she continues to emphasize her life as active subject, and in my view, this should be seen as an extension of her aim in *Memoirs of a Dutiful Daughter*.

I think we can conclude this is what Beauvoir had in mind with her art of living: through her own life, she wanted to prove a woman could live as subject. Her own life was to form a refutation of Freud's theory; it would give other women a successful example of life as an active woman and thus mean something for them. Beauvoir herself said:

In this transitionary period, when women are on their way to emancipation but have not yet achieved it, I think it is important to show the life of a woman. (ME: 450)

Through my novels and my biography, many women have more or less identified with me, or have attempted to introduce a specific line in their lives which was borrowed from my life. So, at that level, I think I accomplished what I set out to do. (Dayan and Ribowska, 1979: 77)

Thus, the first answer to our question, what did Simone de Beauvoir want? has emerged: Simone de Beauvoir wanted to be an exemplary woman, operating as subject within culture; she wanted to be *a subject as a woman*.

What moved Simone de Beauvoir?

However, for a complete characterization of Beauvoir's personal art of living, we should not only examine what she herself had in mind, but also apply a broader perspective. But we do not want a Freudian explanation here, not least because Beauvoir herself would have been radically opposed to such a project: her personal, specific choice as a woman would not emerge from a Freudian psychoanalytical framework. According to Beauvoir, psychoanalysis applies—incorrectly—the notion of normality and considers everyone who deviates from the prescribed norms as inhibited or a failure.

> This it is, among other things, that makes the psychoanalysis of great men so shocking: we are told that such and such a transference, this or that sublimation, has not taken place in them; it is not suggested that perhaps they have refused to undergo the process, perhaps for good reasons of their own; it is not thought desirable to regard their behavior as possibly motivated by purposes freely envisaged. (TSS I: 82)

It would seem as though here Beauvoir was resisting a priori any explanation of her own life in Freudian terms.[4] This "great [wo]man" insists we include the dimension of choice in our analysis. But in its turn, this dimension has to be placed in a social context if we are to do justice to Beauvoir's own perspective, we are obliged to examine "her total situation."

We will therefore have to turn to the social context of her life. Only against that backdrop can we gain insight into the meaning of her life. Beauvoir herself believed a writer is "unable to depict the facts of a life and its meaning at one and the same time" (FoC: 512; see also Jeanson, 1966: 206). Elsewhere she also argued that

> it may seem strange for an author not to know exactly what he has written. But it is a fact that he follows a specific line and is more or less blind for the background against which this line unfolds. ("Préface au livre d'Anne Ophir," 1976: 12)

> The background, tragic or serene, against which my experiences are drawn gives them their true meaning and constitutes their meaning. (FoC: 288)

We will first go back to her early years in order to dig out the roots of her ethical project. Our examination is based primarily on parts one and two of her autobiography, *Memoirs of a Dutiful Daughter* and *The Prime of Life*.

Simone was saddled by her parents with contradictory expectations and demands. The Catholic milieu in which she was raised was stifling. The predominant norms for women and girls were traditional: girls had to be virgins when they married, and bring in a considerable dowry. Marriages were arranged by parents, and love rarely played a role. Girls were not allowed any independent relationships with the outside world. Mother sat in on school lessons and also read any letters. Going out alone at night was strictly prohibited. Simone lived at home until she was twenty, and was almost suffocating under her mother's all-seeing eye.

Humility, self-sacrifice, and physical purity were the Christian virtues her mother impressed upon her. Simone's aesthetic father, however, represented different values. From an early age, he treated her as an "esprit." He read to her, guided her through literature, and was proud of his elder daughter's intelligence. Simone adored him.[5] She wanted to be his interlocuter and his lover. Her rivalry with her mother took on overt forms at the start of puberty (see MDD: 71–72, 110).

But the war brought about a real change in the Beauvoir family fortunes—Georges was ruined financially and was declared bankrupt. Thus, a new door opened for Simone, leading to a future very different from her mother's. Georges de Beauvoir was now unable to give his daughters a dowry, and from then on he impressed on them the need for a profession to earn their livings. If a girl in this milieu went into further education to learn a profession, this meant the family had declined socially. Usually, girls from this class went to university only for "finishing." Thus, Simone's friend Zaza attended lectures, but her parents would not have dreamt of giving her permission to take part in examinations. In contrast, Simone's whole university education was aimed from the start at a future profession. She rejected what she saw as "amateur" female students and called herself a "professional" (pp. 178–79).

But her situation as the well-brought-up daughter of a less than wealthy family was contradictory. "My parents, by helping to push me, not into marriage, but into a career, were breaking with tradition; nevertheless they still made me conform to it" (p. 174). Beauvoir herself has suggested that her parents' contradictory values were the cause of her development into an intellectual. The values of her father and the values of her mother differed from each other so much that she was *obliged* to learn to think for herself. However, in my view, the root lies more in the contradictory nature of her social position. Both parents held the same views on a woman's true calling (marriage and a family), and both were equally distressed at the fact that their socioeconomic circumstances forced them to provide Simone with professional training. Her parents gave Simone a task that they both abhorred, and this double standard shook her view of the world, thus nudging her toward intellectual development. She simply could not identify with the values that obtained at home.

From her early puberty, her father ridiculed her eagerness to learn. He reproached her for having bad skin and being clumsy, and shifted his attention to her younger sister, Poupette, who remained a "sweet child." Mother de Beauvoir distrusted Simone's education because she suspected Simone was lapsing from her religion, and sister Poupette no longer worshiped her. Simone, who had counted on her father's support and sympathy, who had identified with the status of brilliant student, innocent soul, and loved elder sister, felt rejected and tumbled into deep loneliness. "I had made myself freely; and, with the approval of one and all, I thought I had made myself into an eager, hard-working student: and there I was, turned into a monster" (ASD: 23).

Gradually, she began to opt for the strategy of exaggeration. She pursued her studies to extremes, even learning Greek verbs during meals and proudly indulging in a strict ascetic attitude. Her unhappiness ultimately became open rebellion, and the conflicts intensified. Once, her father had said proudly, Simone has the brains of a man, Simone is a man! Now he rejected her absolutely. He made clear his disappointment in all manner of ways. Simone's teacher-training course at the university filled him with disgust. Teachers belonged to

> the dangerous sect that had stood in defence of Dreyfus: the intellectuals. Blinded by their book-learning, taking a stubborn pride in abstract knowledge and in their futile aspirations to universalism, they were sacrificing the concrete realities of race, country, class, family, and nationality to those crack-pot notions that would be the death or France and of civilization: the Rights of Man, pacifism, internationalism, and socialism. (MDD: 178)

Her family considered the books she read as morbid, wrong, or unnatural, and Simone became increasingly and horribly isolated. Over time, she became aware of the contradiction in her situation and of the conflicting messages from her father. "I was obeying his wishes to the letter, and that seemed to anger him; he had destined me for a life of study, and yet I was being reproached with having my nose in a book all the time" (p. 179). Her father was ashamed of his daughter because she was a constant reminder of his social failure. He also adhered to the traditional double standard applied to the fair sex, which Beauvoir would expose in The Second Sex. A woman had to be chaste, modest, and virtuous, but she had to be sexually attractive, charming, flirtatious, and witty as well.

Her father was a confirmed antifeminist, as Beauvoir herself noted. He praised women who gave up their professions as lawyers or doctors to devote all their time to family. But he also enjoyed the company of beautiful and flirtatious women. If her father cultivated Simone's "esprit," this was initially solely in line with his notions of charm; a woman not only had to be beautiful, she also had to be entertaining and witty. Simone was very badly dressed by her mother—her father valued well-dressed women, and praised her vivacious cousin Jeanne: "my father never tired of telling everyone that his brother had a delightful daughter;

then he would give a sigh" (p. 175). Girls who were intelligent and still glittered at salons were held up as examples for Simone (pp. 178–79).

Nor could Simone find any kind of self-affirmation in literature. There was one book with which she believed she could identify—Louisa May Alcott's *Little Women*.

> I identified myself passionately with Jo, the intellectual. . . . I shared her horror of sewing and housekeeping and her love of books. She wrote: in order to imitate her more completely, I composed two or three short stories . . . the relationship between Jo and Laurie touched me to the heart. . . . The thing that delighted me most of all was the marked partiality which Louisa Alcott manifested for Jo. (p. 90)

But what a disappointment when, in the sequel *Good Wives*, the author married Laurie off to Jo's younger sister Amy:

> blonde, vain, and stupid. I threw the book away from me as if it had burned my fingers. For several days I was absolutely crushed by a misfortune which had seemed to strike at the very roots of my being: the man I loved and by whom I had thought I was loved had betrayed me for a little goose of a girl. (pp. 104–5)

Simone's whole circle cautioned her against becoming too learned. Her philosophy teacher warned her not to become too engaged in logical argument: she would "dry up" and begin to resemble her women teachers. One examiner asked her—ironically—if she hadn't got enough diplomas (p. 156). Zaza's mother fought tooth and nail against Simone's influence: "she was afraid her daughter might become an intellectual" (p. 277). Nor is Zaza herself a support for her friend. Beauvoir recalled Zaza "took no part in the conflicts that set their mark on my adolescence" (ASD: 17). Even fellow students at the Sorbonne warned Simone, "twenty is too young for a blue-stocking, and if I went on like this I'd turn into an ugly little spinster" (MDD: 288). Her adored cousin Jacques talked continually of girls who, in spite of examinations, still managed to play tennis, go dancing, and dress well (p. 147). Her parents sometimes brought in friends to help in their attacks on Simone: "they would then all join in denouncing the charlatanism of modern artists, the intellectual snobbery of the public, the decadence of France, and the civilized world" (pp. 225–26). Simone became used to not responding to such provocations, an attitude that irritated her parents intensely.

Unsurprisingly, she became depressed in this atmosphere of enmity and stifling mistrust. No one loves me, no one values me for who I am, she sighed frequently. She wondered if she really was so ugly, and if she would ever find a man who could love her. She believed she had to relinquish the hope of love for all time and spend her days in loneliness as a philosophy teacher somewhere in the provinces. She felt like an exile, an outcast (see pp. 191, 240, 146, 248, and 260, respectively). It is also hardly surprising that Simone used pride and a sense of superiority as a defense. Vocation is a recurrent theme in *Memoirs of a Dutiful Daughter*. From an early age she had felt exceptional. "I was convinced that I would be, that I was already, one in a million" (p. 91). She sought the heights of perfection through the Catholic faith, identifying with Saint Bernadette of Lourdes and Jeanne d'Arc, while waiting for visitations and planning a future as a Carmelite nun. Simone invented penances to purify herself. "Locked in the water-closet—my sole refuge—I would scrub my flesh with pumice-stone until the blood came, and fustigate myself with the thin gold chain I wore round my neck" (p. 134).

When her interests shifted to her father's more worldly attitudes, this sense of vocation was transformed into a desire to become a writer. "In my view, writing was a mission, a salvation; it was a replacement for God," she said later (LE: 383). Indirectly, she compared her life as writer to a religious vocation when she wondered why people were so surprised she had no children—after all, Carmelites never became mothers (PoL: 78). The themes of vocation and service to humanity remain leitmotivs in *Memoirs of a Dutiful Daughter*: "I had to be of service; to what? To whom?"; "I was somebody, and I would do great things"; "[I had] the certainty of vocation" (MDD: 227, 241–42, and 331, respectively). It is clear Simone's vocations are proud reactions to her sense of exclusion from the group of girls around her. Her doubts about whether she was the kind of woman who could be loved, her sense of being different, special, were transformed into a decision to *do* something special.

Her decision to become a writer, a "vocation" she began to pursue seriously during her first year at university, can be seen as the result of her father adoration. He had always valued writers above scholars. Moreover, her milieu—with papa leading the field—had made more than clear that scholarship marred a woman. It is no coincidence that we find Simone sighing, "I wasn't interested in dry-as-dust erudition" (p. 160). Even during her philosophy studies she preferred literature: "I wouldn't have been at all pleased if someone had prophesied that I would become a kind of female Bergson; I didn't want to speak with that abstract voice which, whenever I heard it, failed to move me" (p. 208). By the age of fifteen, Simone had already realized it was easier for women to gain fame through writing: "the most celebrated women had distinguished themselves through literature" (p. 141).

Her teachers were impressed by her philosophical talents, but she herself did not value them highly (see chapter 1). We now understand why:

the abstract, "dry-as-dust" voice of philosophy would not enhance her status as a woman. Filled with pride at passing her examinations, she had proclaimed she had the heart of a woman and the mind of a man (see p. 296), but her identity as a teacher of philosophy was far from secure. After completing her course, she decided to give private lessons rather than accept a permanent job. When, two years later, she finally took a post in Marseilles, she felt as though she were living a masquerade (see PoL: 20). She could not identify with this role: "I discharged the duties of a philosophy teacher without really being one" (p. 346).

It was different for Sartre. "To acquire a teacher's certificate and have a profession was something he took for granted" (p. 212). Beauvoir knew her girls'-school education meant she lagged behind male students. Even during her school years, she felt this keenly:

> Whenever I passed by the College Stanislas my heart would sink; I tried to imagine the mystery that was being celebrated behind those walls, in a classroom full of boys, and I would feel like an outcast. They had as teachers brilliantly clever men who imparted knowledge to them with all its pristine glory intact. My old school-marms only gave me an expurgated, insipid, faded version. I was being crammed with an ersatz concoction; and I felt I was imprisoned in a cage. (MDD: 121–22)

She was impressed by the head start enjoyed by fellow students Sartre, Aron, Nizan, and Politzer:

> their culture had a much more solid grounding than mine, they were familiar with hosts of new things of which I was ignorant and they were used to discussion; above all, I was lacking in method and direction; to me the intellectual universe was a great jumble of ideas in which I groped my way blindly; but *their* search was, for the most part, well-directed. (p. 344)

An education at a general lyceum would not only have given her "intelligent teachers" and "open-minded companions," but most of all she would not have been obliged to "hide my intellectual development as though it were a deformity" (ASD: 19–20). *Memoirs of a Dutiful Daughter* is all about Simone's lonely battle to develop, as a girl, into an intellectual, as she herself reiterated. "Becoming an intellectual, a writer, brought other problems for a girl from my generation than for girls today, and that is why I wrote *Memoirs of a Dutiful Daughter*; I thought it might be interesting to tell that story" (LE: 383).

Beauvoir spoke in terms of a struggle to lead the life of an intellectual (p. 48). This struggle, her experience of the irreconcilability of the two destinies—that of future professional woman and of dutiful daughter—

is, in my view, the basis of her sense of fulfilling a mission: if she was going to be criticized from all sides, she would justify *herself* and thus she would render the world a service. Many authors have perceived Beauvoir's urge for justification as a desire for immortality or as an urge for the absolute.[6] But these explanations miss the point of Beauvoir's enterprise. The fifteen-year-old Simone decided that, "By writing a work based on my own experience I would re-create myself and justify my existence. At the same time I would be serving humanity" (MDD: 142). In many different phrasings, Beauvoir reiterated the issue of her work: "I wanted to show my life as it had been recreated by myself in freedom" (ME: 439). "My life would be a beautiful story come true, a story I would make up as I went along" (MDD: 169).

Beauvoir wanted her life to be joyful and happy. She stated, "I have never met anyone, in the whole of my life, who was so well equipped for happiness as I was, or who laboured so stubbornly to achieve it" (PoL: 28). Later, influenced by the dramatic events of World War II, she would put the importance of personal happiness into perspective, but it always remained a major theme: "In point of fact I never discarded it altogether" (p. 370). In an early letter to Sartre we find,

> I've always wished for happiness but without thinking I had any right to it: thought of it as something constructed by me, rather than as manna fallen from on high. It would never have occurred to me to *complain* about my parents, for example. You had to win your happiness, as I saw it, amid conditions some of which were burdensome, others favourable. (LS: 170)

If, according to her parents and her whole milieu, it was impossible to be both a woman *and* an intellectual, Beauvoir saw this as a challenge and wanted to build up a happy life as intellectual woman in order to prove them wrong. She wanted to meld her two supposedly irreconcilable identities into a new, positive synthesis. This is the story which, by its telling, became true, the story of the possible compatibility of being both girl *and* subject, woman *and* active creating being, woman *and* intellectual.

Rather than accusing Beauvoir of making false representations, which is in vogue in feminist interpretations, because she was said to have sketched a far too positive image of her life,[7] we find the opposite is actually the case. The true merit of Beauvoir's work is that it constructs a female subject in the form of an intellectual woman. In her autobiography, she wanted to give us an image that had formerly been inconceivable: a woman who lives a successful life as intellectual and who experiences herself positively as both woman and intellectual.

If we recall what Beauvoir said of de Sade, i.e., his merit was his acceptance of his singularity which he then transformed into an identity, then it applies almost literally to herself. If we replace de Sade's name with Beauvoir's in the following quotation, we see how clearly she sketched the outlines of her own project:

> But what is his place? Why does he merit our interest? Even his admirers will readily admit that his work is, for the most part, unreadable. . . . The fact is that it is neither as author nor as sexual pervert that de Sade compels our attention: it is by virtue of the relationship which he created between these two aspects of himself . . . ; [with] this act, in which he assumed his separateness, he attempted to make an example and an appeal. It is thus that his adventure assumes a wide human significance (MS: 10–11).

Beauvoir set to work in an analogous fashion. She wanted to interlink being a woman *and* an intellectual and turn this identity into an example and a challenge. This is at issue in her life.[8] Her autobiographical work, in which she attempts to create this reconciliation, can thus be seen as the core of her oeuvre.

Commentaries

Francis Jeanson also considers Beauvoir's autobiography as the core of her work (Jeanson 1966: 10). He, too, notes that her autobiography is essentially "a continual attempt at unifying herself" (p. 209). Other authors, such as the Dominican monk Henry in his *Simone de Beauvoir ou l'échec d'un chrétienté* (1961), also conclude Beauvoir was trying to forge herself into a unity. However, the reason why she had to unify herself and which elements had to be shaped into a unit remains vague in Jeanson ("different moments, different levels"), and all too obvious in Henry ("the believing with the unbelieving part"). In contrast, to us the reason is patently clear: Beauvoir had to model her "masculine" intellect and her "woman's heart" into a new, livable synthesis.

Sartrist Francis Jeanson applied a purely existential psychoanalytical approach to Beauvoir and thus has a blind spot where her social situatedness is concerned—her socialization as a woman—and this is why he cannot properly understand her autobiographical project. Because he does not involve her social situation, and particularly her position as woman, in his research on her project-for-life, he gets no further than its hardly shocking characterization as "*l'entreprise de vivre*," which is also the title of his book. Although Jeanson does remark a number of times how nice it is that Beauvoir, with all her intellectualism, remains "*une vraie femme*" (sic) (p. 214; see also p. 213), he misses the true *entreprise*:

the fact that it was the goal of her project to create an identity as both an intellectual *and* a woman.

In comparison, the approach used by Anne-Marie Lasocki, who characterizes Beauvoir's project as "*l'entreprise d'écrire*" (also the book title), is far more interesting. She notes that the uniqueness of Beauvoir's work lies in the open assumption of being-woman-and-writer (see Lasocki, 1971: 5). However, she fails to elaborate further on this point and remains bogged down in descriptions and representations via quotations, thus taking Beauvoir too much at her word. For example, Lasocki's book begins with an extensive exposition on the death theme in Beauvoir, as Beauvoir herself raised it, but without placing it in a broader context. (I will come back to this in chapter 10.) However, Lasocki does argue that Beauvoir's oeuvre should be considered the work of a writer who is busy making herself into a writer before our very eyes. The uniqueness of Beauvoir's project is seen to lie in her explanation for the fate of a "*femme écrivain*" (p. 5). But the fact that this is no explanation but a conquest, the fact that Beauvoir attempts to design an identity as an intellectual woman, eludes Lasocki.

The actual purport of her project also eludes Beauvoir, but this is totally in keeping with her belief that an author cannot oversee the sense of his work and life. The fact that this sense lay in the creation of an art of living as an intellectual woman, and thus had a gender-specific content, escaped her. Using different words, she continually stated that her authorship was her life's fulfillment (see FoC: 377, 275; ASD: 47, 129). Borrowing a term from Sartre, she even called this her "original project" (see ASD: 38).[9] She considered herself an intellectual *tout court*, someone who wants to know and who frames his life in words. The gender element played no role in her self-conception as writer. She stated, "The fact is that I am a writer—a woman writer, which doesn't mean a housewife who writes but someone whose whole existence is governed by her writing" (MDD: 664). When Sartre asked her what it was like to be a "*dame de lettres*," she exclaimed, "what a strange expression." For her, a woman who writes is "first and foremost a writer who devotes his life to writing and has no time for other, so-called feminine occupations" (Dayan and Ribowska, 1979: 79).

Nor did she question her authorship in the light of her situation; she made no connections with the fact that her surroundings considered her intellectuality irreconcilable with her gender. We have seen that her decision to proclaim herself a writer rather than a philosopher had everything to do with this. But she herself believed she would have become a writer anyway. When asked if her womanhood had ever placed inner obstacles in her path, she replied, "I cannot give you a real answer because

I have never been able to find a real answer for myself. It would be interesting to examine that thoroughly" (LE: 391).

Beauvoir herself stated that true understanding of a person's life requires full understanding of the time in which he lives (ASD: 49). In *L'amérique au jour le jour*, she argued that there is always "a gap between the subjective truth and the objective reality of an action; everyone who acts is also an actor and he cannot know the role his private world plays within the world of others" (Am: 332–33). In my view, Jeanson (1966) argues rightly that Beauvoir also provided her autobiography with a chronological order because she understood the meaning of her life did not coincide with her self-image. And in the foregoing, we did not extract the meaning of Beauvoir's life from this self-image, but from the whole of her situation as *jeune fille bien—et mal!—rangée*.

Many authors have failed to see that Beauvoir's autobiographical project was broader than her small world alone, or that she had a much more general goal in mind. For example, Elaine Marks considers narcissism as the most important factor in Beauvoir, and Strickland believes it is pure egoism (Marks, 1973; Strickland, 1966). Winegarten *reproaches* her for her interest in self-creation; Beauvoir should have written an authentic account (Winegarten, 1988).

In opposition to these conceptions of Beauvoir, I believe she was not engaged in a private project; her task was broader based. Willems calls her a "born pedagogue" and argues that "her prose is always demonstrative and utilitarian. It is an evocation and a communication" (Willems, 1972: 14). Beauvoir wanted to provide other women with handholds they could use to lead a professional life like her own. The autobiography was written as an exemplary work. It can be considered her most important ethical contribution.

Singularity

If we characterize Beauvoir's art of living as an ethics in which she wanted to unify her identity as intellectual with being a woman, can we then conclude she was attempting to create a model for female intellectuality? Wouldn't this be a flagrant contradiction of her own ideas? In *The Second Sex*, she opposed any generalizations on The woman or The feminine. In later life, her biggest indictment was against those—including present-day feminists—who believed "the female body provided some kind of new view of the world"; you should not give it a value in itself on pain of lapsing into "the irrational, the mystical, the cosmic" (Schwarzer, 1986: 114).

The eternal feminine is a lie, according to Beauvoir. She did not believe "there are specifically feminine qualities, values or ways of life" (ASD: 494). The idea that something like a feminine thinking, or a feminine intellectualism could exist was essentially alien to her. Although she did see differences between men and women, and also recognized the existence of a number of specific traits in women (e.g., a "relative identity," desire for subjection to a superior being), she considered these the effect of a very specific sociocultural power. Without it, or after it, there would only be slight differences between the sexes.

Thus, it is within existing relations that we should characterize Beauvoir's project as speaking *of* a woman, without attributing her with speaking *on behalf of* femininity. Beauvoir asked, "Have I ever written that women were the same as men? Have I ever claimed that I, personally, was not a woman? On the contrary, my main purpose has been to isolate and identify my own particular brand of femininity" (PoL: 367).

We have seen her striving was to capture a subject position for herself. More specifically we have seen her attempts to style herself into an intellectual woman based on the girl's socialization imposed upon her. We have also seen that Beauvoir felt it was important to show others her life at a time when women's emancipation had only just begun. From the enormous numbers of letters she received, it is apparent that many women could identify with her novels and her autobiography, and that they had mapped out their lives in parallel to hers (see Dayan and Ribowska, 1979: 77). Beauvoir points out the fact that her autobiography generated a great response from women who, like her, practiced an intellectual profession: "In contrast, other readers are women of my own age who have had to go through the same struggle in order to lead the life of an intellectual. I have received many letters from women working in education" (LE: 387).

Yet, she continued to stress her primary concern was with *her* truth, and she remained faithful to the existential-philosophical point of departure that claims every consciousness can speak only for itself. In *The Mandarins*, Henri wants to express the "flavour" of his life, "as if such a thing were a perfume, labelled, trade-mark registered, always the same, year after year" (M: 160). Beauvoir also wanted to pass on her life's element of originality. Both her novels and her autobiography were written as means of communication with her readers. "By addressing my readers directly I hope to perform this service" (PoL: 8). "[I]f you tell the truth about yourself scrupulously, (you help) others . . . to plumb the depths of their own truth" (LE: 395).

A 27-year-old woman wrote to her, "What a disappointment to find you are writing your memoirs! What we want to know is how to fight our way through life, with our husband, our job, our children, our desire to prove ourselves, and you come up with your memories which are only of interest to yourself!" (p. 395). But, according to Beauvoir, the opposite is true: "At this point in time, writing about myself is the most appropriate way of talking to others about themselves" (p. 395).

Through the description and construction of her own life, she wanted to give other women guidelines for organizing their own lives. But, true to her conceptions of the singularity of positive ethics, she kept her distance from statements on who or what a good woman is, or what real femininity is. She stated emphatically that feminism is *"une manière de vivre individuellement, et une manière de lutter collectivement"* (Jeanson, 1966: 264).

8

A PHILOSOPHER AS WOMAN

In the previous chapter we concluded Simone de Beauvoir attempted to develop an art of living as intellectual woman. In this and the following chapter, we shall take stock of the practical expression of that art of living and chart the concrete ethical subject she created in words and deeds. In this chapter we will look at how she organized her life as intellectual woman. The next chapter will examine the form she gave to her intellectual work.

Beauvoir herself pointed out that her formative years ended with World War II; thereafter "the point was no longer to educate but to fulfill myself" (FoC: 5). For this reason, I have based my inventory of her art of living, in this and the next chapter, primarily on the third and fourth parts of her autobiography—*The Force of Circumstance* and *All Said and Done*, which cover the periods 1944 to 1962 and 1962 to 1972, respectively.

In her attempts to style her life, Beauvoir clearly encountered boundaries. In chapter 10 we will look more closely at them and will find there is a reverse side to the life she created for herself. However, here we will concentrate on the values she tried to "live" and "exemplify" for others. Keeping faith with her rejection of a so-called inner life, in her autobiography she described primarily her relations with the world. In chapter 6 of the present volume, we found that she thought man is what he does and that action in the world formed the "substance" of her ethics. In *The Second Sex* she described how women's socialization leads them to imprison themselves in the subjective moment and to cultivate an inner life. She thought of this as an unhealthy life-style. According to Beauvoir, women have to focus actively on the world around them, thereby creating themselves simultaneously. She organized her own life according to this point of departure. It is no coincidence that in both the third and fourth parts of her autobiography, she provided an extensive report of her contacts and activities, the books she read, her travels, and so on.[1] She emphasized the fact that she did not use her life as pretext for literary flights and that she tried to show it as a finite reality (see FoC: 5; ASD: 10). Her aim was to chart her behaviors.

Professional practice

The first thing that strikes us in Beauvoir's life as intellectual woman is that she practiced her profession independently, rather as if she was self-employed. Following a brief career as teacher of philosophy at various schools, which was terminated involuntarily, she never again sought permanent employment. As a self-employed writer, she withdrew from the world of institutions, both academic and otherwise, and from the daily struggle for prestige and positions that are inherent to them. She set up her own *practice*, her own store.

She wrote at least six hours a day and organized her days around the writing with extreme precision. At the beginning of her career especially, she chose to do her writing and researching in (semi) public places (libraries, cafes, hotels). She enjoyed looking up from her work and seeing people around her. If her choice of writing outside her home was born initially out of necessity — a stove still burned at cafe de Flore during the war — she continued this habit in the postwar years. Only when the cafe became too busy and her writer's identity was firmly established did she move her "office" and begin writing at home or in Sartre's flat.

The magazine *Les temps modernes* acted as a platform for continual and essential discussions with contemporaries. Beauvoir did a lot for the magazine, especially in the early postwar years when Sartre was often absent. She evaluated articles, edited, wrote, and saw people at the editorial office at Gallimard, and had meetings twice a week with the permanent staff. Later, when the extent of her activities decreased, she still remained closely involved with the magazine. Editorial meetings were then often held in her home. This basis to her existence as intellectual was supplemented by her own "business," consisting of, among other things, contacts with publishers and readers and a never-ceasing flow of correspondence. With the exception of secretarial help in typing out her manuscripts, she never employed anyone to look after her affairs, al-, though Sartre's secretaries provided occasional support.

Over time, she developed a stable professional identity. After the publication of *She Came to Stay* (1943), she no longer doubted herself as an author. "I had grown used to living inside a writer's skin and nowadays scarcely ever caught myself looking at this new character and saying: It's me" (FoC: 54; see also PoL: 606). Her professional identity lent her a sense of security. She said that, in contrast to Anne in *The Mandarins*, she had "the autonomy that has been bestowed on me by a profession which means so much to me" (FoC: 280). She wasn't worried by the fact that for some time she was financially dependent on Sartre. She knew she could always fall back on her teaching, and her professional identity guaranteed a moral independence (see p. 21). Beauvoir considered herself an autonomous intellectual.

Even if she had not met Sartre, she would still have been a writer, she argued, because her intention predated their meeting. She saw her career as her own product. There was certainly mutual help insofar as each criticized the other's work, often unmercifully (see p. 480). But she stressed the independence of her research and her constant and direct contact with the world around her, without living *through* Sartre (see ASD: 33; FoC: 661). From 1954, her books brought in a lot of money and she considered her position financially privileged.

In the early postwar years, she enjoyed her role as "real Parisian figure," without experiencing the kind of skepticism Sartre felt. She was not troubled by doubts about her political role as writer. As she was saddled with a lot fewer pretensions than Sartre, she was gratified by her new status. In her eyes, one of the advantages was the contacts she had with prominent people all over the world: through these she felt she "had a grip" on history (see FoC: 49, 55, 667). As the years progressed, her world took on wider proportions, also in a political sense. At the age of sixty-four, she wrote, "On the whole I see where I stand in the world more clearly than when I was forty. I understand the structure of society and the course of history better than I did before; and I am better at making out people's intentions and their reactions" (ASD: 229).

Beauvoir worked hard. On several occasions, she herself mentioned the perseverance and struggle her work entailed (see FoC: 661) and the fact that her sense of vocation was essential in generating the energy this required. In discussing a friend, she remarked that this person was talented but lacked vocation: "I think she wasn't interested enough in other people to have the patience to keep on talking to them page after page" (p. 240). She saw herself as a person who was able to concentrate and who pursued and completed plans. If people called her stubborn, obstinate, and dogged, she reformulated these comments as strong-willed, tenacious, and determined. In spite of criticism, she retained confidence in herself.

When her first book was rejected by Gallimard, she simply began a new project. Nor was she fazed by the stream of criticism evoked by the publication of *All Men are Mortal*. In fact, this criticism stimulated a desire for revenge. She defined herself as a still-"dutiful" student who became restless when idle for two or three weeks. In the long term, idleness bored her. It made her days colorless (see ASD: 47, 150). In spite of the fact that her sense of mandate and vocation faded—this is understandable because her aim, styling herself into and justifying herself as an intellectual woman was gradually realized—she remained true to her professional identity as writer. She no longer believed writing "justified" her existence, but without it "I should feel mortally unjustified" (FoC: 666).

Writing—confronting the empty page and formulating sentences—was an effort. She was overcome by dejection at the start of each new book. All appeared enterprises of colossal proportion. Writing *The Mandarins* cost her at least as much effort as her first work. More than once she decided to give up on the project, especially because Sartre came up with serious criticisms. But her friends Bost and Lanzmann persuaded her to persevere. The final two years of the project were years of "labor" (see FoC: 299, 266). She stopped drinking alcohol in order to concentrate more fully and took long walks so that she could maintain the six- to seven-hour writing days. Disturbances during her work infuriated her. Even Sartre was sent away (see Bair, 1990a: 427). Her punishing work routine continued also as she grew older. She got through a lot of her writing work in the mornings while still in bed and no one, not even a lover, could keep her from it.

The work itself was difficult to describe, she said, but she tried. How do you transform rough notes into actual writing? "When I feel ready, I write three or four hundred pages straight off. This is arduous work: it requires intense concentration, and the rubbish that I accumulate appalls me. At the end of a month or two, I am so sickened I can't go on. I begin again from scratch" (FoC: 285). Based on all this accumulated raw material, she then writes one definitive page per day. Subsequently, she revises and rewrites it all:

I begin again at page one, read it through and rewrite it sentence by sentence; then I correct each sentence so that it will fit into the page as a whole, then each page so that it has its place in the whole chapter; later on, each chapter, each page, each sentence, is revised in relation to the work as a whole. (p. 285)

This was "the most exciting part, doing the second draft and seeing it take shape" (p. 89).

In general, and with the exception of *The Mandarins* which took four, writing a book took her two to three years. Articles for *Les temps modernes* were also time-consuming because they required a lot of preparation. Beauvoir claimed that all the writers she knew had to work very hard. People often tend to think too lightly of the investment writing requires. When *Memoirs of a Dutiful Daughter* appeared, many women said they could have written it themselves, but the fact they did not do so was no coincidence (see pp. 334, 285). People have to realize what work is; it is not about trying to achieve literary fame on the cheap. Nor is making discoveries the same as picking up on a flash of insight that no one else has had, but "driving straight for your goal, and damn everything else" (PoL: 42; see also FoC: 125).

But apart from the sweat and tears, writing was also fun, adventure, freedom for Beauvoir. Even the physical side of writing attracted her: "especially in the afternoon when I come back at half past four into this room that's still thick with smoke from the morning, the paper already covered with green ink lying on the desk; and my cigarette and fountain pen feel so pleasant in my fingers" (FoC: 93; see also p. 444). She enjoyed sitting at her desk in a room permeated with work. Research at the Bibliothèque Nationale was also enjoyable: "it is pleasant and restful to fill one's eyes with words that already exist, instead of having to wrest sentences from the void" (p. 177; see also p. 444).

Work became increasingly important. As she grew older, the need to get out into the world declined, and desire for work increased. Beauvoir recalled developing the sense of urgency Sartre always mentioned. Writing dominated her life. It occupied her not only when she confronted a blank sheet of paper, but also at night. "It often happens that a sentence suddenly runs through my head before I go to bed, or when I am unable to sleep, and I get up again and note it down" (p. 286; see also p. 444). When she was conceiving a new book, she made notes continually, even during walks and other activities (see p. 185).

When she wrote, Beauvoir felt she had something to say. She valued words and truth, and was surprised that people often failed to understand her intellectual drive (see pp. 93, 378, 200). "I was for clear-cut opinions" (p. 70), she stated, but her intensity often shocked people.[2] She herself suggested that, at the beginning of an intellectual career, women especially should close themselves off somewhat from people, because a certain struggle is needed if one is to succeed intellectually and affirm oneself. She stated she was later able to open up more to other people when work and profession no longer entailed a major struggle, but on a political level she always remained very abrupt and rigid in her dislikes (see Jeanson, 1966: 276).

She didn't like public speaking. She felt intimidated by the audience who transformed her into an object: "I am afraid I may not measure up to their expectations or to my own intentions. I talk too fast, terrified by the length of the silence I must fill and by the quantity of things to be said in such a short time" (FoC: 593; see also ASD: 48). But she enjoyed positive public responses (see FoC: 208). On her travels with Sartre to, for example, Japan and Brazil, she began giving lectures on the situation of woman. Yet she often spoke of her lack of interest in the role of public "personality." She refused to exhibit herself on television and radio, and rarely gave press interviews because she wanted her success to be the exclusive product of her work, and not of publicity or notoriety. When 40,000 prepublication orders had been received for *The Prime of Life*, she wondered anxiously whether she had become a producer of best-sellers with a readership that was guaranteed and for whom the quality of the work no longer played a role (see pp. 664, 589).

She wanted to be loved for the content of her books alone. Thus, she was highly gratified by the voluminous correspondence they generated. "The majority of my correspondents tell me of their fellow feelings, confide their difficulties, ask for advice or explanations; they encourage me and sometimes enrich my experience" (FoC: 488). *The Second Sex*, *Memoirs of a Dutiful Daughter*, and *The Mandarins* were all immediate successes, not only in France but in other countries, such as the United States. And when a book on her life and work appeared (Gennari, 1958), Beauvoir exclaimed, "At the moment, everything seems to be encouraging me to be narcissistic" (FoC: 425), but she really saw it as fulfillment of her girlhood dream to acquire the affection of others through her work (see p. 328).

Day-to-day life-style

Beauvoir has often been accused of leading a purely intellectual life. That image is correct insofar as writing certainly dominated her life. But at the same time we also find that she elaborated her intellectual existence into a comprehensive life-style. In contrast to the then-current privatist way of life of women of her class, she created for herself a relatively public life-style. Hotels, cafes, restaurants, terraces, bars—she was often to be found in public places, not least during her continual travels.

Of the Sartre-Beauvoir duo, it was she who determined the ingredients of daily life. The journeys, the bicycle, walking and later automobile tours, the meetings with friends, the practical organization of their relationship (such as working in each other's flats, the long vacations together), this was all her doing and resulted in an unconventional life-style.

As we have seen in chapter 6, Beauvoir's ethics comprised a self-styling through the technique of a fixed daily schedule. The seven-day working week was organized according to an established pattern: for example, going out in the morning for breakfast and reading the papers in a cafe or on a terrace. After picking up the essential cigarettes, she worked for around three hours. Then followed a lengthy lunch with Sartre or others in a restaurant before another three to four hours work and dinner, again with people. Whiskey in a cafe or—in later years—listening to music, with or without Sartre, in her apartment rounded off the day. When she and Sartre began spending the summer months in Rome from 1953, their life there also followed a set routine: "Up at 9.30, long breakfast with the newspapers in the Piazza San Marco. Work till 2.30. A snack. Sightseeing or a museum. Work from five till nine" (FoC: 429). "And then we drink a little bit too much whisky in the Piazza Santi Apostoli or the Piazza del Popolo," to wash down hours of conversation (p. 438, see also p. 367).

If, in the early postwar years, she maintained a student life-style, by the time she reached her forties, she had begun to tire of hotel living. In 1948, she rented an apartment, and in 1954 she used the money brought in by the Prix Goncourt to buy the house she would live in until her death. From the moment she had her own flat, she changed her life to some extent. She stayed home more, bought furniture and a wardrobe. In the mornings she worked at home and in the afternoons at Sartre's apartment—a habit she retained, even during periods when other lovers played a major role in her life. However, she continued to eat in restaurants, where she met all kinds of people, and to go out with friends. She always remained somewhat aloof from Paris's nightlife, not least from the so-called "existentialist" scene in the jazz cellars and cafes of the Quartier Latin, which flourished in the early postwar years. During a visit to the Tabou club, she remarked that both conversation and respiration were impossible due to the noise and smoke (see p. 152).

Parties occupied an important place in her social life, especially in the late 1940s. Beauvoir organized a "*réveillon*" (festive meal) at her home every Christmas Eve. There were also numerous posttheater suppers following performances and rehearsals of Sartre's plays. Both Beauvoir and Sartre drank heavily, especially in their younger years. Parties with friends from the resistance, and meetings with writer friends, such as Koestler and Hemingway, lasted until dawn. Alcohol played a major role in those "fleeting moments of eternal friendship" (p. 61). After an evening with Koestler and Camus that had got out of hand, Camus asked them, "Do you think it's possible to go on drinking like that and still work? No. And in fact such excesses had become very rare for all three of us" (p. 150).

Beauvoir was always surrounded by a permanent circle of friends and intimates. If writing was her life's fulfillment, she emphasized that friends and love were nevertheless the most important. There was great continuity in her friendships, some of which had begun as love affairs. She called her friends her family and stated that with them she thought, and exchanged information and opinions on events, books, films, and so forth (see ASD: 52). The fact that this circle was relatively small met with her approval. "I should rather spend more [time] with those who are close to me. I have put so much of myself into their lives that their projects, their successes and their failures have become mine" (p. 52).

She maintained friendships with women much younger than herself (for example, pupils Olga Kozakiewitch and Nathalie Sorokine were both ten years her junior, and Sylvie Le Bon was thirty-three years younger) and with women who needed her. The latter category included, for example, the writer Violette Leduc, who adored her passionately. From 1963 until Beauvoir's death, the relationship with Le Bon was intense. She adopted Sylvie as her daughter to safeguard the legacy of her oeuvre.

Yet, her relationship with Sartre endured. Beauvoir called the fact she had met him "the most important event in my life" (ASD: 29) and spoke of their relationship as a "success" (see FoC: 659). She did not regret not having had children because her vocation was that of writer (see PoL: 77–78). All her life, she remained fascinated by "the genius" Sartre. During periods when she lived with other lovers, she continued to spend afternoons and evenings with Sartre. They wrote side-by-side in his apartment. "I continued to see Sartre as much as before" (FoC: 297). She worked out complete schedules in order to accommodate her other lovers. "The equilibrium . . . was durable and endured" (p. 309, see also p. 510). In chapter 10 we will see what price she paid for this equilibrium.

Her assurance that "since I was twenty-one I have never been lonely" (ASD: 39) sounds almost defiant, but it is certainly true that her existence was filled with close ties within a small circle of people, and contacts with many others. As her fame increased, her contacts became less free and uninhibited. People approached her differently. But she no longer cared for fleeting meetings. Outside her own circle, she wanted where possible to talk on a one-to-one basis "since we could often get through the small-talk stage very quickly then" (FoC: 476; see also pp. 298, 476).

If the price of fame was a certain isolation, it also opened many doors. Although she hated the salons of Parisian women, there were certainly invitations she looked on with pleasure. Beauvoir remarked that the international intellectual circle to which she now belonged was relatively small. If she wanted to meet someone, she always had the opportunity (see ASD: 45, 67; FoC: 129). Meetings were arranged for Sartre and Beauvoir during their travels, through various intermediaries and by local French cultural institutes. Professional contacts through other sources also continued to be widely available to Beauvoir, not only through *Les temps modernes*, but also as a result of Sartre's and Beauvoir's political activities in later years. Only when the Algerian war was at its height did they lead a retired life, reducing to a minimum their professional and social contacts. This forced seclusion was a direct result of open public hostility to their support for the Algerian struggle for independence.

Reading occupied an important part of their time, especially during their summers in Rome.

> There is no occupation that seems more natural to me. . . . I am still wonderstruck by that metamorphosis of little black marks into a word—a word that projects me into a particular world or that brings this world within the four walls of my room. The most lumpish text is enough to bring the miracle about. *Yng lady, 30, exp. sht-typ. seeks work three days a week.* My eyes scan this advertisement and all at once France is peopled with typewriters and young ladies out of work. (ASD: 154)

Reading is enjoyable. It creates new and durable relations between yourself and the world (FoC: 147). Compared to visual images, words are much more powerful. "For a moment the image is enchanting; but then it fades and loses strength. Words have this immense privilege: you can take them with you" (ASD: 211–12). Beauvoir devoured the books she read for pleasure: sometimes reading them so quickly that, once finished, she had to begin again. Apart from purely recreational reading, as a way of passing time—detective stories, science fiction, novels—there was also the thirst for knowledge and information: "Above all I try to understand my own period" (ASD: 157).

She read studies on the Soviet Union, the United States, Latin America, Cuba, the French working class, the Italian proletariat. When important events took place, she read everything on the subject she could get her hands on—the Six-day War, May '68, the Czech invasion, the Chinese Cultural Revolution. Historic events during her own lifetime fascinated her and she searched out information "on Franco's Spain, the Greek resistance and the tragic failure of the partisans' war, the Third Reich, the French Milice and Gestapo, the extermination of the Jews, and the wars in Indochina and Algeria" (pp. 157–58). In addition, she read reportage, works on ethnology and psychiatry. She followed the work of so-called "anti-psychiatrists" such as Szasz, Cooper, Laing, and Basaglia with great interest and was captivated by Bruno Bettelheim's work. Biography, especially of writers, was fascinating: "That is what interests and puzzles me most—the link between the daily life of a writer (a link so different for each) and the books in which he expresses himself" (p. 161). She reread Proust and Rousseau's *Confessions* time and again. Another theme that fascinated her was, "how does a woman adjust herself to her womanly state, her female condition" (p. 161). She sympathized, for example, with the work of Lou Andreas-Salomé. In more general terms, she valued "those works that throw new light upon the human state" (p. 160).

When tired of reading, she also enjoyed checkers, crossword and other puzzles, and American movies especially. She loved Buster Keaton, Westerns, James Bond, but also Visconti and Pasolini films (see p. 197 ff). Gradually, music began to play a greater role. On three or four nights a week, she would listen to her classical records. "Of course, I could read; but when the evening comes, I feel I've had enough of words, my mind is swimming with them. . . . Music takes me into another universe" (FoC: 498).

Traveling and taking trips also occupied a lot of her time. During her younger years, she had practiced being alone through her departure for Marseilles and through the long, solitary walks she took while there. From that time on, she felt she could count on herself. Throughout the rest of her life, she would often travel and go on walking tours by herself. In a certain sense, she experienced the identity of a woman alone positively. Inspired by the work of Katherine Mansfield, she perceived aloneness as romantic (PoL: 100). But the initial stages of such a solitary period remained difficult for her (FoC: 251, 131, 480). She dreaded them, but always rediscovered her ability to enjoy her aloneness to the full, and found the days were too short. "My first night alone was spent in Merano; it remains one of my most precious memories. I ate dinner and drank white wine in a courtyard hung with ivy, opposite a copper-faced clock" (FoC: 113).

Beauvoir had a "taste for the immediate." She loved "all the pleasures of the body, the feel of the weather, walks, friendships, gossip, learning, seeing" (p. 55). She loved her trips through France, discovering churches, abbeys, castles, and landscapes en route. Traveling around, arriving at a "charming" hotel, eating the local cuisine—all were pleasures. More than once, she recounted her love of food. "There is another pleasure in which I indulge when I am traveling in France, and that is eating. In their fashion the cooking and often the wine are an expression of the province that produces them" (ASD: 263). She ate with pleasure on her foreign travels. She believed "one learns to know a country to a large extent through the mouth" (FoC: 525).

When she bought a car in 1951, she was thrilled by her ability to "sort of" drive it. Sartre appeared unmoved by the fact Beauvoir was not a particularly good driver: he never criticized her lack of prowess behind the wheel and encouraged her to overtake as many other vehicles as possible. She often made long car journeys alone, and felt an intense satisfaction afterward. On her arrival at her sister's in Italy, she noted, "I should never have enjoyed the immobility, the silence and the tinkle of ice in my glass so much if I had not had that long day of urgent striving behind me" (ASD: 268).

On her first-ever plane trip, she had managed to get a place in the cockpit: "how marvellous, I thought, not only that there should still be first times left for me, but that they should be happening" (FoC: 62). She wanted to explore the whole planet and "chart" every country as much as possible. Her oeuvre comprises a number of travelogues (on China, the United States, and Brazil: see FoC: 522–83). She threw herself enthusiastically into a new "strange" land and tried to penetrate its secrets. Sartre, who did not share this particular obsession, protested increasingly against her compulsive travel programs, and they finally worked out a compromise: mornings were devoted to exploration, with work commencing midafternoons. Beauvoir would also go out alone and return to their hotel at the end of a busy day to find Sartre at work shrouded in a cloud of smoke. During her own skiing holidays, she combined relaxation with mornings spent working on a terrace, "surrounded by the vast, glittering landscape of the mountains," which was a pleasure in itself (FoC: 62).

She claimed her relationship to the large amounts of money she earned remained ambivalent: on the one hand, she did not want to become infected with social injustice, on the other she benefited from the advantages it brought, particularly the expensive trips it made possible. She got round the problem to some extent by using her money impulsively and letting herself be led by her mood. She did not dress expensively, but certainly looked the "lady." She visited the hairdresser—in spite of her penchant for turbans—used makeup, and varnished her nails diligently throughout her life.

Beauvoir was more than aware of her bourgeois origins. She compared herself, for example, with writer Christiane Rochefort and noted, "she was a real working-class girl, and there wasn't much she hadn't seen: I envied her daring, her fire, her inner freedom" (p. 596). The spontaneity of her friend Lanzmann was also alien. Most of her friends, and she herself, were puritans: "we kept our reactions under control and externalized our emotions very little" (p. 296).

But Beauvoir certainly had her rebellious side. Her attitude tended to be stubborn and singular, and she was not above trampling over all kinds of established codes. She would show the door to people she did not like[3] and would create scenes in public. Confronted with dangerous situations during her solitary trips, she acted decisively. She threatened to jump from a moving car, fought with an Arab, and offered him money so that she could escape (see PoL: 94; FoC: 63). This kind of experience gave her the feeling she could tackle anything, remarking ironically, "I do not regret having nursed this illusion for so long, since it supplied me with a touch of audacity which made life much easier for me" (PoL: 94). She complained of the fact that her "powers of revolt" had dimmed with age (FoC: 673). But in a political sense, she remained a rebellious lady all her life.

Politics

Beauvoir's attitude to practical politics was rather ambiguous. On the one hand, and based on a somewhat odd rationale, she stated that she agreed so often with Sartre that his presence at a political meeting made her own superfluous; she didn't want to accompany him like a shadow (see FoC: 28). On the other hand, she still felt guilty: "I blamed myself for not having tried to do more. Sartre pointed out exactly what I had always told myself: that I can't very well go round mimicking him all the time; our names are so closely linked we're almost thought of as only one person" (p. 419).

She felt no immediate affinity with the practical side of politics—congresses, committees, manifestos, and discussions were matters that interested her only to a limited extent (see p. 275), and she stated, "I was not active because I am an intellectual" (Dayan and Ribowska, 1979: 62–63). Of friends who worked for the Algerian *Front de Libération Nationale* underground movement, she noted,

I admired those who took part in such action. But to do so demanded total commitment, and it would have been cheating to pretend that I was capable of such a thing. I am not a woman of action; my reason for living is writing; to sacrifice that I would have had to believe myself indispensable in some other field. Such was not by any means the case. I contented myself with giving what help I could when I was asked for it. (FoC: 472)

With regard to the Algerian war, she wrote, "I wanted to stop being an accomplice in this war, but how? I could talk in meetings or write articles; but I would only have been saying the same things as Sartre less well than he was saying them. I would have felt ridiculous following him like a shadow." But she went on to say, "Today (1963–KV), however little it might affect the outcome, I could only throw all my weight into the struggle" (p. 382).

Her attention for the specifics of politics increased in the early 1950s. She recognized the importance of expertise in the field of politics, an expertise that transcended general moral discussions. In *The Mandarins*, Henri formulates this as follows:

the simple fact was that he was particularly ill-equipped for the political life. "Well, I'll just have to start working at it," he said to himself. But if he really wanted to extend his knowledge, it would require years of study. Economics, history, philosophy—he would never be done with it! What a job! And all that just to come to terms with Marxism! Writing would be completely out of the question. . . . There was something unfair in this whole thing. He felt obliged, like everyone else, to take an active interest in politics. That being the case, it shouldn't require a specialised apprenticeship; if politics was a field reserved for technicians, then they shouldn't be asking him to get mixed up in it. (M: 153–54)

In the course of her life, Beauvoir built up a basic general knowledge of politics. She read historical works and immersed herself in the political developments of her time, reading a number of newspapers every day and following the news broadcasts. In her autobiography, she provided reports of the political situation in the countries she visited. As her professional identity became stronger with time, her fear of appearing in public declined, and she became more active politically. But she continued to emphasize she was not a specialist in or an original thinker on practical politics. With a certain equanimity, she claimed always to have followed Sartre's lead in political stances, and that she had shared his view of the communist party and socialist countries (see ASD: 33). She noted that Sartre's philosophical ambition was to produce a fully comprehensive description of existence. This was why he could not confine himself to theoretic reflections, but had to be involved in practical choices: "Hence he found himself committed to action in a much more radical way than myself. We always discussed his attitudes together, and sometimes I influenced him. But it was through him that these problems, in all their urgency and all their subtlety, presented themselves to me" (FoC: 12).

When Sartre was released from prisoner-of-war camp in 1941, he was active in the formation of a resistance group (*Socialisme et Liberté*)—a move that initially surprised Beauvoir. In 1940, there was no room for doubt at an intellectual level: people had to hate national-socialism and collaboration. But she herself had not found a way of expressing resistance to national-socialism (see ASD: 33). Beauvoir joined this group, but its aims remained vague, and establishing political contacts proved extremely difficult; it remained isolated from the real French resistance. Sartre tried to make contact with the communists. "They, however, distrusted any group formed outside the auspices of the Party, and in particular those of the 'petit-bourgeois intellectuals' " (PoL: 500).

The group collapsed under the weight of dejection and impotence. Sartre and Beauvoir threw themselves into work.[4] In 1943, Sartre was invited by communist intellectuals to join the underground writers' union, the *Comité national des écrivains* (CNE). Beauvoir's first novel was published in 1943, with approval from the Comité, but she was not invited to join and her contacts with CNE always went through Sartre.

When Sartre became serious about his affiliation to socialism, he worked his way frenetically through piles of books on economics and history and encouraged Beauvoir to do the same. " 'You should read this!' he would tell me, pointing to the books piled up on his desk; he would insist: 'It's fascinating.' I couldn't; I had to finish my novel. And then, although I too wanted to know more about the world I was living in, it wasn't a necessity for me as it was for him" (FoC: 267).

Their ways parted here, both intellectually and practically. Beauvoir was working on *The Mandarins*. Both had important relationships with others. Sartre's shift toward communism reached its height between 1950 and 1954, although as far as we know, he never joined the party. Partly through the influence of Claude Lanzmann, who was her lover from 1952 to 1958, Beauvoir gradually became more interested in Sartre's political attitudes (see pp. 302–3). She noted,

> I have often wondered what my position would have been if I had not been associated with Sartre in the way that I was. Close to the Communists certainly, because of my horror of all that they were fighting against; but I loved truth too much not to demand the freedom to seek it as I

wished. I would never have become a Party member; since I had less objective importance than Sartre, the difficulties of this attitude would have been reduced, but the attitude itself would have resembled his. I therefore found myself in perfect agreement with him. (p. 53)

From 1955, she chose to become more involved in Sartre's political activities. She accompanied him to conferences and on international trips with a political tint, including visits to China, Cuba, Brazil, the Soviet Union, Poland, Japan, Yugoslavia, the Middle East, and Czechoslovakia. She attended international writers' symposia, participated in the debates and discussions there, and in the Russell Tribunal on the Vietnam War (1967). Following the Soviet invasion of Hungary (1956), Sartre and Beauvoir distanced themselves from the U.S.S.R. Yet, they continued to visit there until 1966; they maintained friendly relations with a number of progressive Soviet intellectuals who were in conflict with "the conformists" (see ASD: 306). However, in 1972, Beauvoir wrote, "I draw no comfort from anything that is happening in the European socialist countries" (p. 438).

During the Algerian war (1958 to 1964), when they were driven into isolation because of their pro-independence stance and anti-Gaullism, they again became closer to the French communist party. In 1960, Beauvoir supported a campaign to help Djamila Boupacha (an Algerian woman who had begun a civil suit against her French torturers) and lent her name to a book on the trial. She was threatened by the OAS as was Sartre, who suffered two bomb attacks on his apartment in his mother's house. During the May revolution in 1968, Beauvoir was frequently to be found in the corridors of the student-occupied Sorbonne. She joined in their demands for educational reform.

From that time onward, her public activities accelerated. She undertook journalistic work for Maoist publications, assumed nominal responsibility for the magazine *L'idiot international* (as Sartre had done for a similar publication, *La cause du peuple*), for which she acted in spite of a government ban. She spoke in public as chair of the association of friends of *La cause du peuple*, hawked the publication with Sartre and others, and allowed herself to be arrested by the police. However, Beauvoir was somewhat ambivalent about the Maoist movement. She considered its belief in the imminent arrival of revolution rather naive and childish. But she did not regret "the few services" she could do for the Maoists. "I should rather try to help the young in their struggle than be the passive witness of a despair that has led some of them to the most hideous suicide" (p. 479). She supported the existence of a left-wing press and felt it necessary to champion its cause (see p. 438).

From 1970, she also took an active part in demonstrations and actions organized by the French women's movement. She signed the so-called manifesto of the 343—in which the signatories said they had had abortions—in support of a right-to-choose campaign. She added her weight to actions of girls in homes for unmarried mothers, and occasionally made her apartment available as the location for an abortion. She assisted in establishing women's refuges in France and became president of the *Ligue des droits des femmes*. When possible, she helped the women's movement, not only by lending her name to initiatives, but also by assuming an advisory role. In her own way, she participated in practical politics—her own way being support at the grass roots level.

Now that we have charted the way Beauvoir organized her life as intellectual, I think we can distinguish the following three "self-techniques." First, we can conclude she integrated enjoyment of the good things in life into her life-style as intellectual. She made sure her life was very pleasant by expanding her intellectual existence into a comprehensive life-style. Her life was in no way ascetic or cerebral, as she herself stressed, but had all manner of pleasurable aspects (see also FoC: 694). It was characterized not only by work and all the social contacts work brought with it, but also by meeting with friends, cafe visits, good food, skiing, trips, whiskey, cigarettes, terraces, and newspapers. A further striking point is that she created her own professional practice by introducing a serious work pattern according to fixed rituals, often in public places. In this way, she lifted her activities and occupations out of the private sphere and gave them the status of labor. Finally, we find she consciously shaped her life in a way that obliged her to continue developing as *individual*. By not marrying, by remaining financially independent and continuing to work, she guaranteed herself an ongoing active involvement with the world and with other people.

9

A WOMAN AS PHILOSOPHER

In this chapter we will take stock of the way Beauvoir structured her intellectual work. We have to go into some of the philosophical background of her work to detect the specific type of intellectuality she developed in the context of her art of living as intellectual woman. Diligent worker that she was—her friends called her "Castor" (beaver) for this very reason—she left an extensive oeuvre. This oeuvre consists of a number of treatises on ethics, a play, a number of novels, the voluminous studies *The Second Sex* and *Old Age*, travelogues, a four-part autobiography, and two books on the deaths of her mother and Sartre, respectively. Recently, a war diary and a collection of letters have been added to the body of her work, but these were not written with publication in mind. In addition, she generated numerous forewords, introductions, book reviews, and such (for an overview, see Francis and Gontier, 1979).

As we have seen in chapter 1, Beauvoir did not bother to profile herself as a philosopher. She claimed to have no philosophical ambitions (see FoC: 12) and to know her limitations in this field (see PoL: 548). Yet, she repeatedly alerted her biographer to the philosophical articles she had written in the 1940s as not only the beginning, but also *the key* to her oeuvre (see Bair, 1990a: 269).[1] We have seen that these articles developed a number of basic principles of an existentialist ethics, with as central thesis the notion that a positive abstract morality has no justification because morals are located at the level of concrete human behavior.

It is this thesis that indeed forms the key to interpreting the rest of her oeuvre. Beauvoir worked outside of the strict boundaries of academic philosophy because it had no place for the themes she was interested in. Based on her own approach in ethics, she worked freely, without worrying overmuch about the academic tradition of her discipline. We will now examine how she went about this.

The philosophical novel

First, we will take a closer look at Beauvoir's literary work. We have seen how she introduced the concept of the metaphysical novel in her article "Littérature et métaphysique." This type of novel would not be aimed at expressing universal and objective truth, but would show the subjective, singular, and dramatic truth of existence (see chapter 5). Beauvoir preferred this mélange of philosophy and literature to the *roman à thèse*, which expresses abstract propositions. This is why she later and in retrospect distanced herself from her early novels, in which she had articulated her philosophical ideas in an abstract way.

The central theme of *She Came to Stay* (1943) is the relationship between Self and Other. Its watchword is a Hegelian notion: "Every consciousness is bent on the death of the other consciousness." In this novel, Beauvoir describes how the eldest woman, Françoise, in a ménage à trois, gradually begins to feel threatened: from *pour-soi*, she becomes an object in the world of the others, Pierre and Xavière. This unbearable experience can only be terminated in one way—Françoise murders Xavière and thus reestablishes herself as subject.

While still writing this novel and influenced by her own more thorough reading of Hegel, Beauvoir concluded that every person lives in relation to a social dimension and has to find a moral solution to it. In her diary she noted she no longer subscribed to the philosophical thesis of *She Came to Stay*. She considered the *repression* of the consciousness of others as juvenile (JG: 364) and solipsistic (p. 362): in future, she wanted the social dimension to be central to her work.[2] Her subsequent novel, *The Blood of Others* (1945), is the expression of this shift in focus.

In the postwar years, this book was greeted as the first existential novel on the resistance. But, in fact, it also treated the philosophical problem of relationships with the other. The main character Hélène, who until the outbreak of war had been a selfish woman, finally concludes she cannot avoid her responsibilities to others. She joins an underground group. The resistance fighter Jean Blomart has to decide whether he can use violence if it will endanger the lives of innocent people. Hélène dies as a result of his decisions. Blomart comes to believe violence, as a means of achieving specific ends, is sometimes justified—a conclusion that concurs with one of Beauvoir's so-called methodological rules in *The Ethics of Ambiguity* (see chapter 5).

The play *Les bouches inutiles* (1945; *Who Shall Die?*) deals with another of these methodological rules from her moral theory, namely the rule that stipluates that means and end in a struggle for freedom have to be consistent with each other (see chapter 5). Beauvoir described the dilemma confronting the inhabitants of a besieged town when food shortages have become pressing. Should women and children or the elderly and infirm still receive food, or should they be sent out of the town because they are of no use to the defenders? Are some people of more value than others? What does it mean to be of no use to society? Her answer to this problem is unambiguous: all people are of equal value. The inhabitants decide to leave the city together and throw themselves into the fight.

All Men Are Mortal (1946) articulates a founding principle of Beauvoir's "ethics of ambiguity." Fosca, who has become immortal after drinking an elixir of life, no longer feels emotion and lapses into indifference. He thus ceases to be human. His existence through the centuries becomes absurd and unbearable, his actions become senseless. Without death, life has no significance, without the finite situatedness of man, his ties with the world disappear. Being human means commitment to other people.

Beauvoir considered her early novels as failures because philosophical ideas are central to them but lack a human guise. Their characters are not flesh-and-blood people, but marionettes of abstract propositions. The crime in *She Came to Stay* is implausible at a subjective level: Françoise has nothing of the murderess in her. Killing Xavière serves no purpose other than to provide a solution for an abstract philosophical problem. In hindsight, Beauvoir called the drift of *Who Shall Die?* no more than sermonizing: "I made the same mistake as in *The Blood of Others* . . . my characters were reduced to mere ethical viewpoints" (PoL: 588). She also believed *The Blood of Others* suffered from didacticism and a prosy style (p. 589).[3] Thus, Beauvoir regretted the fact her early novels carried an unequivocal moral message. They are all moral-philosophical novels (or novels *à thèse*).

Later, she was at pains to articulate the ambiguity of moral decisions in her literary work, and in her view, she succeeded with *The Mandarins* (1954). If the early novels ended in a "morally edifying conclusion," in

The Mandarins "no firm decision is made . . . we are not told who is right and who is wrong, and the condition of ambiguity is preserved" (p. 589). Moral decisions are here made visible as a difficult, subjective process of deliberation.

The subjective level is also at issue in both *Les Belles Images* (1966) and *La femme rompue* (1968; *The Woman Destroyed*). Beauvoir shows here some of the specific subjective basic experiences she had in mind with her concept of a "metaphysical novel." *Les Belles Images* articulates the basic experience of a woman who fights for authenticity and autonomy. It shows the struggle of advertising designer Laurence to find an alternative to her world of pretty pictures, the unfeeling milieu in which only success and status count. Laurence revolts against the safe life-style of her environment and opts to take control of her life. She tries to raise her daughter with the idea that something has to be done about the suffering of her fellow men. *The Woman Destroyed* is a collection of three stories, two of which sketch the experience of a woman who has lived as a secondary being and has renounced her own tastes and occupations in the name of love. The suffering of these women, but also their "bad faith," emerge sharply, precisely because Beauvoir focuses solely on the subjective level.

But her philosophical ideas, especially her concept of "willing oneself free" certainly remain the basic framework for these novels. This is also apparent from her indignation at the reception of *The Woman Destroyed*. She stressed that she was not making judgments and that readers (women) themselves had to decide; however, when they did exactly that and welcomed *The Woman Destroyed* as a book with main characters with whom they could identify, she was incensed. Apparently, this reading did not correspond with the notion she wanted to express in the book:

> I don't like "thesis" books, but the story was that a woman should be independent. The heroine of *The Woman Destroyed* is completely destroyed because she lived only for her husband and children. So it's a very feminist book in a sense since it proves finally that a woman who only lives for marriage and motherhood is miserable. (Simons, 1989: 23)

In conversation with Bair, Beauvoir let slip that she did not think Virginia Woolf's literary work was interesting (this in contrast to her appreciation of Woolf's feminist writings), because "they don't have any center. There isn't any thesis" (Bair, 1990a: 655). We can conclude that all Beauvoir's novels are, in fact, representations and expressions of her philosophic ideas. By using novels to articulate philosophical ideas, she joined a literary tradition many of whose greatest exponents are French.

The literary works of a number of Enlightenment philosophers, including Diderot's *Jacques le fataliste*, Montesquieu's *Lettres persanes*, and Voltaire's *Candide*, rank as so-called philosophical novels, as do some of the works of Rousseau, one of Beauvoir's favorite authors. And Beauvoir's own literary work should also be ranked in this genre, although a distinction should be made between writing from her self-styled "moralistic period" and her later novels.

We have already seen that Irene Selle considers *The Mandarins* a novel *à thèse* (see chapter 5). She also argues that the later *Les Belles Images* and *The Woman Destroyed* express abstract moral ideas, albeit molded in a different, more indirect narrative form, which constitutes a better screen for the all-knowing author. According to Selle, over time Beauvoir only changed her narrative technique (from direct into indirect). In fact, Beauvoir, as all-knowing author, is said to have continued launching her preconceived philosophical principles through her novels, although she did so with more cunning as time went on (see Selle, 1980: 109).

I think Selle's view lacks subtlety. The later novels do not carry a positive moral message the way the earlier ones do. We have already classified the earlier work as *moral-philosophical* literature; to distinguish the two, I would like to qualify the later writings as *ethical* novels because they show people's subjective, normative processes of deliberation, with only a *negative* moral code in the background.

Recent attempts to read the later novels using theories inspired by psychoanalysis (see chapter 1), are justified by the fact that these novels give voice to the singular, subjective level. Thus, a psychoanalytical approach is legitimate and interesting. However, when the philosophical import is totally ignored, then the evaluation is far too one-sided. The literary work of Simone de Beauvoir is closely linked to her philosophical position and should be considered and evaluated as philosophical literature.

The philosophical essay

Besides literary philosophy, Beauvoir also worked in another genre, which she herself called essayistic. "When I am concerned with reason, then I write an essay" (LE: 394). Essays and novels

> correspond to two different orders of experience which cannot be communicated in the same manner. Both sorts of experience are to me equal in importance and authenticity; I see myself reflected no less in *The Second Sex* than in *The Mandarins*, and vice versa. If I have used two different modes of self-expression, it was because such diversity was for me a necessity. (FoC: 332)

I am not interested in making appeals to people's better natures when I think I've got truth on my side. In my novels, on the other hand, I set great store by nuances and ambiguities. That is because my intentions are not the same. . . . My essays reflect my practical choices and my intellectual certitudes. (p. 332)

We shall now consider how Beauvoir's theoretic treatments relate to the tradition of academic philosophy. In doing so, we will concentrate on *The Second Sex*. In chapter 3 we saw how this work utilized philosophical concepts and a philosophical method. We concluded that, in structuring this book, Beauvoir had been inspired by philosophical phenomenology. But can her study also be qualified as a *systematic* philosophic work? Let us take a closer look.

Beauvoir's point of departure was that women's whole situation had to be charted and that economic and social factors were essential elements in that situation (see chapter 3). She not only wanted to provide an exhaustive description of women's experience, but also of their objective circumstances. These were the subject of book one of *The Second Sex*, entitled *Facts and Myths*. In this first book, she dissected scientific theories and myths on women, but also the history of the state, society, and the family. She analyzed as repressive for women the whole social framework in which people live.

But in so doing, did she not explain these phenomena scientifically, thus breaking with the method of describing accurately observed phenomena in their empirical form? Did her analysis of women's oppression not explain the phenomena by defining their underlying structures rather than elucidating them (using *Erklärung* instead of *Aufklärung*, cf. chapter 3)? Some critics believe this is the case, causing Beauvoir to become entangled in hopeless contradictions (see e.g., Moi, 1986: 114).

Is *The Second Sex* truly inconsistent in a methodical sense? To answer this question we will have to dig deeper into the backgrounds to this work. At the beginning of the war, Beauvoir was reading Hegel's work intensively: every afternoon in the Bibliothèque Nationale, from two till five, she set herself to read his *Phänomenologie des Geistes*.[4] In her war diary she noted enthusiastically how his work had led her to the realization that man was embedded in a social dimension (see JG: 361). Beauvoir read the French translation of *Phänomenologie* by Jean Hyppolite, and Jean Wahl's study *Le malheur de la conscience dans la philosophie de Hegel*, published in 1929.

Interest in Hegel's thinking had been revived strongly in the 1930s in France through the lectures of Alexandre Kojève. These lectures were attended by Beauvoir's friends and colleagues, Maurice Merleau-Ponty,

Georges Bataille, and Raymond Aron among them.[5] *Phänomenologie* can be considered as the precursor to the later phenomenology.[6] In this book, Hegel wanted to provide a description of what presents itself to consciousness (the first edition carried the subtitle: *Wissenschaft der Erfahrung des Bewusztseins*) and he definitely had concrete, empiric reality in mind.

In his foreword, he continually emphasized that the philosopher should not concern himself with abstract and empty generalities, but should be involved with concrete reality. Hegel's later work is labeled idealistic by phenomenologists: concrete reality is totally subordinated to the unfolding of concepts.[7] However, in his *Phänomenologie des Geistes* Hegel still adhered to concrete reality. The philosopher is "invited not to put his own thinking in the place of human experience. Thinking here is based strictly on the empirical actuality of history" (Bakker, 1969: 61). Later phenomenologists therefore see Hegel's empirical philosophy of history as a source of inspiration. All of our work is a continuation of this, stated Merleau-Ponty in his *Sens et non-sens* (1966).[8]

Given this background, it is hardly surprising Beauvoir believed an analysis of history within the framework of phenomenology was possible. She wanted to provide, analogous to Hegel's approach, empirical philosophy of history in book one of *The Second Sex*, showing and conceptualizing the logic of concrete social events. Here, she treated objective thinking and humanity's objective social order, which together are covered by the Hegelian term "objective Geist." Thus, book one of *The Second Sex* can be characterized as a phenomenology of the objective mind.

Book two, entitled *Woman's Life Today*,[9] is a phenomenology of the subjective mind. Dealing with the subjective world of woman as Other it meshes fully with the existential-phenomenological tradition that goes back to Heidegger. We have already seen that Beauvoir was familiar with Heidegger's work and said that her ideas on humanity were permeated with his philosophy (see chapter 3). Heidegger saw man as wholly reliant and dependent on the world. Man is also completely dependent for his knowledge on the facticity of the material, historic world. Thus, thinking and knowing are not abstract, logical activities, but an interpretation of the world by the person we are in the world. As Theo de Boer argues, "for Heidegger, the originality of thought lay in careful listening to and the adequate registration of what occurs in the interplay between man and the world around him." In Heidegger, phenomenology conceptualizes "that which is familiar to us on a pre-reflexive level." "It is an illumination and an elucidation of a pre-philosophic experience" (de Boer, 1989: 152). Beauvoir's approach and choice of subject for book two go back to this Heideggerian perception: her treatment of the everyday life of women is precisely this philosophical articulation of prereflexive experiences.

We can now conclude that, in both books of *The Second Sex*, the phenomenological method of describing and articulating empirical phenomena is applied. Given this methodological consistence, Beauvoir saw books one and two as theoretical extensions of each other—she saw her separate treatment of the objective social order in which woman is embedded as part of her description of woman-in-situation, and not as an explanation for it. She ranked the social dimension under the concept situation and thus provided *The Second Sex* with systematics: the phenomenological method was grounded in empirical history of philosophy and existential phenomenology. Thus, in a methodological sense, *The Second Sex* is structured consistently.

If in her conclusion, Beauvoir argued socialism would also bring about women's liberation (see chapter 3), the Marxist body of ideas does not otherwise play a great role in this work. Influenced by Sartre's communist leanings, Beauvoir gradually added a Marxist element to her own thinking in the 1950s. This is most apparent in her study of *Old Age*, in which she explained the oppression of the elderly as a result of the economic law of a market economy based on the principle of profit. "Exploited, alienated individuals inevitably become 'throw-outs,' 'rejects,' once their strength has failed them" (OA: 602). Because he no longer generates profit, the old person becomes the Other.

In *The Second Sex*, however, Marxist influence is still limited. In retrospect, Beauvoir felt her theory on the oppression of woman should have been based on materialistic, economic factors: "I should take a more materialist position today in the first volume. I should base the notion of woman as other and the Manichaean argument it entails not on an idealistic and a priori struggle of consciences, but on the facts of supply and demand" (FoC: 202). But she added immediately, "this modification would not necessitate any changes in the subsequent developments of my argument" (p. 202). And we certainly see the same structure that she applied in *The Second Sex* used again in *Old Age*, even though the explanation of the social oppression of old people is Marxist in orientation. Beauvoir introduced Marxist notions as a supplement to her phenomenological analysis, not as a replacement.

She did not follow Sartre's project to build in existentialism to a kind of ideal Marxism that would represent an all-embracing philosophical anthropology. Sartre's *Questions de la méthode*, his *Critique de la raison dialectique*, and his study of Flaubert (his attempt to apply this all-embracing philosophy of man) did not mean much to her (see also Bair,

1990a: 516–17). In this respect, her approach was pragmatic, and she only used Marxism as a local theory. She stated that people can use Marx's theoretical notions "without totally accepting the system."

If Marxism was introduced as a *supplement* to her phenomenological analysis in *Old Age*, in *The Second Sex* it was only used in connection with perspectives for change in women's situation: "the coming of the machine destroyed landed property and furthered the emancipation of the working class along with that of women. All forms of socialism, wresting woman away from the family, favour her liberation" (TSS I: 143).

We have already seen that Beauvoir considered women's participation in paid employment as an important change, but she also mentioned general access to contraception in the same terms: "The evolution of woman's condition is to be explained by the current action of these two factors: sharing in productive labour and being freed from slavery to reproduction" (p. 152). She also argued that participation in the labor market would only take women "half way": "The woman who is economically emancipated from man is not for all that in a moral, social, and psychological situation identical with that of man. The way she carries on her profession and her devotion to it depend on the context supplied by the total pattern of her life" (TSS II: 691).

Factors other than fundamental access to paid work also played a key role, such as for example the socialization of girls both at home and at school. In *The Second Sex*, Beauvoir showed there is a specific complex of factors that, in history, made it impossible for women to realize their *pour-soi* potential. Thus, she was not concerned with isolating a single factor as determinant in itself. Participation in the paid labor force is not enough to generate improved relations between the sexes.[10] For Beauvoir, an important factor in bringing about change in the situation of women was the dimension of ethics.

We have seen how she developed Sartre's ontology into an existentialist ethics. Ethics even took precedence over ontology: the right moral attitude could put an end to the objectification of the other. But she linked her ethics to a social concept of freedom: a person's social situation was determinant for whether he could realize himself as *pour-soi*, which in turn was a precondition for assuming a moral attitude. Thus, her ethics implied social reform was needed if the objectification of women was to be ended and if relations between the sexes were to be based on something other than hostility. Women had to be freed through concrete measures from total confinement to the sphere of family and sexuality, and should have the opportunity to develop through employment and social activity.

Such social reform requires a moral conversion of all people. It requires men to give up their desire to *be*, and to accept their *manque d'être* (see chapter 3) so they will no longer need woman as their mirroring object. It requires woman to reject whenever possible the position of Other allocated to her. Women too should accept their lack and no longer choose the safety of a supposed object status, insofar as they did so. Beauvoir did not need Marx to provide her theory with a perspective of change. Her own theoretic frameworks developed in the early 1940s were adequate to the task.

If the moral question only existed for Sartre within the framework of a metaphysical or ontological system, and no suggestion of an ethics in the strict sense of the word was present in his work, Beauvoir introduced an autonomous moral dimension analogous to Kant's concept of "good will." Through the concept of "willing oneself free," which was inspired by Kant's notion of good will, she elaborated existential phenomenology into an independent ethics in the Kantian sense and thereby amended Sartre's philosophy. In contrast to Sartre, Beauvoir did not derive the (im)possibility of ethics from ontology, but made morality independent and even brought ontology under the primacy of ethics. If, given the nature of man as *pour-soi*, Sartre concluded reciprocity was impossible, then by bringing in the autonomous moral moment, Beauvoir threw fat in Sartre's ontological fire. Reciprocity and intersubjectivity were possible through the fundamental moral attitude of "willing oneself free," which puts an end to our inherent inclination to transform the other into an object.[11] Beauvoir's ethics introduced a moment of change, and thus the historical perspective made its entrance in existentialism.

In *The Second Sex*, a number of references are made to Hegel's theory on the master-slave relationship (see e.g., TSS I: 96, 110). Hegel argued this relationship would ultimately be reversed because the slave would experience himself as free subject through labor and would vie with the master for supremacy. Beauvoir stated such a conversion had not been possible for women in their relationship with men because they had been made into the absolute Other in history, and thus had had no opportunity to experience themselves as free subject. In Hegel the emancipation of the slave was inherent in the essential development of history, a development that in its turn would be followed by the true emancipation of man, because ultimately each individual would recognize his freedom in the freedom of others, and thus recognize himself in humanity. In Beauvoir there is no essential development, but there is a moral appeal: the mediation of the moral moment is a precondition for improved relations between the sexes. Nor do we find the notion of a general reconciliation between individuals through mutual recognition. Moral conversion is continually demanded because, by definition, man is also always negativity, some-thing for which a social revolution offers no solution. The idea of a fu-ture as *total reversal of history* is nonsensical, according to Beauvoir. A definitive reconciliation between the sexes cannot come about. The other will always also remain the Other. But it is possible for us to relate to the other without enmity if we accept our own lack, and stop trying to use the other sex to make up this lack.

The Second Sex does not discuss how these new relations between the sexes should be organized. The work comprises no social programs, no recipe for the right relations between the sexes, no scenarios or blue-prints for future societies. There are no hints for, say, collective child care, reduced working times, or abolition of the family. And in inter-views Beauvoir often exasperated her questionners by never giving a re-sponse to questions on which concrete forms relations between the sexes should assume. Her systematic reply was always: do as I do. Authors who blame her for this (see Bair, 1990a: 515; Whitmarsh, 1981: 162) miss the point of her philosophy. Rather than forming proof of her theory's deficiencies, it is evidence of her consistent philosophical stance; she re-mained loyal to her notion that a general positive morality was not pos-sible. She did not articulate the alternative at a theoretical level, but at the practical level of her own life. In *The Second Sex*, a social ethics is only present as a criterion of criticism, and is not elaborated into an al-ternative social model.

If we now take the philosophical structure of *The Second Sex* as a whole, we can conclude Beauvoir was doing the following. She applied phenomenological methods to chart reality. She wanted to describe ex-haustively and conceptualize the whole situation of woman, and she pur-sued this aim consistently in *The Second Sex*. It is this idea that is respon-sible for what appears at first sight to be an eclectic jumble of social theory, psychology, cultural studies, history, and philosophy. The autono-mous, ethical moment emerges in this work as criterion for evaluating existing reality, and as opportunity for changing that reality. In terms of structure, *The Second Sex* is a fully consistent work.

All in all, Beauvoir's own philosophizing proves systematic in charac-ter. She used elements from the thinking of various philosophers—for example, in *The Second Sex* we find the names of Sartre, Merleau-Ponty, Hegel, and Heidegger on the same page (TSS I: 32)—but she was able to systematize these into a specific theoretical perspective, a reconciliation of existentialism and ethics. In this reconciliation, her integration of Sartre's intellectual solipsism into the framework of existential phenome-nology proved decisive. She also made use of Kant's notion of the auton-omy of ethics, Hegel's concept of man as social being, Heidegger's view of man as always involved with the world, Sartre's idea of man as *pour-soi*, and Merleau-Ponty's theory of man as unity of body and conscious-ness. Beauvoir took what she needed from academic philosophy and was able to meld these elements into a new systematic whole, as the exami-nation of her theoretic work in chapters 3 through 6 shows.

In doing so, however, she opted for an exposition of her ideas in a form that deviated from systematic academic conventions. In line with her phenomenological orientation, i.e., her point of departure that phi-losophy should deal with the factual world around us, she preferred to tackle the subject of her study in a direct way, without first providing an extensive exposition of the corpus of academic philosophical texts on that particular subject. She certainly referred to other philosophers in her texts, but the structure of her texts was that of an author who defines a particular subject and reflects upon it.

We can classify this structural approach as the philosophical essay. As we have seen, Beauvoir herself talked only of essays, without the quali-fication, but I think this term is not broad enough to encompass the specific work methods she applied in *The Second Sex* and other studies. This also applies to her other theoretic treatises, including those on eth-ics. On further examination, these too proved to be systematically philo-sophic in content (see chapters 4 and 5), but for these studies Beauvoir also chose essay form rather than using systematic academic conventions. By opting for the philosophical essay, Beauvoir was able to reach a broader readership than is usually the lot of academic philosophical trea-tises, and that meant a lot to her.

Autobiography

In her autobiographical work, Beauvoir combined ethics and phenome-nology in a specific way. She herself stated that her autobiography told "her" truth: the truth as she experienced it. In these writings, she was at pains to describe her situation as fully as possible and to provide a com-plete portrait of her life because she believed this could be of use to others. She wanted to chart her whole situation. It is against this back-ground that her continual assurances of the veracity of her autobiogra-phy should be understood. If she omitted events, then this was only to protect the interests of others, she claimed (see PoL: 8; FoC: 7).

However, arguing that Beauvoir used phenomenology's method of unprejudiced description does not suffice. We have already seen that she talked of her autobiography in terms of literature and creation: in auto-biography the author gives himself a "fictional" existence (ASD: 130). In chapter 6, we found the issue of her autobiography was to develop and reveal an individual art of living. The conclusion can be that Beauvoir used the phenomenological method within the framework of her ethics as art of living, and especially within the scope of the "self-technique" of describing and inventorying her actions (see chapters 6 and 8).

Philosophy and method

Our study of the philosophical merits of Beauvoir's oeuvre means reading between the lines of her self-image and her own methodological reflections, because she herself did not consider her work as philosophy. Based on the foregoing, we can conclude her methodological reflection did not keep pace with what she actually did in her oeuvre. She elaborated on an existing philosophical method (phenomenology, and especially existential phenomenology) and combined this with a moral perspective, in both a social and personal sense. Even her use of the journalistic genre is linked to her philosophical position, because her epistemology considered personal perception as irreplacable in observing the truth. Her reportages during the liberation of Paris, articles for the Maoist press in the 1960s, but also her travelogues on the United States and China were all molded into a journalistic form, and written to influence public opinion or establish specific facts. But if the journalistic genre hovers on the extreme edges of philosophy, in terms of content, her theoretical essays can certainly be ranked as systematic philosophy.

In making up the balance, we can state that her total oeuvre can be classified as a philosophical project. Philosophical literature, philosophical essays, the autobiography as art-of-living ethics, the personal report as expression of subjective truth—Beauvoir chose her genres based on her philosophical position, which can be regarded as a specific type of *Lebensphilosophie*. She wanted to articulate her subjective experiences of the phenomena so that they could be of use to others in their own lives.

Classifications of Beauvoir's work that fail to take this into account miss the point and reduce what is actually a philosophic position to, for example, no more than narcissism. Bair considers Beauvoir's essay "Literature and Metaphysics" as introspection (see Bair, 1990a: 321), and *The Mandarins* and *The Second Sex* as different attempts at self-understanding (see p. 451). Eliminating Beauvoir's phenomenological-philosophical position removes from sight the calibre of her oeuvre. Beauvoir is not so much attempting to understand her own experiences through philosophy, but rather making philosophy out of her own experiences. When, for example, she wrote a book about her mother's death, this was not merely a way of "dealing with her own feelings" as Bair argues (p. 490), but primarily an attempt to conceptualize prephilosophical experiences. Beauvoir is trying here to articulate truth, a truth in subjective experience, which can as such offer comfort to others because it breaks down the boundaries of individuality.

If Beauvoir believed articulating experiences was an articulation of a truth, then it becomes clear why in both *The Second Sex* and *Old Age* she made frequent use of ego-documents (diaries, letters, autobiographies) of women and elderly people. She also utilized the countless conversations she had had with women about their lives, including those garnered during her stay in the United States, and also made use of her own and others' personal observations and experiences in *Old Age*. As Bair rightly remarks, this method has been borrowed by many researchers in women's studies (see p. 655). But this approach derives from existential phenomenology and cannot, therefore, be regarded as a specifically "feminine" method launched by Beauvoir.

She herself argued that, although language may be permeated with male prejudices (see FoC: 195), this does not mean women have to create their own "feminine" language. It was enough to use caution and to be continually alert to the presence of male bias, she stated (see *Préface au livre d'Anne Ophir*, 1976: 11). Her conclusion is that women have to make the best of it (see Bair, 1990a: 384).[12] The language of science is also full of male prejudice, so we have to

> carefully distinguish between those things which have a universal nature and those which are marked by their masculinity. . . . I think it is perfectly safe to study mathematics and chemistry: biology is suspect; psychology and psycho-analysis even more so. From our point of view it seems to me that what is called for is a revision, not a repudiation, of knowledge. (ASD: 495)

When, in this respect, we make up the balance of Beauvoir's work method within philosophical tradition, then we can conclude she made frequent use of the ideas of male philosophers, but in doing so, continued to follow her own propositions and her own agenda. By synthesizing these theories into her own context, she succeeded in creating her own philosophy which, especially through *The Second Sex*, influenced contemporary history. At the very least, this book can be considered a motor behind the women's movements that evolved in recent decades in the United States and Europe (see also Le Doeuff, 1979: 48).

From this we can conclude that a specific feminine method is not necessary to write a book with a positive impact on women's emancipation. Morris (1981) also reached this conclusion with respect to *The Second Sex*. She argues it is not the intrinsic value of the philosophical texts, but their functioning in a social context that is decisive for their meaning.

But her point of departure is that Beauvoir applied Sartre's misogynistic philosophy without modification, and only amended it through her specific political project (i.e., women's emancipation). Morris fails to see that Beauvoir developed her own systematic philosophy. Beauvoir not only broke down Sartre's theory of internal negation through her concept of emotion and man incarnate as positive ways of living, she also shifted the emphasis from ontology to ethics and thus from ontology to history. In other words, she was engaged in changing contexts in the level of theory itself, and not only in its application.

Commitment

Beauvoir perceived herself as an intellectual and was not ashamed to be one, as we will discover: "It does not worry me to be called an intellectual or a feminist: I accept what I am" (ASD: 47). In *The Mandarins* Henri expresses it as follows: "And besides, being an intellectual is no disgrace. . . . I'm an intellectual, period. And it annoys the hell out of me when they make that word an insult" (M: 178). In a commentary on this novel, Beauvoir stated,

> we were intellectuals, a race apart with whom novelists are advised to have nothing to do; merely to describe a collection of peculiar animals whose adventures would have been interesting as a series of anecdotes but nothing more—that was a project that could never have held my interest; but, after all, we were human beings, just a little more concerned than most people with giving our lives an integument of words. (FoC: 275–76)

She put the role of intellectuals into perspective, as is also clear from the title *The Mandarins.* She was certainly aware of the negative connotation of the word "mandarin," one of whose meanings is a pompous, self-conscious person. (For example, she protested when the press reported Sartre had been received in China as a "mandarin" [*La longue marche*: 350].) She explained the choice of title as follows: "there is a little irony in the word, but also a lot of sympathy. It is true intellectuals have their own problems and preoccupations. But they should not deny their destiny; that destiny is difficult, they have to assume it" (Rolland, 1954: 360).

Given her practical nature, Beauvoir soon saw the French intelligentsia's pretension of making world history as rather naive; it took Sartre a lot longer. Whitmarsh (1981) remarks that Beauvoir had begun to doubt the effectiveness of French intellectuals as early as 1948. Her travels to the United States in 1947 and the years of contact with American intellectuals that followed would play a decisive role in this realization (see

Whitmarsh, 1981: 168). Stuart Hughes, who devoted a book to the self-overestimation of the French intelligentsia, suggests Beauvoir also had the pretension of giving humanity a voice through her work (Hughes, 1987: 166–67). But she was fully aware of her limitations from the very start. In the previous chapter, it appeared that, unlike Sartre, she was not tormented by existential questions on her authorhood. She was happy with her success, and was not worried about her role in world history. Sartre worked continuously on a solution to his dilemma: how can an intellectual from a bourgeois background be on "the right side," i.e., the side of the oppressed? He believed the role of intellectuals had to be fundamentally redefined. In comparison, Beauvoir's stance was much more pragmatic: "I do not believe in the universal and everlasting value of Western culture, but it has been my food and I love it still. I should like it not to vanish entirely but to be handed on to the rising generation—most of it, at any rate" (ASD: 229–30).

In spite of its universal goals, language is only understood by a limited audience: "At the present time many of the young, whom I should particularly like to reach, look upon reading as pointless. So I no longer see writing as a privileged means of communication" (p. 229). Words are a part of history and as such have their own, relative place. In *The Mandarins*, Henri says, "You don't prevent a war with words. But speaking was not necessarily a way of changing history; it was also a certain way of living it" (M: 752). If words are a specific way of experiencing history, then intellectuality is more a way of life than a privileged relationship to reality. The intellectual is no philosopher-king in Beauvoir; he lives his life like everyone else. On her own life as writer, Beauvoir stated, "It's as good a life as any other" (FoC: 664). If an intellectual makes a constructive political commitment, he does so within the framework of his individual art of living. We will now look more closely at this aspect of Beauvoir's personal art of living.

Beauvoir held the same political views as friends who were sometimes much more active, such as Sartre and Lanzmann. Her political opinions were antibourgeois right up until the end. She continued to oppose the class that had produced her, but which she considered as privileged and exploitative. When *The Prime of Life* was too well received by the bourgeoisie, partly because of the optimism it exudes, she was appalled (see FoC: 593). Thus, she was out to shock with the subsequent part, *The Force of Circumstance* (see p. 595)—which goes some way to explaining why it is so pessimistic in tone. However, this book is dominated by her criticism of the French bourgeoisie for their repression of the Algerian rising. She also attacked the technocratic Western world in which only organization and tools counted for anything and were only "the means of attaining other means with no end ever in sight" (p. 654). For her, the United States was the prime example of this development, a consumer society in which values are only measured by success (see p. 385). She described her disgust at the American middle classes, who lacked all inner motivation for their actions: "they were incapable of thinking, of inventing, of imagining, of choosing, of deciding for themselves; this incapacity was expressed by their conformism; in every domain of life they employed only the abstract measure of money, because they were unable to trust to their own judgement" (p. 133).

While adhering closely to her own judgment, she detested political dogmatism that has an answer to all problems and demands blind faith in the creed.

> I regret that the non-Communist left should have grown as monolithic as the Party itself. A left-winger must necessarily admire China without the least reservation, take Nigeria's side against Biafra and the Palestinians' against Israel. I will not bow to these conditions. Yet this does not prevent me from being very close to the gauchistes in the area in which they are most directly concerned—in the action they carry out in France. (ASD: 437).

Politics should be a continual creative process and should not be derived from doctrines. Dogmatism and technocratic thinking are therefore taboo. Beauvoir continually opposed the "technical," the utilitarian and organized life (see p. 174). "Doesn't man (which man?) need aggressiveness in his environment as much as calm, doesn't he need resistance, the unexpected, and to feel when he looks about him that the world is not just a big kitchen garden? Must we really choose between hovels and high-status subdivisions?" (FoC: 439).

When she lived for a time in a newly constructed part of Paris (because of their position on the Algerian war, she and Sartre had to move house temporarily), she noted,

> The whole life of the "Organization Man" and his wife was on display there—the French product copied from the American model. He left for work, she went out shopping; in the morning she took the dog out (the husband walked it in the evening), in the afternoon her children. On Sunday, he would clean the car, then the family would go off to church or on a picnic. (p. 628)

She welcomed Solzhenitsyn's view of human life: "the more intensely aware one is of the world and the more one is concerned with helping others, the better one lives. I fully agree with these conclusions" (ASD: 185).

As we saw in the previous chapter, her own contribution to practical politics was limited to rendering "some services" to political movements with which she sympathized. She emphasized that it was not in her nature to take initiatives in collective action, but that she truly sympathized with them.[13] She did not take up a position *opposite* the masses in the name of humanist individualism, as the prometheism of many intellectuals dictated.

In this respect, her view of writer-philosopher Albert Camus speaks volumes. Camus and Sartre were friends in their youth. During the Algerian conflict, their ways increasingly parted. As a Frenchman born and raised in Algeria, Camus refused to take the side of the Algerian freedom fighters against French domination, as Sartre and Beauvoir had done. Beauvoir shared with Camus a love of life and a preference for the concrete rather than the abstract, for people rather than doctrine (see FoC: 119). But she blamed him for placing man's individual happiness *against* all collective action in his *L'homme révolté* (1951) (see FoC: 182, 377, 396). In the name of an "abstract morality," Camus was judging all too easily (pp. 138, 362). Whereas Sartre's books were banned in Franco's Spain, those of Camus merited store window displays (see p. 509). According to Beauvoir, Camus stayed far away from politics because he had "no taste for the deliberations and the risks entailed in political thought; he had to be sure of his ideas so that he could be sure of himself" (p. 116).

Anna Mostovych claims both Sartre and Beauvoir saw the intellectual purely as critic (see Mostovych, 1982: 225). Anne Whitmarsh also believes the two thought intellectuals should not make constructive suggestions or political programs (see Whitmarsh, 1981: 96, 73). But after World War II, neither Sartre nor Beauvoir was of the opinion that intellectuals should remain on the sidelines while the future was under construction, or that they should refrain from participating in political scenarios.[14] Beauvoir stated emphatically that she and her friends not only wanted to criticize, but also to offer something constructive—which is why they rejected the name *Grabuge* (quarrel, spat) in favor of *Les temps modernes* for the magazine they started. "The title was to convey a positive commitment to the present" (FoC: 22; see also p. 12).

In *The Ethics of Ambiguity*, Beauvoir said a critical attitude was too easy: "The return to the positive encounters many more obstacles" (EA: 132). We have seen that in this work she was still trying to reconcile ethics and politics at an abstract level and introduced methodical rules for moral, politically constructive actions. By rejecting her moralism, she distanced herself from that attempt, but the notion of moral politics returned at the level of the intellectual's art of living.

Sartre had given up his project to reconcile politics and ethics at the end of the 1940s (see chapter 6). According to Beauvoir, he swung continuously between constructiveness and negativity; if he had emphasized the need for intellectuals to act constructively one week, he would then turn against it the next because it was "discipline" (FoC: 235). But his swings culminated in the direction of discipline at the end of the 1940s. From then until 1956 he lent his support to the communist party and to socialist countries. At the end of his life, he again chose revolt—along with the youth of the day.

However, Beauvoir continued to think of ethics and constructive politics together. In *The Mandarins* Henri decides to participate in a political "constructive" action: he affiliates his newspaper *L'Espoir* with the political program of the SRL. Now that the paper no longer functions as an underground publication, and the unity of the resistance is no more than a hollow phrase, a lack of commitment cannot be opportune. "The Resistance is one thing, politics another" (M: 17). If the paper fails to make a political choice, it will lapse into insignificance. However, Henri realizes he will become so intensely involved in politics that his literary writing will suffer. At the same time, he also thinks politics should no longer be left to politicians (see p. 15). "[H]is concerns about war, peace, and justice weren't just idle nonsense" (p. 192). So you have to be involved with politics "to try to change conditions" (p. 179). Henri realizes France has become a fifth-rate nation, Paris a village, and *L'Espoir* "a local sheet on the same level as a village weekly" (p. 205). The SRL still believed France had a part to play if it did not remain isolated: "All hope was on their side; elsewhere, nothing but emptiness" (p. 206). "The SRL needed a newspaper and it stood for something he had to help. The world was wavering between war and peace, the future depended perhaps on an imponderable: it would be a crime not to try anything and everything to sway the balance in favour of peace" (p. 190). "Constructiveness" now gains the upper hand. Henri immerses himself in political studies, and works hard to fill the gaps in his knowledge of politics and to increase his insight.

Beauvoir's commentary was, "After his trials in the resistance, this intellectual was no longer satisfied with the role of writer alone. He accepts his responsibilities, takes park in actions, runs a daily paper, sets up a movement" (Rolland, 1954: 359). Yet, Henri remains faithful to the role of intellectual as critic. He publishes information on the existence of camps in the Soviet Union, which displeases the SRL. He makes this decision based on his personal art of living and not on the grounds of technical political discussion, an objective truth, or political doctrine. Henri keeps politics and ethics together, although he does not manage to reconcile them. We have seen how his decision means that he loses the paper and that Dubreuilh's SRL collapses. Nevertheless, both writers again take political initiatives: they start a political weekly and ultimately remain faithful to their political engagement and to positive, constructive politics. The character Anne in *The Mandarins* goes through a similar process. She also chooses—in the end—a return to positiveness. Her lover in America had signified hope for her; losing him had led to despair. But in the end she nevertheless opts for life.

Beauvoir said of *The Mandarins*,

> One of the principal themes that emerges from my story is that of *repetition* in the sense in which Kierkegaard uses that word: truly to possess something, one must have lost it and found it again. . . . Instead of being content with facile optimism, they [the main characters] take upon themselves all the difficulties, the failures, the scandal implied in any undertaking (FoC: 282).

Some authors consider *The Mandarins* as saturated with skepticism and pessimism on the role of intellectuals (see Mostovych, 1982: 236; Whitmarsh, 1981: 94). But they are missing the point: the so-called difficult optimism. Beauvoir argued this book was about "a resumption of hope when hope which is too easy has gone, a difficult optimism which is simultaneously a contested optimism; that is what I wanted" (LE: 395).

Besides criticism, intellectuals can certainly raise constructive political alternatives and scenarios if they do so within the framework of a personal art of living, and not on behalf of an objective truth or fixed doctrine. Beauvoir herself formed part of the commission to advise Yvette Roudy, the French minister for women's emancipation, through concrete proposals for the improvement of the position of French women (see Bair, 1990a: 603). However, the core element in her constructive political contribution was her writing, as she herself also claimed. In this sense, what emphases can we distinguish in her oeuvre?

The practitioner

Beauvoir's thinking is characterized by an emphasis on the life of individuals. Her engagement as intellectual is, therefore, aimed primarily at lightening the suffering in the lives of real individual people. Action is only relevant to her if it can bring about concrete change in people's lives. She rejected the idea of relying on a social revolution sometime in the distant future. The here and now is more relevant than an abstract ideal. In *The Force of Circumstance*, she recalled, "I gave a lecture at the Ecole Emancipée and was told that once the Revolution had been achieved, the problem of woman would no longer exist. Fine, I said; but meanwhile? The present apparently held no interest for them" (FoC: 201).

Asked what she considered the problems of our time, she mentioned the position of women, underpaid and exploited immigrants, the homeless, the elderly, juvenile delinquents, prisoners, and psychiatric patients. The struggle for justice and humanity has to be pursued at all those levels. "That is the essential struggle" (Teitelbaum, 1973: 28). If she was after an improvement in the quality of life of individual people in the here and now, through her writing she attempted to contribute to that improvement in a number of ways.

We have already seen that in her writing, she attempted to establish direct communication with her readers. She has been accused of pessimism because, in her novels and in *The Force of Circumstance* and *Old Age*, she gave despair a voice. She was subjected to countless reproaches, especially from the left wing, for the way she ended *The Force of Circumstance* by articulating her feelings of impotence and despondency. Beauvoir was angered by the so-called "socialist optimism" which, according to these critics, she should have applied in her work. Such optimism was similar to that of technocrats who are all too eager to suppress human suffering. It was literature's task to protect the human dimension against technocrats and bureaucrats (ASD: 499).

Writing about failure, about fear, pain, and sorrow—all can help readers because it can break down loneliness. By speaking about the things we usually keep locked up inside us, literature can save people from despair. Words "wrench tears, night, death itself from the moment, from contingency, and then transfigure them" (FoC: 666). In a commentary on the book she wrote about her mother's death, *A Very Easy Death*, she formulated her aim:

> All pain is shattering; but what makes it unbearable is the fact that the person who undergoes it feels cut off from the rest of the world; when the pain is shared, at least it is no longer a banishment. It is not out of morose delectation, nor out of exhibitionism, nor out of provocation that writers often tell of hideous and deeply saddening experiences: through the medium of words they render these experiences universal and allow their readers, deep in their private unhappiness, to know the consolation of brotherhood. (p. 135)

And in her lecture "Mon expérience d'écrivain" (1966) she stressed that the protest from both left and right against so-called *littérature noire* was totally misplaced. Talking about fear, loneliness, the deaths of loved ones, is a way of meeting one another and of taking away the darkness. After all, when people go through a hurtful experience, they suffer in two ways: first, through the misery, and then because sorrow isolates: you are separated from others because you are unhappy. Beauvoir considered the accusation of pessimism as an impotence and an unwillingness to see the negative aspects of human life: there *is* no recipe for life that will spare you from pain, sorrow, and loneliness. Rather than telling people fairy tales, literature should disseminate this truth. Only on this basis can optimism truly exist (see ASD: 499).

Beauvoir also wanted to assist her readers in another way. With *The Second Sex* and *Old Age*, she attempted to make oppressed people aware of their situation and to give them weapons to improve it. Beauvoir came to the conclusion that the fate of old people today is scandalous. This has nothing to do with biology, but with economic and social factors: poverty and loneliness are too often old people's fate. *Old Age* (1970) was an immediate success, but Beauvoir was most happy with the approbation of a number of gerontologists. "Generally speaking, specialists do not much care to see others treading upon their preserves. These, on the contrary, congratulated me for having broken what they too called the 'conspiracy of silence'; and several of them offered me their collaboration" (ASD: 150).

She gave radio interviews so that she could reach as many people as possible, and subsequently received letters that confirmed her somber conclusions (see p. 149).

The Second Sex also generated correspondence that emphasized her thinking on women's position: "A series of extracts from the letters I have received since the book came out would make a very moving document" (FoC: 429). This book also helped people:

> Self-knowledge is no guarantee of happiness, but it is on the side of happiness and can supply the courage to fight for it. Psychiatrists have told me that they give *The Second Sex* to their women patients to read, and not merely to intellectual women but to lower-middle-class women, to office workers and women working in factories. "Your book was a great help to me. Your book saved me," are the words I have read in letters from women of all ages and all walks of life. (p. 203)

Women who wanted to discuss their problems with Beauvoir were received at her home. She supported them, for example in their attempts to write, but she considered herself ill-equipped at giving personal advice because "I have no exact knowledge of the person who asks for it" (ASD: 68). She also opened her door for political activists who appealed to her for assistance (see p. 69), for instance members of the women's liberation movement.

Yet, the creation of her own art of living can be considered her prime contribution to constructive politics. By giving other women a positive "scenario," she wanted to help them organize their own lives. She was continually occupied in finding practical answers to the question of how to live. Whitmarsh argues that Beauvoir's philosophy as a whole could be considered political philosophy "in the same way as that of Plato or Aristotle because it is about how we should live and about our relationships with others" (see Whitmarsh, 1981: 52). Yet, at the same time, she calls Beauvoir's commitment no more than philanthropic and apolitical in nature. This distinction is hardly satisfactory in Beauvoir's case. After all, she managed to turn the personal into the political: she saw her own life as a woman as a public event long before a similar perception under the slogan "personal is politics" came into vogue among feminists. From this point of view, Beauvoir's commitment is certainly political.

When we come to take stock of the core thematic elements in her oeuvre, we find giving meaning to life is one such element, which also comprises themes that have now become known as medical ethics (such as euthanasia in *Old Age* and *A Very Easy Death*). Another main theme is the psychological problems of women who lose themselves in others (in *The Second Sex, The Woman Destroyed*, and others, but also in the autobiography insofar as it offered solutions in the form of a positive art of living). Finally, the social emancipation of oppressed groups in general is a core element in her oeuvre. She wrote on the position of Jews (in a foreword to Steiner's *Treblinka*, and other writings), about Blacks in *L'Amérique au jour le jour*, on women, on old people, on women laborers (in the journal *J'accuse*), on Algerians during the Algerian war (in the foreword to *Djamila Boupacha*). As I see it, on an intellectual level, Beauvoir was trying to unite the two forms of commitment represented by Henri and Anne in *The Mandarins*, i.e., that of writer-politician and of physician–social worker respectively. As a result, I believe she developed a specific, exemplary type of intellectuality.

My feeling is that the old concept of practitioner can serve to characterize this type of intellectuality. According to *The Oxford Dictionary*, the practitioner is "one engaged in the practice of any art, profession or occupation" especially in medicine and in law. He provides practical legal, medical, and other support and acts on behalf of others, but is also someone who "practices anything; one who carries on a practice or action." These meanings seem tailored to suit Beauvoir's specific brand of intellectuality. As an intellectual, she not only wanted to be a doctor of life, through her writing, for both herself and others, she also provided (sometimes legal) assistance to others and offered practical political support and encouragement. Moreover, as we have seen in chapter 8, she expanded intellectuality into a practical lifestyle and established her own "practice" as intellectual. As a philosopher, Beauvoir was not interested in building theoretical systems, or in building up a personal erudition.[15] She was more interested in life itself and with all her intellectualism was a perfectly practical person. The type of intellectuality she developed as intellectual woman can rightly be characterized as that of a "practitioner."

10

PHILOSOPHY AS PASSION

In this chapter, we make up the final balance of the life and work of Simone de Beauvoir. First, we evaluate her contribution to ethics, along with her main work, *The Second Sex*, and her personal art of living. Then we will take stock of her life, specifically by questioning whether her attempt to organize it along the lines of her philosophical ideas was successful.

Relevant philosophy

In the course of this study, we have seen that Beauvoir's oeuvre was philosophical in content. She not only enjoyed a sound philosophical education, but also continued to work close to philosophical traditions. She belonged to a group of philosophers, which included Sartre and Merleau-Ponty, who were involved in the magazine, *Les temps modernes*, and she wrote systematic philosophical works, among them a number of treatises on ethics and the philosophical-phenomenological studies *The Second Sex* and *Old Age*. But her literary works, novels *and* autobiography also proved to be part of a philosophical project: a philosophy that aimed at expressing reality should, according to Beauvoir, also articulate the subjective aspect of that reality. During this exploration of her work, we discovered ethics formed a constant theme in her oeuvre. As a student she was already planning to write on ethics, and she remained faithful to that early interest.

In *The Ethics of Ambiguity*, she concluded morality resided within the situated dimension of human existence—the area where emotion and personal judgments play a role—and at the same time introduced the idea that only a specific type of philosophic literature could do justice to the situated dimension. From that time on, her literary work proved to be ethical-philosophical in nature. In the same *Ethics of Ambiguity* she underpinned the insight that social circumstances can impede the assumption of an ethical attitude. In *The Second Sex* and *Old Age*, she analyzed how the social circumstances of women and the elderly made it impossible for them to develop as free ethical subjects. She thus placed moral action and judgment in a social context. At the same time, this perspective led to a general normative criterion on man's social circumstances: those circumstances have to be such that he can realize his (ontological) freedom and assume an ethical attitude based upon it (see chapter 5). Man may not be oppressed is the basis of the "negative" moral code, i.e., a prescriptive rule formulated in a negative way. Beauvoir's conception of a positive ethics as art of living, however, can be considered the central notion in her philosophy, with her elaboration of a personal art of living as intellectual woman at its heart.

All of these aspects of her philosophy have maintained their relevance in the light of current theoretical debates. Martha Nussbaum recently dusted off the concept of philosophical literature. In her influential *The Fragility of Goodness* (1986) and in *Love's Knowledge* (1990), she raises the idea of moral judgments as subjective processes of deliberation for which literature (e.g., Greek tragedy) is the most appropriate form of expression. Beauvoir shared this view, and we also find the concept of philosophical literature in her work.[1]

Contemporary, so-called postmodernist philosophers also argue that philosophy and literature are interwoven. Some even suggest philosophy as a whole could be replaced by literary philosophy.[2] In this respect, I think Beauvoir's perception is much to be preferred—she distinguished between pure philosophy and literary philosophy and believed each complemented and supplemented the other and that both could very well exist *alongside* each other. In the area of ethics, pure philosophy can elaborate on general negative moral codes, as did *The Second Sex*, while literary philosophy can do the same for positive ethics, as did, for example, *The Mandarins*.

Beauvoir's notion that people can only be moral subjects if they meet a number of social preconditions is, in fact, the still-topical sting or barb in her thinking. In her pure philosophical work, she showed people cannot, by definition, act freely based on conscious and intentional considerations. Their social circumstances can be such that they could not assume this form of individuality. A number of preconditions have to be fulfilled for rational and free action. Beauvoir's thinking thus implies a criticism of social theories that presuppose *all* people are free beings gifted with reason. These theories assume something that still has to be captured by the majority of people, and thus they enhance fundamental inequality. People are not moral subjects by definition; the issue here is providing people with the opportunity to develop as such.[3]

Beauvoir's idea that a positive ethics can only exist in the form of a personal art of living is also relevant today in the light of contemporary discussions. In my view, her answer to the question, what remains of a positive ethics now that "God is dead"? is especially relevant given postmodernist skepticism on the very existence of morality. Through its criticism of Truth, postmodernism has swept away all foundations for a positive ethics (see notes 1 and 2). Beauvoir's idea of ethics as art of living can fill the hiatus that is left. Various postmodern philosophers have also confronted this problem. Where political and moral Truth are missing, they often turned to Beauty as a basis for ethics. The option of making one's life into a work of art then becomes the criterion: everyone should be the artist of his own existence (see e.g., Ignatieff, 1990).

The body of ideas of the late Michel Foucault, who, in contrast to Sartre, certainly wanted to bequeath an ethics (as Eribon [1989] also argues), has a similar purport. In chapter 1, we saw how his last books on the history of sexuality exposed a type of ethics he called aesthetics of existence. He alerted us to the so-called prescriptive texts on sexuality in Greek and Roman culture, which held up the ideal of a beautiful life, and he suggested the reintroduction of this typically Greek form of ethics. He argued these were certainly *ethical* texts as care of the self was a condition for good citizenship. Even so, it seems to me that maintaining the brilliance of one's own life takes precedence over care of fellow man. And it also seems to me that the primary motivation in Foucault's ethics is, therefore, the Beauty of one's own existence, which is why his thinking suffers from a certain aestheticistic elitism. Beauvoir's idea of ethics as art of living distinguishes itself from the way today's postmodern authors embrace aesthetics. In chapter 6 we saw that for her the aesthetic moment represented the form but not the content of ethics—art of living for her is the art of life and not living as work of art. Her concept of positive ethics as personal art of living does not suffer from aestheticism and is, therefore, the preferable solution.

I also think we can still use Beauvoir's notions on ethics to solve the theoretic dilemmas of today's feminism. From the 1960s, modern feminism has developed as a primarily Hegelian type of thinking; a variant on Hegel's master-slave theory. This type of thinking is characterized by the notion that the slave (read woman) is the better, unalienated person; that the slave/woman is oppressed by the master/man; that the slave/master conflict will be solved in a Utopian phase at the end of history. In the feminist epistemology applied by numerous researchers in the field of women's studies, this Hegelian system is referred to: the assumption is that from their oppressed position, women have a more complete and more objective view of reality.[4]

This feminist epistemology can be considered the core of contemporary feminist thinking on women's oppression. For its underpinning, frequent reference is made to Beauvoir's classic study on woman, *The Second Sex*, which also applies the Hegelian master/slave dichotomy to analyze the male/female relationship. However, as we have seen, because of her affinity with Sartre's philosophical anthropology, Beauvoir's theory deviates on essential points from the Hegelian system. In this respect, feminist theoreticians have appropriated and interpreted it incorrectly. First, Beauvoir rejects out of hand the dialectic surpassing of oppositions and the existence of a utopia; second, in her perception, woman acquiesced partially in her own oppression; and third, woman's oppressed position does not make her better than a man or a more complete human being.

Beauvoir's perception actually implies a reformulation of the Hegelian aspect of the modern feminist body of ideas, i.e., the Hegelian form that is responsible for that body of ideas' bad name. More than ever before, feminism appears to have been discredited, whereas it seems as though goals are increasingly being realized in the Western world, i.e., in a material sense through women's legal and political emancipation, and on the level of ideas insofar as notions from feminism have been adopted— albeit often implicitly.

As reaction against Hegelian political thinking, feminist theoreticians have introduced a postmodern perspective. However, it is becoming increasingly clear that postmodern thought is an impediment to the development of a useful feminist body of ideas. It actually makes a feminist point of departure impossible because any form of unification, either in word or deed, is considered repressive. However, a defense of women's rights will always be essential in the same way as all people's basic human rights need continual reiteration and defense (currently against fundamentalists and large-scale racist movements). Beauvoir's concept of ethics certainly meets these criteria. On the one hand, it means general norms

can and should be applied in the form of the *negative* moral code of freedom for all. On the other, it means *positive* normative propositions
should present themselves as contingent choices, or rather as concrete,
elaborated arts of living.

The critical problem

The foregoing chapters have led us to the conclusion that Beauvoir's creation of an art of living as intellectual woman can be considered the heart
of her oeuvre. As such, this project also forms a clue to her main work,
The Second Sex. By placing the life of Simone de Beauvoir in its social
context, we have seen how she tried to mold her two, so-called irreconcilable identities, that of woman and that of intellectual, into a unity (see
chapter 7). We have seen how, in her autobiography, she claimed always
to have lived as a female *subject*, but also admitted she had been raised
stereotypically as a girl. In her study of woman, she characterized this
socialization as molding for an '*être relatif*' (LDS I: 15), or rather as
training for a person who lives *through* others.

On her analysis of the female situation in *The Second Sex*, she said:
"that is how *I* experienced it" (Schwarzer, 1986: 158), and emphasized
that her emotional and mental training had been different from that of
men (LE: 385). She exclaimed, "Have I ever claimed that I, personally,
was not a woman?" and stated, "I received a young lady's education and
when my studies were finished, my position was still that of any woman
in a society where the sexes are divided into two embattled castes. In a
great many ways I reacted like the woman I was" (PoL: 367).

In *Memoirs of a Dutiful Daughter*, she described how her mother
monitored and controlled everything she did, calling their relationship
"symbiotic": "any reproach made by my mother, and even her slightest
frown was a threat to my security; without her approval, I no longer felt
I had any right to live" (MDD: 39).

Beauvoir also reported terrible mortal fears in her youth. She herself
classed these as "metaphysical incursions" and as confrontations with
death and nothingness. I see those fears as evidence of her extremely
close ties with her mother, her sister, and their nurse. When they were
absent, the young Simone experienced an immense, dizzying emptiness:
there was no longer anyone for whom she existed. And in puberty, her
psychological stability was also totally dependent on others: "[to] be
loved, be admired, be necessary; be somebody" (p. 231)—for Simone
these were all one and the same. Her psychological training was aimed
at making her dependent on the love of a sovereign subject in whose eyes

her existence would be justified and with whom she could live in an extremely close relationship (as Madeheim [1966] also pointed out).

We can conclude her socialization as woman was definitely "successful" in this sense. She was tormented by mortal fears at times when she was alone and did not live symbiotically with another—be it mother, sister, friend, lover, or adopted daughter.[5] Loneliness was a real problem all her life, and her repugnance for old age was related to this. The thought of never having another intimate relationship was unbearable (see e.g., FoC: 673). Her assurance that she had never been alone since she was twenty-one (ASD: 39) seems almost imploring, and appears to indicate a strong need for close relationships with others.

But Beauvoir had no intention of resigning herself to life equipped only with this psychological baggage. Her situation had also destined her for a professional life, as we saw in chapter 7, and her education and socialization in this area came into conflict with her tendency to lose herself completely in a beloved other. Her art of living, in which she styled herself into an independent professional woman, was her solution to this inclination. Her professional training had formed her into a subject, i.e., into an active and speaking individual. Through this training, she experienced her traditional female tendency as immoral.

When, after completing her studies, she realized she was vanishing in Sartre and was losing her own ambitions and plans, she felt as though she was some kind of "parasite" (PoL: 61). "The difficulty nagging at me was not so much a social as a moral, almost a religious, contradiction in terms. To accept a secondary status in life, that of a merely ancillary being, would have been to degrade my own humanity; and my entire past rose up in protest against such a step" (p. 62). "Obviously," she added, "the only reason for the problem presenting itself to me in these terms was because I happened to be a woman." She knew that an act of will alone would not give her back her self-confidence and independence, so she decided to accept a job in Marseilles. This is how she fought against her "parasitic" inclinations, and she felt with success. The world became "richer and fuller," she again saw countless tasks awaiting her (PoL: 112). Based on this, she concluded, "I was emerging triumphant from the trials to which I had been subjected: separation and loneliness had not destroyed my peace of mind. I knew that I could now rely on myself" (pp. 112–13).

Yet, the tendency to cling to Sartre remained. "Ever since Sartre and I had met, I had shuffled off the responsibility for justifying my existence on to him. I felt that this was an immoral attitude, but I could not envisage any practical way of changing it" (p. 316).

The stereotyped representation of woman and her education into an *"être relatif"* is, therefore, the perfect butt for *The Second Sex*. Beauvoir protested against this in the name of her ethics, but also because she had personally been hindered by it.

> The independent woman—and above all the intellectual, who thinks about her situation—will suffer, as a female, from an inferiority complex; she lacks leisure for such minute beauty care as that of the coquette whose sole aim in life is to be seductive; follow the specialists' advice as she may, she will never be more than an amateur in the domain of elegance. Feminine charm demands that transcendence, degraded into immanence, appears no longer as anything more than a subtle quivering of the flesh; it is necessary to be spontaneously offered prey. But the intellectual knows that she is offering herself, she knows that she is a conscious being, a subject. (TSS II: 694)

> Women of like situation may, through man's mediation, come to have very different fortunes.

Married girl-friends are, therefore, a curse for the woman who is trying to achieve her goals by herself.

> she feels she is arbitrarily condemning herself to take the most difficult roads; at each obstacle she wonders whether it might not be better to take a different route. . . . her gait is also timid and uncertain. The more she seems to be getting ahead on her own the more her other chances fade; in becoming a bluestocking, a woman of brains, she will make herself unattractive to men in general (pp. 707–8).

In my view, we should see *The Second Sex* project against the background of Beauvoir's personal struggle to develop herself into an independent, professional woman. With this work, she became the pioneering voice of those women who, like herself, had been socialized stereotypically, but who also (had to) le(a)d a life within one of the professions. *The Second Sex* is an expression of a period of transition. Seen in this light, the fact that the book was such a hit in the United States—by 1969, 750,000 copies of the paperback edition had been sold—is not so surprising because women's participation in the professions there was already relatively extensive. Beauvoir's study is an indictment not only against the stereotypical socialization of the girl, which makes a professional life difficult if not impossible, but also against the dominant ideas on femininity, which oppress professional women as well.

The relevance of The Second Sex *today*

Beauvoir's indictment against the stereotypical straitjacket of femininity is topical insofar as the old patterns of femininity are still imposed on women. But *The Second Sex* also wanted to be an analysis of the situation of woman throughout history and in all cultures. We have seen that the book was structured as a philosophical-phenomenological study, and it professed to chart and analyze the total situation of woman.

Corrections to Beauvoir's analysis have emerged from various academic disciplines. Cultural anthropologists and historians have pointed out the vast differences in the position of women at different times and in different places that are not visible or conceivable under the general heading of oppression. Speaking in terms of structural, asymmetrical power relations between the sexes allows more nuances than the term oppression. Beauvoir's idea that woman's biology, i.e., her greater share in reproduction, was a major factor in the origination and development of these asymmetrical relations is still generally accepted today. Psychologists and cultural theorists have come up with new insights into the socialization of men, which proves just as stereotypical as the socialization of women. But contemporary feminist theory has been especially productive in its contributions to psychoanalytical theory.

In chapter 6, we saw that *The Second Sex* parallels Freud's diagnosis of the female position, but rejects pertinently his ideas on the role of the unconscious and the structure of sexual desire. At the end of her life, Beauvoir appeared to have come to think more kindly of Freud: "Although I challenge some of his theories, particularly those concerned with women, Freud is one of the men of this century for whom I have the greatest admiration" (ASD: 164). Although she rejected vehemently Freud's theory of penis envy and the castration complex, she certainly reevaluated her aversion to his perceptions on another area. In her thinking, childhood had now become "the key to every life" (p. 45). Beauvoir cited studies that showed major differences between children as young as three years old who had been stimulated and those who were not. The attitude of caregivers is determinant: their prejudices appear to have a self-fulfilling effect. "So all that is required for important differences between boys and girls to appear as early as three or four years of age is a failure on the part of the parents to 'stimulate' male and female babies in the same manner" (p. 485).

Beauvoir now believed a person's earliest formation is all he can build on (see p. 12). She thus realized emotions are anchored at a deeper level and cannot simply be influenced by consciously chosen behaviors (see also Whitmarsh, 1981: 183). However, rather than Freud's emphasis on sexuality in the form of the Oedipus complex, Beauvoir preferred the concept of existential psychoanalyst Bruno Bettelheim, who argues that the first twenty-four months are determinant for psychological formation (see ASD: 160).[6] In *The Second Sex*, Beauvoir overestimated the freedom and thus the notion that life is "makeable." Women's social conditioning is more deeply anchored than she realized, namely on the level of the unconscious. In this light, *The Second Sex* should be brought up to date. Freud's theory on the essential female position need not be accepted in order to see the importance of his discovery of the unconscious dimension.

But this does not mean *The Second Sex* has become obsolete as philosophical framework for academic research. Supplements and adjustments, including those related to the role and workings of the unconscious, are possible within the ethical framework of *The Second Sex*; the demand for room for women to develop still stands. The claim that only a total overview can provide insight into the situation of woman also remains important. Beauvoir considered disciplinary reductionism in the study of woman's position as fundamentally wrong—for example, she believed psychoanalysis could only find its truth in a historical context. As cross-link between the various academic disciplinary approaches to gender relations, *The Second Sex* is still topical and unsurpassed in terms of structure and execution.

The absence of a general positive morality in *The Second Sex* on the organization of relations between the sexes, at political *and* subjective level, is also a positive point. Beauvoir only opposed a specific *complex* of meanings, practices, and institutions, especially the link between marriage and family and education for subordination, woman's economic dependence, and the cultural representation of woman as the Other. This complex had to be disaggregated because it took away women's chances of developing into a subject. If Hatcher (1984) claimed *The Second Sex*'s argument was that women should not be allowed to be housewives (see chapter 9, note 10),[7] others claimed Beauvoir meant women should avoid motherhood.

But such ideas miss the point of *The Second Sex*. The central theme throughout is the total situation of woman. The central aim throughout is to show the social context of matters such as motherhood and marriage. It is not motherhood itself, but a specific material realization and representation of it that is criticized in *The Second Sex*, and this also applies to marriage, economic dependence, and so on. If other social arrangements emerge, each and every one of these practices can acquire a different meaning. Beauvoir herself argued she had nothing against motherhood as such. "Oh, no. I have nothing against it! I have something against the ideology which demands motherhood from all women and against the circumstances in which women are obliged to be mothers" (Schwarzer, 1986: 108).

Nor does *The Second Sex* offer concrete positive alternatives for the organization of love between the sexes on a personal level. Only Beauvoir's general perception of our relationship with the other emerges on this point, a perception that is still relevant, especially when compared with, for example, that of Elisabeth Badinter, whose *Man/Woman: The One Is the Other* (1989) created a furor in Europe. Badinter claims passion is passé. As differences between the sexes will become increasingly more vague, comradeship and tenderness will take the place of romantic love and passion. Beauvoir's response would have been that every person is always separate from the others because he is also always pure consciousness, i.e., a nothingness (see chapters 3 and 4). People, men *and* women, are separate beings by definition. If they live as free individuals, they will always be the other for each other; passion will therefore always be possible. Against the backdrop of our existence as separated individuals, becoming one with the other in love will always remain a special, unique experience: "the one will never be the other" would probably have been Beauvoir's response to Badinter.

The relevance of Beauvoir's art of living

The Second Sex offers no positive ethics. For this we have to turn to Beauvoir's art of living. Her notion of ethics as art of living has retained its importance as solution to the problem of many women who want a professional life or in some other way want to lead the life of an independent individual, but have been socialized traditionally. Art-of-living ethics is no luxury for women and other disadvantaged groups. It can be a useful and necessary tool for dealing practically on a daily basis with the effects of a bifurcated consciousness. The content of Beauvoir's personal art of living, i.e., her concrete "self-techniques," and her strategies to make herself function as an autonomous individual, still appeal to numerous women.

Her specific creation of an identity as intellectual woman, which I characterized as that of the "practitioner," can also be a source of inspiration for women today. It can contribute to combatting a certain duality many intellectual women still experience. Recent research has shown that, in spite of their high performance, women in science often lack self-esteem and suffer from self-doubt. In their eyes, the ideal academic or scientist is still a man (see Widom and Burke, 1978; Noordenbos, 1987;

Widdnall, 1988). Most studies are limited to showing causes in the academic world itself—informal and hidden recruitment practices and the shortage of female role models have emerged as major factors (the always primarily male staff recruits male students and researchers, and male students have positive role models). But other causes also lie at the root of women scientists' problems with identification, such as their gender-specific education as girls.

The decisive factor, however, in the problematic self-image of intellectual women is the culturally transmitted notion of the irreconcilability of femininity and intellectualism, noted in chapter 1. It would appear this idea is so deeply anchored in our culture that it cannot be changed within the space of one, two, or even three generations. Although overt discrimination against women in the Western world has almost become culturally unacceptable, transmitted meanings are so entrenched, so covert, so diverse, and so numerous, they cannot be easily transformed. Thus, the theme of the subjective experience of the woman intellectual still demands attention. If the presence of positive role models is important, then it would seem to me useful to develop these also at a symbolic level, whereby being a woman and intellectualism are extensions of each other and not at opposite ends of the spectrum.

Hopefully, it will have become clear that I do not mean the clichéd image of the woman as-just-different, or the idea that all women intellectuals simply work in a different way than men. Attempts by contemporary feminism to formulate a so-called feminine science and epistemology are based on a general stereotype that, it seems to me, should be combatted rather than encouraged.[8] Yet, feminism not only wants the total equality of men and women, it also wants to be an instrument of cultural criticism and to enrich the dominant culture with *several alternatives*. Influenced by the postmodern body of ideas (see notes 2 and 3), contemporary feminists all too often consider these two strategies as conflicting. They maintain that either equality with men has to be sought, or the difference between women and men has to be emphasized. In my view, both strategies could exist side by side without any problem if cultural feminism were to present itself in the form of feminist "arts of living."[9] Beauvoir's notion of a positive ethics as art of living makes it conceivable to speak as a woman (thus *creating* oneself as such) without speaking *for* or *on behalf of* women. Positive norms can certainly be introduced if they are not presented in the form of a *moral system*. Beauvoir's personal art of living is precisely such a way of creating oneself as intellectual woman without trying to create a female model of intellectuality (see also chapter 7).

The limits of art of living

Although in many ways we can consider Beauvoir's art of living as a successful project, it still has specific boundaries and limitations. These become visible through her own, later realization of the deep anchoring of early emotional development. Based on this, it becomes clear that her concept of an own identity as totally makable by means of an art of living was too optimistic.

What becomes clear is that her art of living is the fight of "the conscious" against the "unconscious." Thus, we can understand certain obsessive traits in her personal art of living, such as for example its restless freneticism. Beauvoir herself said, "Live with no time out: . . . I am still faithful to it" (ASD: 38). But her friend Lanzmann suggests she escaped her fears through *"cette espèce de projet constant"* (Dayan and Ribowska, 1979: 14). And her need to write every day—a day without writing had for her "the taste of ashes"—seemed to derive from this. There were times when fear hit her as soon as she got up from her desk (see FoC: 671).

She called her travels a flight forward[10] (see ASD: 233). Traveling was a means to escape loneliness and not to have to experience emptiness. Her urge for action tended to take on almost maniacal proportions: while traveling she had to do everything and see everything. When she discovered music, it had to be studied exhaustively (see PoL: 143–44, and others). Nevertheless, severe anxiety attacks continued to haunt her, and she never managed to come to grips with those feelings except through alcohol, sleeping pills, and tranquilizers.

Moreover, in other areas, real life proved more unruly than the creed. This was the case in her love life especially. Our conclusion that the art of living is subject to the limits defined by early development explains why it could not offer Beauvoir real solutions in this area. Throughout her life she held firm to her ideal image of being part of "The Writer Couple," but Sartre's permanent Don Juanism was traumatic for her. To understand her relationship with Sartre, we must again go back to *The Second Sex*. In this work, she concluded girls develop a desire for a superior man as replacement father. We have seen that, in *Memoirs of a Dutiful Daughter*, she explained her own desire for a superior man in a different way: as an intellectual woman, she had to make up such a backlog in comparison with men that a man had to be superior if he was to be her equal (see chapter 7). However, if we read between the lines of this part of her autobiography, everything indicates that she was unable to escape from an internalization of the stereotyped female position in culture.

"All my imagination was devoted to the fulfilment of my destiny as a woman," she herself concluded (MDD: 56). "The day would come when I would swoon in the arms of a man" (p. 166). The young Simone was completely convinced women were inferior to men. Her parents had explained repeatedly that a woman is what a man makes of her (see p. 146; p. 36). Thus, she would only "be in love the day a man came along whose intelligence, culture, and authority could bring me into subjection" (p. 145). Simone's father loved books, and thus her lover also had to love books, and moreover be more learned than herself. Cousin Jacques was not eligible, but Sartre seemed the perfect candidate. He was better read than she was, and more adept at debate; Beauvoir saw in him the superior lover for whom she was looking. Until the end of her life, she remained infatuated with what she saw as Sartre's superior "genius." Bair describes how Beauvoir would not even question putting aside her own work to help Sartre. She revised and edited his manuscripts, and even wrote journalistic articles under his name so he would be free to devote his time to philosophical work (see Bair, 1990a: 516, 567, 228). She rejected his marriage proposal also because she thought marriage would hinder his creative work.[11]

Various authors have noted Beauvoir often lapsed into docility in Sartre's presence. She herself argued that her faith in his thinking was so great she felt she could draw a sense of infallible security from it, as she had done earlier from God or her parents (PoL: 27). And the fact that throughout the years she continued to address Sartre as "*vous*" underlines this aspect of their relationship.

Her childlike adoration of Sartre is also apparent from her urge to imitate him. Her letters to him written at the beginning of World War II even express a tendency to imitate his relationships with women (see chapter 2). When Sartre began an important relationship while on a trip to America, Beauvoir followed suit some years later. When Sartre adopted his lover Arlette Elkaïm, Beauvoir also adopted a daughter, as we have seen. Beauvoir's imitative behavior was so extreme she even developed the same aversion to raw shell fish (see ASD: 277). Her relationships, with Nelson Algren and—for about ten years—with the much younger Claude Lanzmann, become comprehensible against the backdrop of the father-daughter relationship with Sartre: the relationships could easily exist side-by-side. Beauvoir herself pointed this out implicitly: "there could be no question of trying to duplicate the understanding I had with Sartre. Algren belonged to another continent, Lanzmann to another generation" (FoC: 296).

Even her intense relationship with Sylvie Le Bon in the final decades of her life did not unseat Sartre. Beauvoir recognized her own history and felt reincarnated in Sylvie: "She too was an intellectual and she too was passionately in love with life" (ASD: 75). Sylvie had also had terrible rows at home about her intellectual career: her mother even destroyed her favorite books. She taught philosophy at the same lyceum in Rouen where Beauvoir had once been a teacher, she lived in the same hotel there, and took coffee in the same bar.

Beauvoir and Le Bon were very close on a daily basis. But Beauvoir tried to remain faithful to Sartre, in spite of his many affairs and his relationship with Arlette Elkaïm, which drove a wedge between them. Her own peace of mind continued dependent on his condition. For a long time, Sartre took handfuls of stimulants in order to continue working. His obsession with work took on irresponsible proportions, especially during the writing of *Critique de la raison dialectique*. When he escaped a coronary by a whisker, she noted in her diary, "Nothing else counts. My book, the criticisms, the letters I get, the people who talk to me about it, everything that would otherwise have given me pleasure, rendered utterly void" (FoC: 463). Right until the end, she considered her relationship with Sartre as the successful enterprise of her life. Every attempt to evaluate her work as independent philosophical oeuvre was resolutely dismissed by her in one word: Sartre (see Simons, 1986: 204).

Her description of Sartre's illness and deterioration during the last ten years of his life in *Adieux, A Farewell to Sartre* (1981) shocked many. The French press suggested she was out for revenge on him. Jardine (1986) even talks of literary "murder." But the disgust at Sartre's decline is wholly in accordance with Beauvoir's abhorrence for any kind of reduction of man to a passive existence, an abhorrence that also forms the main tenor of *The Second Sex*. At the same time, *Adieux* is also characterized by an undertone of admiration for the resilience with which Sartre managed to struggle back and pick up his activities.

Now, there would not be much wrong with the father-child aspect of their relationship as such, if it were not for the fact that, through it, Beauvoir remained encapsulated in a youth trauma. Beauvoir claimed their sexual relationship lasted fifteen to twenty years (Schwarzer, 1986: 156). But even on her deathbed, she would not and could not accept Sartre's countless lovers and her own limited role in this aspect of his life.[12] She suffered under Sartre's indifference to her as a *lover*; in her autobiography, we find numerous indications. These are not only her own remembered feelings of jealousy but also her depressed moods, which always coincided with periods when Sartre was absent.[13] He never cohabited with her, but he did share his room with girlfriend Wanda, and he did move into his mother's house at the age of forty, following the death of his stepfather (his mother referred to the move as her third marriage, see ASD: 104). When Beauvoir heard he was planning to marry Elkaïm, she exclaimed he could not do that to her. So, in spite of Sartre's indifference, where did this stubborn Sartre-love come from? For an answer we will have to go back to Beauvoir's youth and look more closely at the specific nature of her relationship with her father.

Trauma

If in later life Beauvoir accepted the importance of a happy childhood, she continued to stress that her own had been very happy indeed. Her sister Hélène's way was seen as far more difficult. In comparison with Simone, she had had an anxious childhood (see p. 13). Beauvoir talked of her own sense of security in the cradle, and called her infancy tranquil (see p. 13) and herself "a happy, well-adjusted child, self-confident and open" (p. 15).

Her biographers, Francis and Gontier and Bair, copy these recollections diligently and without question, and Bair only mentions in passing that there was little love in the Beauvoir home. But when, for example, we hear Beauvoir recall being locked repeatedly in a dark closet, or being humiliated and laughed at by her parents in the presence of others (see MDD: 12–14), it seems sensible to take the idealized image of a happy childhood with a handful of salt.[14] Beauvoir spoke disapprovingly of the way George Sand raised her daughter because she gave only a "conditional" love, "a terrifying thing for children, for whom emotional security is so necessary" (ASD: 169). In fact, she was also characterizing her own childhood. She had to match the image of a dutiful daughter in every respect, or love and approval would be withheld.

Her mother was not a positive role model. Françoise de Beauvoir was ten years younger than her husband, and he dominated her in every respect. Thus, Simone oriented herself totally to her father, but was subject to one rejection after another, both as a child and in puberty. This father, whose intellectual and spiritual gifts his daughter so revered and admired, was rarely to be found chez Beauvoir. He was a womanizer who was openly unfaithful to his wife, and he spent much of his time outside the home enjoying Paris's cafes and nightlife. In her puberty, he overtly and continually brutalized Simone. He never tired of telling her she was ugly, as sister Hélène, whom he openly favored at the time, recalled indignantly.[15] Simone would never be able to shake off her negative self-image as an unattractive woman.[16] In a general sense, she remarked, "if a man has been ill-loved in childhood, and if he adopts his parents' view of him, then he builds up a disagreeable image of himself that he can never throw aside" (p. 47).

In my view, this applied to Beauvoir herself. Her father's preference for the younger, nonintellectual sister is the blueprint for Beauvoir's relationship with Sartre. In this relationship she relived time and again the pain of her father's rejection, a pain that emerges most poignantly in her first published novel, *She Came to Stay*. This novel was written based on her experiences of a ménage à trois that she, Sartre, and her former pupil Olga maintained over a period of some years. Beauvoir said *She Came to Stay* was written with damp palms because the theme of a Françoise fighting for her self-worth was so closely interwoven with her own life.[17] She would repeat this pattern time and again.

In my view, she was attempting to exorcize the youth trauma generated by her father through its repetition in her relationship with Sartre. That Sartre was her necessary love goes back to the fact that, like her father, he was a womanizer who preferred nonintellectual women and whose love had to be recaptured time and time again. As superior man = replacement father, he had to approve of her as intellectual *woman*. If we consider her life in this perspective, then the melancholy tone of the final two parts of her autobiography becomes clear: Beauvoir never received the unconditional love of the (replacement) father she so desperately wanted. Sartre had stopped loving her. The rest was unimportant.

The real reason Beauvoir persisted in the notion of herself and Sartre as a couple is, I think, rooted in her insecure self-image as a woman. Her whole environment, with father at the forefront, had inculcated in her the notion that she could not be a woman *and* an intellectual. Beauvoir wanted to prove them wrong. Thus, she certainly wanted to belong to the "second sex," and not to a third. This is why I believe she refused to profile herself as a lesbian: in her view, homosexuals were the third sex (see Bair, 1990a: 389).[18]

We can also ultimately trace her difficulty with growing old back to her insecurity as a woman. Beauvoir did not recognize herself in the image of an old woman. "One day I said to myself: 'I'm forty!' By the time I recovered from the shock of that discovery I had reached fifty. The stupor that seized me then has not left me yet" (FoC: 672). In her eyes, the old woman was a mutilated woman, a sexless being (see p. 493). She hated her old face "as it was attacked by the pox of time for which there is no cure" (p. 673). Mentally, she felt about thirty years old right up until the end of her life. It was essential for her to be seen as a *woman*, and her status as Satre's life-companion had to guarantee this womanhood.

Her youth trauma is, I think, also the reason Beauvoir hestitated in

profiling herself as a philosopher. At the end of her life, her self-conception in this respect was more subtle. "I'm not a philosopher in the sense
that I'm not the creator of a system, I'm still a philosopher in the sense
that I've studied a lot of philosophy, I have a degree in philosophy, I've
taught philosophy, I'm infused with philosophy, and when I put philosophy into my books it's because that's a way for me to view the world"
(Simons, 1989: 20). Simons believes Beauvoir was modest in this respect
because of her admiration for Sartre's philosophical genius (see Simons,
p. 13 ff). But as I see it, Beauvoir hesitated to apply the philosophy label
to her oeuvre because she thought a philosophical identity would detract
from her identity as a woman. She felt more comfortable in the company
of the female writers who had gone before her. Her self-image as writer
and her relationship with Sartre acted as a safeguard for her gender identity. They were the cover under which she could develop her intellectual
work. Her intellectual development flourished in this environment, but
she paid a price in her personal life. She lived continually with fists
clenched (see PoL: 292), and she continually struggled against the stub-
bornness of unconscious patterns.

Intellectual passion

Our recognition of the importance of a person's earliest formative years
does not refute Beauvoir's art-of-living ethics. After all, it is important
what we make of what we are made of. If certain limitations of Beauvoir's art of living have become clear, at the same time its importance has
also been emphasized. When the position of "*être relatif*" is so deeply
inculcated, it is obvious no simple or immediate solution can counter it.
This demands continual and permanent effort and the application of numerous techniques. People are not solely an unconscious; they are also
conscious beings and need theories, ideas, and tools at this level.[19] Beauvoir's art of living was her attempt to direct her life by means of "self-
techniques." Countless women worldwide still value and pore over her
work, not because her attempts were totally successful, but because she
made them. Her art-of-living ethics is a passionate answer to a problem
many recognize. Although feminist critics have a tendency to claim Beauvoir stood outside the position of women, and was thus unable to analyze
that position adequately (see e.g., Evans, 1985), I believe she lived the
most stereotyped trait of the situation of women, i.e., her socialization as
a "relative" being, "from within."

   Many feminists today consider her relationship with Sartre a blemish
on *The Second Sex*, a work that ranks as one of feminism's classics.[20] But
the other side of the coin is equally valid—Beauvoir's penetrating philo-

sophical questioning of the relative identity of woman is due to her own experiences in her relationship with Sartre.

Deirdre Bair wanted to write an intellectual biography of Simone de Beauvoir and to treat her life and work as interwoven elements (see chapter 2). Her enterprise stranded completely because her point of departure was that the life and work of Beauvoir had to be understood from Beauvoir's orientation on Sartre. Bair failed to see that Beauvoir *actually oriented herself on her orientation on Sartre*. Her work and life revolved around the problem of woman's relative identity, and it is this theme that made it—and her—an original.

If, in chapter 2, we concluded the equal relationship with the other was the main theme in her work, the critical problem behind this theme was to reconcile the emotional structure of a "relative woman" with an education as professional woman. Moral treatises, novels, autobiography, *and The Second Sex* all were the products of that drive. Time and again, although in different words, Beauvoir worked on the solution to the same problem. This makes her philosophizing into a passion. Her own words on de Sade typify her philosophical project most clearly:

> His wearisome repetitions are tantamount to a purification rite whose repetition is as natural to him as regular confession is to a good Catholic. De Sade does not give us the work of a free man. He makes us participate in his efforts of liberation. But it is precisely for this reason that he holds our attention. His endeavour is more genuine than the instruments it employs (MBS: 58).

Beauvoir thought it strange that people did not want to believe in "intellectual passions" (FoC: 200). As Sartre once said, she was capable of shedding "metaphysical tears," and her passion was sometimes infectious:

> I found myself alone with Sartre in the streets of Paris at dawn. I began to sob over the tragedy of the human condition; as we crossed the Seine, I leaned on the parapet of the bridge. "I don't see why we don't throw ourselves into the river!" "All right, then, let's throw ourselves in!" said Sartre, who was finding my tears contagious and had shed a few himself. (p. 119)

But they simply continued on their way over the Seine.

NOTES

1. Introduction

1. Recent American publications especially express a kind of personal fascination with the life and work of Beauvoir (see e.g., Wenzel, 1986). A Simone de Beauvoir Society is located in the United States, which publishes a newsletter for members (see Y. Patterson, ed., *The Simone de Beauvoir Society Newsletter*, 1983–).

2. For an anthology of the most important philosophic passages on women and the difference between the sexes, see Stopczyk (1980).

3. The philosopher Hegel formulated this as follows:

> It is possible for women to have a certain maturation, but they are not formed for the higher sciences, philosophy and the higher arts. Women can have flashes, taste and decorative qualities, but the ideal is out of their reach. The difference between man and woman is comparable to that between animal and plant. The animal corresponds more to the character of the man, while the plant, destined for a more uniform development, corresponds more to the female nature. (Hegel, 1979: 319)

4. With very few exceptions, universities were closed to women from the institutions' beginnings in the twelfth century until the end of the last century. Training for medicine and independent practice of medicine were open to women in certain periods, although not based on university education (see e.g., Hemelrijk, 1988; Kristeller, 1984).

5. Rang (1988) discovered numerous catalogs of seventeenth- and eighteenth-century intellectual women—lexicons with short biographies of educated, often aristocratic women—containing pleas from men for the development of women's intellectual capacities. A positive image of learned women emerges from these catalogs but the petit bourgeoisie put an end to it in the second half of the eighteenth century: the dominant image became that of learned women tortured

by nerves. However, it appears that there were far more educated women than had previously been supposed. Rang concludes, albeit tentatively, that intellectual women were more "normal" within a specific group than we had assumed. Yet, the very existence of these catalogs seems to me an indication of an ongoing so-called *problem*. Apparently, the notion of women as intellectuals was not widely accepted.

6. Van Bruggen wrote a philosophical work called *Prometheus* (1919) which received absolutely no attention from professional philosophers. Under the pseudonym Justine Abbing, she produced *From the Life of a Thinking Woman* (1920), lamenting the position of intellectual women.

7. The notion that science is not a purely rational occupation has been under discussion especially since the publication of Thomas Kuhn's influential *The Structure of Scientific Revolutions* (1970). Kuhn points out the fact that social processes within scientific disciplines are a determinant of the behavior of researchers. This means that factors other than the rational play a role in scientific research.

8. Kraüs (1989) also notes that we should not take Beauvoir at her word. She too believes Beauvoir's work should be studied as independent philosophical oeuvre.

9. Any further reference to Sartre's existential philosophy concerns his pre-Marxist period.

10. There are some authors who argue that of the two, Beauvoir was the real creative philosopher. Fullbrook and Fullbrook (1994) claim that the whole philosophical system of *Being and Nothingness* was in fact borrowed from Beauvoir's novel *She Came to Stay*. However, one need not go as far as this to prove the independence of Beauvoir's work.

2. The Life of a Thinking Woman

1. Bair says she was allowed to read selected passages only, and then under Beauvoir's supervision. In retrospect, she felt this had impeded her writing of the biography, in which she concludes Beauvoir put her sex life on a back burner in the period from 1939 through 1941. Further, Bair reproaches Le Bon for publishing the letters without due consideration. She claims their publication only gave more ammunition to those who wanted to defame Beauvoir and Sartre. Taken out of historical or biographical context, the publication "is a sorry way to remember one of this century's most influential literary couples" (Bair, 1990b).

2. Sartre emerges from the letters as an amoral Don Juan. We begin to suspect the level of censorship Beauvoir applied in the *Letters to Castor* (Sartre's letters to her), whose editing she oversaw. We search here in vain for the intrigues of both which are so apparent in the unedited Beauvoir letters.

3. The man in question was philosopher Maurice Merleau-Ponty. For reasons Beauvoir could not understand but which she labeled cowardly betrayal, he ended the relationship with Zaza. She only discovered the real reason thirty years later when her biographers Francis and Gontier told her that Zaza's parents had threatened to make public the fact that Merleau-Ponty and his brother and sister were illegitimate unless he agreed to forget marrying Zaza. He was so worried about his sister's own chances of marriage that he acquiesced, albeit reluctantly.

4. Girlfriends came and went in rapid succession, and he often had a "harem" of five or six at the same time (Cohen-Solal, 1987: 303). According to

Cohen-Solal, Sartre did not experience a lot of pleasure in physical love (see also Beauvoir, in: Schwarzer, 1986: 156; Bair, 1990a: 397). His countless conquests appear to indicate a more Don Juan–like seductive urge.

5. According to Poster, a sense of guilt led Beauvoir to give a distorted view of her youth when she wrote this in 1960 during the Algerian war. Sartre and Beauvoir's pre–World War II life-style, with all its (sexual) experimentation, cannot be seen as petit bourgeois in any sense, Poster argues, but should be considered "the slowly developing freedom of a new kind of radicalism which is typical of the New Left" (1975: 78).

6. Bair believes Beauvoir felt uncomfortable about her job with German-occupied radio for the rest of her life (see Bair, 1990a: 280; chapter 8, note 4).

7. *"J'ai perdu beaucoup de temps avec des femmes qui ont bâclé leur travail"* (*Le Matin*, 16 December 1985).

8. By publishing Beauvoir's letters to Sartre just before Bair's biography appeared, Sylvie Le Bon provided a counterbalance to the image sketched by Bair. Hazel Barnes notes that the letters contradict Bair's new myth of Beauvoir as totally oriented and subordinated to Sartre (see Barnes, 1991: 25).

3. The Second Sex *and Philosophy*

1. To be precise, she wrote it between October 1946 and June 1949, with interruptions for a four-month stay in the United States and the writing of *L'amérique au jour le jour* which took her five months.

2. Judith Okely refutes Beauvoir's claim that women are always equated with nature. Indians in the Bolivian highlands equate the married couple with "culture" and all unmarried people with "nature." "The opposition nature-culture is not simply linked to a gendered opposition" (Okely, 1986: 82). Beauvoir's notion of a universal menstruation taboo has also been proved untenable by cultural anthropological research (see pp. 84–85).

3. The *pour-soi* exists *"à titre d'être qui n'est pas ce qu'il est et qui est ce qu'il n'est pas"* (EN: 177).

4. This quotation is omitted from the English translation.

5. This is confirmed by Françoise Collin, editor-in-chief of the Franco-Belgian feminist journal *Cahiers du Griff* (Collin, personal communication).

6. I was told this by the American philosopher and Beauvoir-specialist Margaret Simons.

7. Parshley also cut the text by about 10 percent. He scrapped from the "Myths" section Beauvoir's examination of the work of a number of writers and also skipped a number of passages from "History."

8. Alice Schwarzer notes that, in the first French collective feminist publication, which appeared in 1970 under the title *Libération des femmes année zero*, the editors could not come up with anything better to write about than a demolition job on Beauvoir (see Schwarzer, 1986: 14–15).

9. " . . . *fréquemment, en effet, le mari révèle . . . que sa femme a donné des signes objectifs de plaisir et ce sont ces signes que la femme, interrogée, s'applique farouchement à nier"* (EN: 90).

10. Le Doeuff (1979) and Collins and Pierce (1976) have already gone into the following passages from *Being and Nothingness* at length.

11. This is also clear from the structure of *The Second Sex*, book II, dealing with the "lived experience" of woman as absolute Other.

4. A Place for Love

1. For example, when Beauvoir argued that people often found the use of contraceptives a disruption of the fusion process (see TSS II: 408). When she raised the question of differing sexual experiences between men and women, fusion is brought in implicitly: "The erotic experience is one that most poignantly discloses to human beings the ambiguity of their condition; in it they are aware of themselves as flesh and as spirit, as the other and as subject" (p. 423). Beauvoir went on to explain that women are less inhibited in giving themselves up physically to love, while men more often remain imprisoned in their lonely role as sovereign subject. On the other hand, it is harder for women to develop and experience themselves as subject in love because of their tendency to make themselves into object.

2. In *The Prime of Life*, Beauvoir talked in terms of a "delight": "when heart, head, and body are all in unison, there is high delight to be had from the physical expression of that oneness" (p. 62).

3. Elsewhere she wrote, "We detested the idea of eroticism—which Malraux used so plentifully in *Man's Fate*—because it implied a specialized approach that at once over-inflated sex and somehow cheapened it" (PoL: 138).

4. In *The Ethics of Ambiguity*, Beauvoir argued repeatedly that existentialism should not be equated with a solipsism.

5. In the early 1950s, an article appeared in the journal *Combat* under this ironically intended title (see FoC: 242). Whether someone should be put to the stake appears to have been a popular question in Beauvoir's France. The magazine *Action* launched a readers' survey under the title, "*Faut-il brûler Kafka?*" (see FoC: 52).

6. Beauvoir was referring here to the Plutarch story of Pyrrhus, king of Epirus (318–272 B.C.), and his advisor Cinéas. Pyrrhus informed Cinéas of his plans for conquest. The latter asked what his further plans were. When Pyrrhus replied he would then take a rest, Cinéas asked why he didn't do that straight away. At first sight, Cinéas appears the wiser, but the opposite proves the case: being a human being means we have to be involved continually with projects, Beauvoir concluded in her prologue to this essay (PC: 233–37).

7. Beauvoir was referring to the ideas of philosopher Descartes, who made a sharp distinction between matter and consciousness and considered one's own consciousness the only irrefutable certainty. This Cartesian body of ideas had major influence on French thinking.

8. Beauvoir defended especially the politico-philosophical consequences of Sartre's theory. Here we only examine the view of man that emerges from this article.

9. By Sartre's phenomenology, we are meant to understand his descriptions of man as situated to indicate that the unity of body and consciousness is of primary importance—I live my body, I am in the world through my body. His ontology should be seen as the theory of the absolute opposition of *en-soi* and *pour-soi*, with internal negation as central proposition (see chapter 3).

10. " . . . *car à travers le développement de son oeuvre Sartre a insisté de plus en plus sur le caractère engagé de la liberté, sur la facticité du monde, l'incarnation de la conscience, la continuité du temps vécu, le caractère totalitaire de toute vie* (MPps: 271). It should be noted that Beauvoir used the term "incarnation"

here for the situatedness of man, and thus did not reserve it for becoming a psycho-physiological unity in physical love.

11. Sonia Kruks also noted that Beauvoir colored her representation of Sartre in *Merleau-Ponty et le pseudo-sartrisme* (see Kruks, 1990: 115; Kräus, 1989: 95).

12. Kräus (1989) sees Beauvoir's view as an unintended cocktail of the ideas of Sartre and Merleau-Ponty, especially those of the latter (see Kräus: 86).

13. Beauvoir summarized her critique of Hegel as follows: "The essential moment of hegelian ethics is the moment when consciousnesses recognize one another; in this operation the other is recognized as identical with me, which means that in myself it is the universal truth of my self which alone is recognized; so individuality is denied" (EA: 104). This is problematic because, "if one denies with Hegel the concrete thickness of the here and now in favor of universal space-time, if one denies the separate consciousness in favor of Mind, one misses with Hegel the truth of the world" (p. 122).

14. "That universal moral theories of Kant, of Hegel, lead to optimism is caused by the fact that through their denial of individuality they also deny the failure" (PC: 363).

15. This difference is well illustrated in Beauvoir's description of their visit to psychologist Van Lennep at his institute in Utrecht, the Netherlands.

> We also took some visual tests invented by Van Lennep, and still not widely known. He showed us pictures of a galloping horse, a motorboat, a train and a man walking: which one gave us the most immediate impression of speed? The man, I said, without hesitation; his was the only case in which speed seemed to me consciously experienced. Also without hesitation, Sartre chose the motorboat, because it *tears itself away* from the surface it devours. My answer made him laugh, and I laughed at his, each of us seeing the other's reaction as a naive self-disclosure. (FoC: 127)

16. An argument for this division is Beauvoir's formulation when she talked of our concept of the world: "*Dans le monde réel le sens d'un objet n'est pas un concept saisissable par le pur entendement: c'est l'objet en tant qu'il se dévoile à nous dans la relation globale que nous soutenons avec lui et qui est action, émotion, sentiment*" (LM: 91). She placed pure rational understanding (*pur entendement*) against action, emotion, feelings. We indicate this pure rational understanding with the term "intellectual."

17. Margaret Simons shows how Keller (1985) incorrectly represents Beauvoir's ethics as an ethics in which man's transcending activity and his absolute freedom are central (Simons, 1987: 2 ff.).

18. Arntz himself states, "emphatic pronouncements are, however, rare" (1960: 284). There is only Sartre's note toward the end of *L'être et le néant*: he advances there the necessity of an *Ethique*, which treats the nature and role of the "*réflexion purifiante*" (EN, 1990: 642). In addition, a footnote about two-thirds of the way through the book refers to the necessity of an ethics: "*Ces considérations n'excluent pas la possibilité d'une morale de délivrance et du salut. Mais celle-ci doit être atteinte au terme d'une conversion radicale*" (p. 463). Finally, in the final section of *L'être et le néant*, Sartre raises the question of whether it is possible that freedom considers itself a value and has as ideal "to be always at a distance from itself" (BN: 627). Sartre concludes: "All these questions, which refer us to a pure and not an accessory reflection, can find their reply only on the ethical plane" (p. 628).

19. Bair revealed that Beauvoir attempted to obtain the unpublished *Cahiers* after Sartre's death. Beauvoir was on very bad terms with Sartre's adopted daughter and executor, Arlette Elkaïm, but she was so eager to have the manuscript that she actually went and begged Elkaïm for it at the door. However, Elkaïm refused and published it herself later (see Bair, 1990a: 589–90).

5. Forms of Ethics

1. Beauvoir stated that, when Sartre was writing his book on Genet in 1952, he began to see the fact that social circumstances determined the individual and could even take away all choices (see FoC: 209–10).

2. Not only social but also physical factors are determinant for the fact that man can exercise his ontological freedom. Through illness a person can be reduced to a totally passive existence. Beauvoir's books about her mother's deathbed and Sartre's deterioration are permeated with repugnance at such a fate.

3. In *Pyrrhus et Cinéas*, Beauvoir still distinguishes dimensions rather than steps in human freedom. "*Liberté*" and "*puissance*" as ontological and social freedom, respectively, are placed *alongside* each other so that Beauvoir becomes embroiled in a twisted reasoning: in spite of social impediments, you *are* still *always* free (see PC: 327). Later, Beauvoir criticized her own argument on this point (see PoL: 550). However, in *The Ethics of Ambiguity*, social freedom and ontological freedom are linked: although our ontological freedom is always potentially present, its realization is dependent on a certain level of social freedom. Thus, we *are* not automatically free, but we can become so.

4. In hindsight, Beauvoir's own comment on this article was, "In *Oeil pour oeil*, I justified the purges after the Liberation without ever using the one solid argument: these mercenaries, these murderers, these torturers must be killed, not to prove that man is free, but to make sure they don't do it again; for one Brice liquidated, how many lives would have been spared!" (FoC: 77). Later, it was generally recognized that the question of punishing war criminals requires a moral stand, and the enormity of the crime is attributed a central role. The enormity of the crime even justified the retroactive application of new legislation, i.e., penalization for crimes against humanity. But the objection against Beauvoir's original argument on this point is that the problem is approached using a moral formula without bringing in the relevant legal debates (my thanks to Ton Dekker).

5. She considered not only her articles from this period as moralistic, but also her literary work—the novels *The Blood of Others* (1945) and *Tous les hommes sont mortels* (1946), and her play *Les bouches inutiles* (1945). These novels are so-called thesis novels and still articulate specific moral formulas.

6. Beauvoir emphasized this repeatedly (see also e.g., PoL: 547; FoC: 274).

7. In conversation with her biographer Bair, Beauvoir emphasized that the collection of essays entitled *L'existentialisme et la sagesse des nations*, including "Littérature et métaphysique," formed a prelude to *The Mandarins* and her autobiography (Bair, 1990a: 321).

8. "Most of the 'action' of *Les Mandarins* in which Henri is involved in fact consists of moral crises and the making of choices" (Faillaize, 1980: 225).

9. Beauvoir stated: "*C'est à propos d'Henri Perron que j'ai tenté de formuler les vrais problèmes*" (Rolland, 1954: 359).

10. This has been added because the English translation does not follow the original French here.

11. Again, in this and the next quotation, we do not follow the English translation because it imprecisely translates *"une morale"* and *"art de vivre"* as "a set of principles" and "an approach to life" respectively (see *Les mandarins*: 134, 136).

12. Celeux (1986) points out a difference between Sartre and Beauvoir: the former was influenced more by Faulkner and Dos Passos, and the latter by Hemingway. Celeux thought it fitting that Beauvoir would be more influenced by a writer who remained close to day-to-day reality because, in contrast to Sartre, Beauvoir was not interested in philosophy but in everyday life. Celeux failed to pick up on Beauvoir's own concept of philosophy.

13. Cottrell (1975) called the narrative style of *The Mandarins* vulgar and inelegant.

14. In my view, this is ridiculous if only because Henri is the book's pivotal character. Moreover, he is also represented as a very respectable person. See also note 9.

6. Ethics as Art of Living

1. Sartre introduced this concept in the chapter on existential psychoanalysis in *Being and Nothingness* (see p. 557 ff).

2. Sartre comes very close here to the "nomadic" strategies of contemporary French thinkers, such as Gilles Deleuze and Félix Guattari. An aversion to psychology and psychoanalysis is also common ground.

3. Cohen-Solal was a personal friend of Sartre's adopted daughter Arlette Elkaïm with whom Beauvoir was seriously at odds (see chapter 4, note 19). In Cohen-Solal's account of Sartre's final years a major role is played by Benny Lévy, who was also a friend of Elkaïm's.

4. For this reason, the words used by Bair to indicate Beauvoir's motivations are less than well chosen. Bair talks about "introspection" (p. 320), "self-examination," "self-scrutiny" (p. 473), "self-understanding" (p. 451), and "self-discovery" (p. 320). I think the term "self-creation" would be far more appropriate.

5. The study of the deeper self only became current with the rise of Christianity, according to Foucault. The deepest areas of secret desires of the flesh had to be explored through self-examination techniques and confession. He believed that this, and especially confession, was the start of the "will to know" that is so characteristic of our culture (see also chapter 2).

6. It can be assumed this also applies to *The Mandarins*. When it appeared, Beauvoir said she had incorporated years of her own intellectual and practical experience into the book—so much so that for a while she would not have material for a new novel (see Rolland, 1954: 361).

7. This was a lecture Sartre gave in 1945 to a packed hall. The audience fought to gain admittance; people said it was a disgrace or fainted dead away—in short, it was a real happening. Sartre later called the publication of this lecture *"une erreur"* (see Jeanson, 1947: 36, 284–85).

8. In this quotation, we do not follow the English translation where it incorrectly translates *"comme on sent"* as "as you see fit" (see *Les Mandarins*: 135).

9. Francis Jeanson attempted to use the same method to reveal the hidden unity in Sartre's life and work. Sartre's fundamental choice is said to have been being a bastard: someone who finds himself alone in opposition to a society that he needs to conquer. According to Jeanson, the experiences of the fatherless Jean-Paul Sartre—he was two when his father died and his mother remarried when he was twelve—are also evident in his focus on Baudelaire and Genet: the former's

mother remarried when he was seven, and as a child, Genet was deserted by his parents (see Jeanson, 1955).

10. The selection of this specific work is also prompted by Sartre's own preference. When he was asked, "Which of your books do you hope the next generation will read?" he replied, "*Situations, Saint Genet*, the *Critique de la raison dialectique* and *Lucifer and the Lord*. . . . and then *Nausea*" (*Le nouvel observateur*, 1975).

11. Poster (1975) claims there is a difference between Sartre's theoretical and political work in the early 1950s. His political writings imply the necessity of a supraindividual political perspective for deliberations on our actions, while the basis of his theoretical work remained the individual's perspective. Sartre's abstract theoretical perspective and his practical engagement differ in this period.

12. See note 10.

13. "*Aucune morale n'est impliquée dans l'existentialisme. J'ai cherché pour ma part à en dégager une*" (LE: 134).

14. "He rejected my Kantian standards, fearing they would become notions within my writing and thus harmful to my expression. It irritated him to discuss this" (Bair, 1990a: 271).

15. According to Beauvoir, *Lucifer and the Lord* illustrated Sartre's definitive acceptance of political commitment. Goetz's antagonist Nasti was said to embody the perfect man of action for Sartre. Nasti accepts the discipline of action, but holds on to subjectivity (see FoC: 249 et passim).

16. See also Hughes, 1966: 225.

17. See e.g., Todd, 1983.

18. "[In *The Second Sex*] I place myself much more on a moral plane whereas Sartre dealt with morality later on. In fact, he never exactly dealt with morality" (in: Simons, 1989: 18).

7. Simone de Beauvoir's Art of Living

1. An extensive exposition on Freud's theory on femininity can be found in Mitchell, 1975.

2. For example, Salomé emphasized the major place occupied by narcissistic autoeroticism in women. She was also responsible for causing Freud to doubt his theory on woman's desire.

3. Juliet Mitchell also notes Beauvoir borrowed many insights from Freud, and subsequently placed them in a historical perspective. However, she argues, "Freud would not have disagreed," before going on to reprove Beauvoir for failing to accept the primacy of sexuality, i.e., Freud's a-historical assumptions. Beauvoir is accused of not recognizing the science behind Freud's theory, and of treating it as philosophy (Mitchell, 1975: 318). But Mitchell's plea for science is, in my view, part of the problem rather than a definitive solution; it assumes what still has to be proven.

Beauvoir herself remarked,

Not being a philosopher, Freud has refused to justify his system philosophically; and his disciples maintain that on this account he is exempt from all metaphysical attack. There are metaphysical assumptions behind all his dicta, however, and to use his language is to adopt a philosophy. It is just such confusions that call for criticism, while making criticism difficult. (TSS: 70)

4. As we have seen in chapter 2, such attempts have been made from a feminist psychoanalytical perspective. Heath (1989) and Moi (1990) are examples, but also Jardine (1986) uses a Freudian-Lacanian feminist approach. (Sartre is said to have been Beauvoir's "phallic mother.") Later, Beauvoir would become more subtle in her thinking on psychoanalysis, but she continued to reject out of hand any reduction of man to his unconsciousness (see chapter 10).

5. In *The Second Sex* she wrote,

It is noteworthy that the worship of the father is to be met with especially in the eldest of the children, and indeed a man is more interested in his first paternity than in later ones: he often consoles his daughter, as he consoles his son, when their mother is monopolized by newcomers, and she is likely to become ardently attached to him. On the contrary, a younger sister never can have her father all to herself, without sharing him; she is commonly jealous at once of him and of her elder sister ... almost all the cases I know of confirm this observation on the different attitudes of the older and younger sisters. (TSS II: 315; note 20)

6. For example, Lasocki (1971) sees a connection with Beauvoir's preoccupation with death. See also Jeanson (1966: 51).

7. See Evans (1985), Appignanesi (1988), Heath (1989), Ascher (1981), and numerous others.

8. Moi (1994) also approaches Beauvoir's life and work from the intellectual woman theme. Her book offers rich material with respect to Beauvoir's French educational background. However her (Kristeva-semiotic) approach to Beauvoir's texts in fact leads her to deal with Beauvoir from a psychoanalytical point of view only and more or less as a victim and suffering woman (see also my chapter 2). In contrast I would consider Beauvoir's work and life primarily as a philosophical enterprise: the enterprise being the creation of an art of living as a woman intellectual. This results in a much more positive picture of Beauvoir as an active, powerful woman.

9. For an explanation of Sartre's concept of a *"projet originel,"* see chapter 6.

8. A Philosopher as Woman

1. Critics who reproach her for this structure miss the point of Beauvoir's art of living: the "externalization" that is diametrically opposed to a *"vie intérieure."*

2. "[H]er decisiveness shook the arondissement," remarked her American lover, Nelson Algren (Marks, 1973: 131).

3. Jeanette Colombel recalls how Beauvoir slammed the door in Michel Foucault's face, saying Sartre was not at home. Foucault did not recognize her and thought she was Sartre's cleaner. On the stairs Colombel and Foucault met Sartre, and their subsequent reception was warm (Colombel, oral communication).

4. Sartre and Beauvoir have been accused of passive collaboration because, as intellectuals, they did not cease writing during the Nazi occupation, and allowed their books and plays to be published. Deirdre Bair says the same applied for most French writers; the number who did stop writing can be counted on the fingers of one hand. In taking stock of both their wartime attitudes, Bair states

neither Beauvoir nor Sartre had major slurs on their reputations, which is also apparent from the fact that no charges were laid against them (see Bair, 1990a: 260).

9. A Woman as Philosopher

1. While noting that this is striking (see Bair, 1990a: 639), in philosophical terms Bair continues to consider Beauvoir as no more than Sartre's exegetist.

2. *"Mon roman. Hâte de le finir. Repose sur une attitude philosophique qui déjà n'est plus la mienne. Le prochain sera sur la situation individuelle, sa signification morale et son rapport avec le social. Importance de cette dimension métaphysique"* (JG: 363).

Merleau-Ponty compares the attitude of Françoise in *She Came to Stay* with the egocentrism of children: they believe themselves the center of the world and cannot distinguish between their subjective world and reality (Merleau-Ponty, 1948: 60–61).

3. Only *All Men are Mortal* could still claim her partial approbation because it does not treat the death theme unambiguously. Death not only emerges as that which gives life meaning, but also as absurd loneliness and separation.

4. We have already seen how Hegel occurs regularly in Beauvoir's ethical treatises of the early 1940s, and he is also present in *The Second Sex*. She cites him approvingly in her introduction, but also uses a long quotation from his *Phänomenologie des Geistes* in the section on marriage (see TSS II: 454).

5. However, interest in Hegel reached its height in Paris in the early postwar years, especially through the lectures given by Jean Hyppolite and through his thesis *Genèse et structure de la Phénoménologie de l'Esprit*, which was published in 1947 (see Eribon, 1989: 30 ff).

6. Bakker argues, "The *Phänomenologie des Geistes* is a work whose significance for later phenomenology cannot be overestimated" (Bakker, 1969: 62).

7. Husserl's teacher Franz Brentano rejected Hegel's idealistic *"Begriffsdichtung"*: a so-called penetration of the inner nature of things without taking seriously their empirical manifestation (see de Boer, 1989: 47).

8. Merleau-Ponty continued, *"si le Hegel de 1827 est sujet au reproche d'idéalisme, on n'en peut dire, autant du Hegel de 1807."* Further on he stated, *"Ce qui est sûr en tout cas, c'est que la* Phénoménologie de l'Esprit *ne cherche pas à faire entrer l'histoire totale dans les cadres d'une logique préétablie, mais à revivre chaque doctrine, chaque époque, et se laisse conduire par leur logique interne avec tant d'impartialité que tout souci de système semble oublié"* (Merleau-Ponty, 1966: 111–12).

9. The literal translation from the French would be "women's life as they experience it."

10. Hatcher (1984) claims incorrectly that *The Second Sex* demonstrates that life as full-time housewife would be immoral by definition. The background here is his interpretation of the book as a work in the Marxist tradition. Beauvoir is supposed to have adopted Marx's ideas on labor as liberation. Hatcher fails to recognize Beauvoir's emphasis on the total situation of woman. He also attributes the position she adopted against the imposition of an inflated inner life on girls and women to the body of ideas of another philosopher—Nietzsche (see Hatcher, 1984: 55 ff). Here again, he fails to perceive the individual systematics of her thinking. Beauvoir's rejection of the inner, spiritual world is completely in accordance with her own phenomenological vision of man, which perceives man

as always focused on the world, and with her objection to the social impediments that prevent women from developing in this way.

11. Some critics claim *The Second Sex* is contradictory because it is not clear how the situation of woman as Other can be ended (see e.g., Okely, 1986: 79–80). They fail to see the crucial role of moral conversion in Beauvoir.

12. Beauvoir did not believe in the so-called *écriture féminine* (see Bair, 1990a: 653).

13. Beauvoir argued that the Anne character in *The Mandarins* was certainly not apolitical, in spite of the fact that she took no active part in politics—she is simply not a specialist in that field. But the fact that she adheres to the same notions that motivate her friends to action means she is not apolitical (see Rolland, 1954: 359).

14. We have already seen that, for example in her article, "Oeil pour oeil" (An Eye for an Eye), Beauvoir attempted to make a positive contribution to the debate on trying war criminals.

15. When Beauvoir was attacked because she did not know the work of Confucius, Boehme, and others but still had the audacity to hold philosophical opinions, she commented, "I tried to explain that he was confusing thinking with erudition" (Am: 44).

10. Philosophy as Passion

1. One of the consequences of this perception is that the philosophical tradition is enriched by a group of authors, including a large number of female writers (a conclusion which neither Nussbaum nor Beauvoir extrapolated from this perception). Criteria for inclusion should be that the authors in question are well trained in the philosophical debates of their time, and through their chosen literary genre, essay or novel, attempt to articulate truths. Based on these criteria, it would seem to me that in addition to Beauvoir, authors such as Belle van Zuylen, Carry van Bruggen, Marguérite Yourcenar, Hannah Arendt, Iris Murdoch, and Ingeborg Bachmann would be eligible for recognition as philosophers.

2. Postmodernism can be classified as a "neo-Nietzscheanism." Following Nietzsche's line, God, Truth, Man and Morality, Progress and Reason are brought down: the notion that these are absolutes that could form guidelines for our actions is denied. If for Nietzsche the realization that God is dead formed the backdrop to his "unmasking" of all fixed points of reference, in philosophical postmodernism this is primarily the realization that language is not an expression or description of reality. Language is not seen as a transparent neutral descriptive medium, but as a field in which terms only refer to each other. Thus, Truth has been knocked off its pedestal. After all, we can no longer claim that a series of terms can describe or reflect reality. All language has become narrative, or rather "discourse," and we now no longer have at our disposal a criterion to call one narrative more true than another. Philosophy is one system of narratives among others. Some postmodernists believe contemporary philosophers should take this into account and present themselves as narrators. Others conclude scientists and philosophers should not construct new narratives. If they do so, new meanings will be created, and the heavy burden of meanings and straitjackets that already weigh down modern man will only increase. The only useful course is to unravel and deconstruct fixed meanings wherever possible so that an open

space is created that would make possible the development of new ways of thinking and living on a practical level.

3. Here, Beauvoir's thinking is diametrically opposed to that of postmodern philosophers whose aim is to abolish moral man and, following Nietzsche, to propogate a thinking "beyond good and evil" (see also note 2). According to this neo-Nietzschean thinking, ethics and morality are themselves already a very specific power mechanism: they limit man to being a creature with a so-called inner life. Man is thus made into a creature who can and must continually give account of his actions. In this way, he becomes predictable and controllable and, as "*ordre intérieur*," is a pillar of the dominant social order. Other ways of living, other forms of subjectivity have to be developed that no longer imprison man in an individual identity. Beauvoir's negative moral code, however, is fully in line with the Enlightenment tradition. She was concerned with enlarging man's freedom to enable him to experience and realize himself as an individual.

4. See also note 9.

5. According to biographer Deirdre Bair, Beauvoir's mortal fear is wholly derived from her fear of desertion (see Bair, 1990a: 541). However, it would seem to me that the fact that Beauvoir wrestled with death was partly due to the death of Zaza, with whom she had a long symbiotic friendship. Zaza's death forms a recurrent theme in Beauvoir's work, as Audet (1979) and Marks (1973) demonstrate.

6. Beauvoir's earlier aversion to psychoanalysis appears to be due in part to the fact that, at the time, it tended to be no more than adaptation to or insertion into prevalent social norms. For example, she had serious objections to the electroshock therapy to which her friend and protégé Violette Leduc was subjected. Keefe (1979) points out that Freudian psychoanalysis plays a great role in her post–*Second Sex* novels and that Beauvoir appears to be aware of the importance of the context of psychoanalytical therapies. Psychiatrist Anne, the female main character in *The Mandarins*, initially wonders why she should cure people. What is normal? But when people begin returning from concentration camps after the war, she no longer wonders. It is important to help that young, grey-haired woman to sleep a little better, or to see that young child make happy drawings (see Keefe, 1979: 126).

7. See also Hatcher's article "Existential Ethics and Why It's Immoral to Be a Housewife" (1989).

8. Feminist theoreticians have been searching for feminine methods and epistemological points of departure. A feminist epistemology should be developed that would comprise an alternative model for acquiring knowledge and would thus signify a change in the very core of science. Feminist science would be characterized by a subject-subject model of knowledge in place of the dominant subject-object model. In socioscientific research, women would (should) apply the method of participating observation. Also their natural sciences research would be characterized by a relational involvement with study material. However, in executing a feminine epistemology, general definitions of femininity inevitably emerge of which neither equality-feminists nor postfeminists are particularly fond (see also Vintges 1988a and 1988b).

9. See Vintges, 1991.

10. Cayron (1973: 36–37) has calculated Beauvoir made 143 journeys between 1929 and 1962.

11. This attitude shows a striking similarity to that of Héloïse, the beloved of the twelfth-century philosopher Abélard. She wrote to Abélard, "It would be impossible for you to devote yourself with equal surrender to a wife and to phi-

losophy. How can one reconcile lessons and servants, libraries and cots, books and spindles, pens and bobbins?" (Le Goff, 1989: 75).

12. In a letter to her lover Nelson Algren, Beauvoir said her sexual relationship with Sartre lasted between eight and ten years (see Bair, 1990a: 397).

13. Terry Keefe asks, "How many of the depressed moods that Beauvoir records in the memoirs are partly attributable to events or people never mentioned?" (Keefe, 1983: 49). However, in my view, we should not be looking for "people never mentioned" to explain her moods, but rather for unreported events in her relationship with Sartre.

14. Carol Ascher argues—rightly I believe—that Beauvoir could not allow herself to delve too deeply into the child she had once been. Her enforced break with her parental milieu had been so radical that she had no space for experiencing her childhood "from the inside" (see Ascher, 1981: 5).

15. "*Et puis Papa était très brutal avec toi. . . . Il te disait toute la journée: 'Comme tu es laide, ma pauvre fille, comme tu es laide!'* " according to Beauvoir's sister Hélène (Dayan and Ribowska, 1979: 36).

16. Bair also notes that Beauvoir believed herself unattractive throughout her life (see Bair, 1990a: 71).

17. Judith Okely believes Beauvoir also identified with the second woman Xavière: the young Simone herself in competition with Françoise (mother Beauvoir's first name) for the love of the main character Pierre = père (see Okely, 1986).

18. Beauvoir explained the title of *The Second Sex* to Bair as follows: "since pansies are called the third sex . . . that must mean that women come in second" (Bair, 1990a: 389). Bair states that Beauvoir would become livid if people suggested her relationship with Sylvie Le Bon was lesbian (p. 508).

19. The insight that the earliest years are decisive for further development leads many women today to analysis or therapy in an attempt to get a grip on their lives. Beauvoir's ethics is also important in this sense; psychiatrists recommend *The Second Sex* as "bibliotherapy."

20. Angela Carter wrote crossly,

We knew she was almost as clever as he was because, at that time, De Beauvoir still thought it worthwhile to tell the world via the autobiographical details on her backflaps that she had come second to Sartre in their university finals. And, goodness me, wasn't coming second to Jean-Paul Sartre—Jean-Paul Sartre!—something to be proud of? . . . What might De Beauvoir not have done had it been objectively proved to her that she was cleverer than Sartre? (Carter, 1982)

BIBLIOGRAPHY

Works by Beauvoir

1943 *L'invitée* (novel). Paris: Gallimard.
      Eng. translation: *She Came to Stay*, 5th ed. Tr. Yvonne Moyse and Roger Senhouse. London: Flamingo, Fontana Paperbacks, 1989.

1944 *Pyrrhus et Cinéas* (essay). Paris: Gallimard.

1945 *Le sang des autres* (novel). Paris: Gallimard.
      Eng. translation: *The Blood of Others*, 1st ed. New York: Knopf, 1948.

1945 *Les bouches inutiles* (play).
      Eng. translation: *Who Shall Die?* Tr. Claude Francis and Fernande Gontier. Florrisant, Missouri: River Press, 1983.

1946 *Tous les hommes sont mortels* (novel). Paris: Gallimard.
      Eng. translation: *All Men Are Mortal*, 1st ed. Tr. Leonard M. Friedman. Cleveland: World, 1955.

1947 *Pour une morale de l'ambiguïté* (essay). Paris: Gallimard.
      Eng. translation: *The Ethics of Ambiguity*. New York: Philosophical Library, 1948.

1948 *L'existentialisme et la sagesse des nations* (four essays). Paris: Nagel. ("L'existentialisme et la sagesse des nations"; "Idéalisme moral et réalisme politique"; "Littérature et métaphysique"; "Oeil pour oeil.")

1948 *L'amérique au jour le jour* (essay). Paris: Morihien.
      Eng. translation: *America Day by Day*. Tr. Patrick Dudley. London: Duckworth, 1952.

1949 *Le deuxième sexe*, 2 parts (essay) Paris: Gallimard.
      Eng. translation: *The Second Sex*. Tr. H. M. Parshley. Harmondsworth: Penguin, 1974, 1984.

1952 *Faut-il brûler Sade?* (essay). Paris: Gallimard.
      Eng. translation: *Must We Burn De Sade?* London: Nevill, 1953.

1954 *Les mandarins* (novel). Paris: Gallimard.
      Eng. translation: *The Mandarins*, 1st ed. Cleveland: World, 1956.

1955   *Privilèges* (three essays). Paris: Gallimard. ("Faut-il brûler Sade?"; "La pensée de droite, aujourd'hui"; "Merleau-Ponty et le pseudo-sartrisme.")

1957   *La longue marche* (essay). Paris: Gallimard.
       Eng. translation: *The Long March*, 1st ed. Tr. Austryn Wainhouse. Cleveland: World, 1958.

1958   *Mémoires d'une jeune fille rangée (1908–1929)*. Paris: Gallimard.
       Eng. translation: *Memoirs of a Dutiful Daughter*. Tr. James Kirkup. Harmondsworth: Penguin, 1977, 1987.

1960   *La force de l'âge, (1929–1944)*. Paris: Gallimard.
       Eng. translation: *The Prime of Life*. Tr. Peter Green. Harmondsworth: Penguin, 1974, 1988.

1961   *Djamila Boupacha* (foreword to collection of essays of the same name with Gisèle Halimi). Paris: Gallimard.
       Eng. translation: *Djamila Boupacha: The Story of the Torture of a Young Algerian Girl which Shocked Liberal French Opinion*, 1st ed. New York: Macmillan, 1962.

1963   *La force des choses (1944–1962)*. Paris: Gallimard.
       Eng. translation: *Force of Circumstance*. Tr. Richard Howard. Harmondsworth: Penguin, 1968, 1987.

1964   *Une mort très douce ("récit")*. Paris: Gallimard.
       Eng. translation: *A Very Easy Death*. Tr. Patrick O'Brian. Harmondsworth: Penguin, 1976, 1983.

1966   *Les belles images* (novel). Paris: Gallimard.
       Eng. translation: *Les belles images*, 1st ed. New York: Putnam, 1968.

1968   *La femme rompue* (three novellas). Paris: Gallimard.
       Eng. translation: *The Woman Destroyed*. Tr. Patrick O'Brian. London: Fontana, 1971, 1987.

1970   *La vieillesse* (essay). Paris: Gallimard.
       Eng. translation: *Old Age*. Tr. Patrick O'Brian. Harmondsworth: Penguin, 1977, 1986.

1972   *Tout compte fait (1962–1972)*. Paris: Gallimard.
       Eng. translation: *All Said and Done*. Tr. Patrick O'Brian, Harmondsworth: Penguin, 1988.

1979   *Les écrits de Simone de Beauvoir*. Edited by C. Francis and F. Gontier. Paris: Gallimard.

1980   *Quand prime le spirituel* (novel). Paris: Gallimard.
       Eng. translation: *When Things of the Spirit Come First: Five Early Tales*, 1st ed. New York: Pantheon, 1982.

1981   *La cérémonie des adieux* (essay). Paris: Gallimard.
       Eng. translation: *Adieux, A Farewell to Sartre*. Tr. Patrick O'Brian. Harmondsworth: Penguin, 1985.

1990   *Lettres à Sartre*. 2 parts. Paris: Gallimard.
       Eng. translation: *Letters to Sartre*. London: Vintage, 1992.

1990   *Journal de guerre* (diary). Paris: Gallimard.

Lectures and Articles Cited

1945   "La phénoménologie de la perception de Maurice Merleau-Ponty." *Les temps modernes* 1, 2. 363–67.

1949   "Les structures élémentaires de la parenté." *Les temps modernes* 7, 49, 943–49.

1950 "It's about Time." *Flair* 1, 3, 76–77.
1959 "Brigitte Bardot et le syndrome de Lolita" (pp. 363–376). In Francis and Gontier, *Les écrits*. Paris: Gallimard, 1979.
Eng. translation: *Brigitte Bardot and the Lolita Syndrome*. London: Andre Deutsch, 1960.
1965 "Que peut la littérature?" (pp. 73–92). In Y. Buin, *Que peut la littérature?* coll. "L'Inédit" 10/18, no. 249 (Union Générale d'éditions).
1966 "Mon expérience d'écrivain" (pp. 439–57). In Francis and Gontier, *Les écrits*. Paris: Gallimard, 1979.
1976 "Préface au livre d'Anne Ophir: Régards féminins." Also in Francis and Gontier, *Les écrits*. Paris: Gallimard, 1979, pp. 577–79.

Interviews Cited

Chapsal, Madeleine (1960). Une interview par Madeleine Chapsal (originally published in *Les écrivains en personne*. Paris: Julliard, 17–37). In Francis and Gontier, *Les écrits*. Paris: Gallimard, 1979, pp. 381–96.
Le Matin, 5 December 1985. "Simone de Beauvoir: le désaveu."
Le Matin, 16 December 1985. "Simone de Beauvoir et ses biographes (suite)."
Rolland, J. F. (1954). Interview de Simone de Beauvoir (originally published in *L'Humanité*, 19 December). In Francis and Gontier, *Les écrits*, 1979, pp. 358–62.
Simons, Margaret (1989). Two interviews with Simone de Beauvoir. *Hypatia* 3, 3, 11–27.
Teitelbaum, Mo (1973). "Women against the System." *Sunday Times Magazine*, 29 April, 28–31.

Works by Sartre Cited

1936 *La transcendance de l'ego*. Paris: Bibliothèque des textes philosophiques.
1938 *La nausée*. Paris: Gallimard.
Eng. translation: *Nausea*. New York: New Directions, 1949.
1939 *Esquisse d'une théorie des émotions*. Paris: Hermann, 1943.
1943 *L'être et le néant*. Paris: Gallimard.
Eng. translation: *Being and Nothingness*. London: Routledge, 1990, 1993.
1944 *Huis clos*. Paris: Gallimard.
1946 *L'existentialisme est un humanisme*. Paris: Les éditions Nagel.
Eng. translation: *Existentialism and Humanism*. London: Methuen, 1989.
1948 *Qu'est-ce que la littérature?* Paris: Gallimard.
1951 *Le diable et le bon dieu* (play).
Eng. translation: "Lucifer and the Lord." In *In Camera and Other Plays*. London: Penguin, 1990, 39–176.
1952 *Saint Genet: comédien et martyr*. Paris: Gallimard.
Eng. translation: *Saint Genet, Actor and Martyr*. London: Heinemann, 1988.
1960 *Critique de la raison dialectique* (précédé de *Questions de méthode*), Tome I. Paris: Gallimard.
1963 *Les mots*. Paris: Gallimard.
Eng. translation: *Words*. Penguin, 1967.
1965 "Que peut la littérature?" (pp. 107–27). In Y. Buin, *Que peut la littérature?* coll. "L'Inédit" 10/18, no. 249 (Union Générale d'éditions).

1975   "Self-portrait in My Seventieth Year." *Le nouvel observateur*, 23 June, 30 June, 7 July.
1983   *Cahiers pour une morale*. Paris: Gallimard (originally written in 1947).

Works on Simone de Beauvoir Cited

Altena, E. van (1983). "Mandaryner peller." In Simone de Beauvoir, *De Mandaryner*. Weesp-Agathon, 713–26.

Anderson, Thomas (1979). *The Foundation and Structure of Sartrean Ethics*. Lawrence: Regents Press of Kansas.

Appignanesi, Lisa (1988). *Simone de Beauvoir*. London: Penguin.

Ascher, Carol (1981). *Simone de Beauvoir: A Life of Freedom*. Boston: Beacon.

Audet, Jean-Raymond (1979). *Simone de Beauvoir face à la mort*. Lausanne: L'Age d'Homme.

Bair, Deirdre (1990a). *Simone de Beauvoir: A Biography*. New York: Summit.

—— (1990b). "Simone's Scarlet Letters." *Guardian* 15 March.

Barnes, Hazel (1990). "Sartre and Sexism." *Philosophy and Literature* 14, 340–47.

—— (1991). "Simone de Beauvoir's Journal and Letters: A Poisoned Gift?" (pp. 13–30). In Yolanda Patterson, ed., *Simone de Beauvoir Studies*, vol. 8. Menlo Park, California: California State University.

Butler, Judith (1986). "Sex and Gender in Simone de Beauvoir's Second Sex" (pp. 35–49). In *Simone de Beauvoir: Witness to a Century*. Yale French Studies 72.

Carter, Angela (1982). "The Intellectual's Darby and Joan." *New Society* 28 January, 156–57.

Cayron, Claire (1973). *La nature chez Simone de Beauvoir*. Paris: Gallimard.

Celeux, Anne-Marie (1986). *Jean-Paul Sartre, Simone de Beauvoir: une expérience commune, deux écritures*. Paris: Nizet.

Cottrell, Robert (1975). *Simone de Beauvoir*. New York: Ungar.

Dayan, J., and M. Ribowska (1979). *Simone de Beauvoir. Un film de Josée Dayan et Malka Ribowska*. Paris: Gallimard.

Evans, Mary (1985). *Simone de Beauvoir: A Feminist Mandarin*. London: Tavistock.

Fallaize, Elizabeth (1980). "Narrative Structure in Les Mandarins" (pp. 221–32). In C. Burns, ed., *Literature and Society, Studies in Nineteenth and Twentieth Century French Literature*. Birmingham: University of Birmingham.

Francis, C., and F. Gontier (1979). *Les écrits de Simone de Beauvoir*. Paris: Gallimard.

—— (1985). *Simone de Beauvoir*. Paris: Perrin.

Fullbrook, Kate, and Edward Fullbrook (1994). *Simone de Beauvoir and Jean-Paul Sartre: The Remaking of a 20th Century Legend*. New York: Basic.

Gennari, Geneviève (1958). *Simone de Beauvoir*. The Hague: Kruseman.

Greene, Naomi (1980). "Sartre, Sexuality and the Second Sex." *Philosophy and Literature* (Fall), 199–211.

Hansen, Linda (1979). "Pain and Joy in Human Relationships: Jean-Paul Sartre and Simone de Beauvoir." *Philosophy Today* (Winter), 338–46.

Hatcher, Donald (1984). *Understanding The Second Sex*. New York: Peter Lang.

—— (1989). "Existential Ethics and Why It's Immoral to Be a Housewife." *Journal of Value Inquiry* 23, 59–68.

Heath, Jane (1989). *Simone de Beauvoir*. Hertfordshire: Harvester Wheatsheaf.

Henry, A. (1961). *Simone de Beauvoir ou l'échec d'une chrétienté*. Paris: Le Signe.

Jardine, Alice (1986). "Death Sentences: Writing Couples and Ideology" (pp. 84–96). In S. Suleiman, ed., *The Female Body in Western Culture*. Cambridge, Mass.: Harvard University Press.

Jeanson, Francis (1966). *Simone de Beauvoir ou l'entreprise de vivre*. Paris: Éditions du Seuil.

Kaufmann McCall, Dorothy, (1979). "Simone de Beauvoir, The Second Sex, and Jean-Paul Sartre." *Signs: Journal of Women in Culture and Society* 5, 2, 209–23.

Keefe, Terry (1979). "Psychiatry in the Postwar Fiction of Simone de Beauvoir." *Literature and Psychology* 29, 3, 123–33.

────── (1983). *Simone de Beauvoir, A Study of Her Writings*. London: Harrap.

Keller, Catherine (1985). "Feminism and the Ethics of Inseparability" (pp. 251–63). In B. Andolsen et al., eds., *Women's Consciousness, Women's Conscience*. New York: Harper & Row.

Kraüs-Kruks, Sonia (1989). "Simone de Beauvoir entre Sartre et Merleau-Ponty." *Les temps modernes* 45, 520, 81–103.

Kruks, Sonia (1990). *Situation and Human Existence*. London: Unwin Hyman.

Lasocki, Anne-Marie (1971). *Simone de Beauvoir ou l'entreprise d'écrire*. The Hague: Martinus Nijhoff.

Le Doeuff, Michèle (1979). "Simone de Beauvoir and Existentialism." *Ideology and Consciousness* 6 (Autumn), 47–57.

Leighton, Jean (1975). *Simone de Beauvoir on Woman*. Rutherford: Fairleigh Dickinson University Press.

Lilar, Suzanne (1970). *Le malentendu du deuxième sexe*. Paris: Presses Universitaires de France.

Lloyd, Genevieve (1984). *The Man of Reason*. London: Methuen.

Madeheim, Helmuth (1966). "Kindheitserinnerungen französischer Dichter." *Die Neueren Sprachen* 15, 30–37.

Marks, Elaine (1973). *Simone de Beauvoir: Encounters with Death*. New Brunswick: Rutgers University Press.

Mead, Margaret (1953). "A SR Panel Takes Aim at 'The Second Sex.'" *Saturday Review of Literature* 21 February.

Moi, Toril (1986). "She Came to Stay." *Paragraph*, vol. 8, 110–20.

────── (1990). *Feminist Theory and Simone de Beauvoir*. Cambridge, Mass.: Blackwell.

────── (1994). *Simone de Beauvoir: The Making of an Intellectual Woman*. Cambridge, Mass.: Blackwell.

Morris, Meaghan (1981). "Operative Reasoning: Michèle Le Doeuff, Philosophy and Feminism." *Ideology and Consciousness* 9, 71–101.

Mostovych, Anna (1982). *The Intellectual in the Works of Simone de Beauvoir*. Ph.D. diss., Indiana University.

Okely, Judith (1986). *Simone de Beauvoir, A Re-reading*. London: Virago.

Ophir, Anne (1976). *Regards Féminins*. Paris: Denoël/Gonthier.

Patterson, Yolanda, ed. (1983–). *Simone de Beauvoir Society Newsletter*. 440 La Mesa Drive, Menlo Park, California 94028.

Schwarzer, Alice (1986). *Gesprekken met Simone de Beauvoir*. Amsterdam: Maarten Muntinga.

Seigfried, Charlene Haddock (1984). "Gender-specific Values." *Philosophical Forum* 15 (Summer), 425–42.

Selle, Irene (1980). "L'Abandon du 'novel métaphysique' dans l'oeuvre de Simone de Beauvoir." *Philologica Pragensia* 116, 46 Praha 1, 23, 108–9.

Simons, Margaret (1983). "The Silencing of Simone de Beauvoir. Guess What's Missing from 'The Second Sex.' " *Women's Studies International Forum* 6, 5, 559–64.

—— (1986). "In Memoriam." *Yale French Studies* 72, 203–5.

—— (1987). "The Moral Philosophy of Simone de Beauvoir." Paper presented at the American Philosophical Association, New York, 28 December.

—— (1990). "Beauvoir and the Philosophical Canon: On Reading Beauvoir's 'The Second Sex.' " *Journal of the History of Ideas* 51, 3, 487–504.

——, ed. (1995). *Feminist Interpretations of Simone de Beauvoir.* University Park: Pennsylvania State University Press.

Singer, Linda (1985). "Interpretation and Retrieval: Rereading Beauvoir." *Hypatia*, Special Issue of Women's Studies International Forum, 8, 3, 231–38.

Stone, Robert (1987). "Simone de Beauvoir and the Existential Basis of Socialism." *Social Text* 17 (Fall), 123–33.

Strickland, G. (1966). "Simone de Beauvoir's Autobiography." *Cambridge Quarterly* 1, 1, 43–60.

Walters, Margaret (1977). "The Rights and Wrongs of Women: Mary Wollstonecraft, Harriet Martineau, Simone de Beauvoir" (pp. 304–78). In J. Mitchell and A. Oakley, eds., *The Rights and Wrongs of Women.* Middlesex: Penguin.

Wenzel, Hélène, ed. (1986). *Simone de Beauvoir: Witness to a Century.* Yale French Studies 72. New Haven: Yale University Press.

Whitmarsh, Anne (1981). *Simone de Beauvoir and the Limits of Commitment.* Cambridge: Cambridge University Press.

Willems, Gilbert (1972). *Simone de Beauvoir.* Uitgeverij Orion. n.p.

Winegarten, Renee (1988). *Simone de Beauvoir: A Critical View.* Oxford: Berg.

Works on Sartre Cited

Arntz, J. Th. C. (1960). *De liefde in de ontologie van Sartre.* Nijmegen.

Cohen-Solal, Annie (1987). *Jean-Paul Sartre.* New York: Pantheon.

Collins, M., and C. Pierce (1976). "Holes and Slime: Sexism in Sartre's Psychoanalysis" (pp. 112–27). In C. Gould and M. Wartofsky, eds., *Women and Philosophy: Toward a Theory of Liberation.* New York: Putnam.

Hughes, Stuart H. (1987). *Between Commitment and Disillusion.* Middletown, Conn.: Wesleyan University Press.

Hunyadi, Mark (1985). "Ma liberté, c'est le meurtre de l'autre. À propos des 'Cahiers pour une morale' de Jean-Paul Sartre." *Revue de théologie et de philosophie* 117, 173–84.

Jeanson, Francis (1947). *Le problème moral et la pensée de Sartre.* Paris: Éditions du Seuil. Eng. translation: *Sartre and the Problem of Morality.* Bloomington: Indiana University Press, 1980.

—— (1955). *Sartre par lui-même.* Paris: Éditions du Seuil.

Kruks, Sonia (1986). "Sartre's *Cahiers pour une morale*: Failed Attempt or New Trajectory in Ethics?" In *Social Text* 13–14, 184–94.

Morris, Phyllis (1975). *Sartre's Concept of a Person: An Analytic Approach.* Amherst: University of Massachusetts Press.

Murdoch, Iris (1953). *Sartre, Romantic Rationalist.* New Haven: Yale University Press.

Nauta, Lolle W. (1966). *Jean-Paul Sartre.* Baarn: Het wereldvenster.

Poster, Mark (1975). *Existential Marxism in Postwar France: From Sartre to Althusser.* Princeton: Princeton University Press.

Schuetz, Alfred (1948). "Sartre's Theory of the Alter Ego." *Philosophy and Phenomenological Research* 9, 2, 181–99.

Struyker Boudier, Cornelis (1967). *Jean Paul Sartre. Een inleiding tot zijn denken.* Tielt, Den Haag: Lannoo.

Todd, Olivier (1983). *De mandarijn van Parijs. Een kritische blik op Sartre.* Tricht: Goossens.

Warnock, Mary (1967). *Existentialist Ethics.* New York: Macmillan.

General Bibliography

Abbing, Justine (pseudonym of Carry van Bruggen) (1985) (originally published in 1920). *In Uit het leven van een denkende vrouw.* Rotterdam: Nijgh & Van Ditmar.

Alic, Margaret (1986). *Hypatia's Heritage. A History of Women in Science from Antiquity to the Late Nineteenth Century.* London: Women's Press.

Bader, V. M., and A. Benschop (1988). *Ongelijkheden.* Groningen: Wolters-Noordhoff.

Badinter, Elisabeth (1989). *Man/Woman: The One Is the Other.* London: Collins Harvill.

Bakker, R. (1969). *De geschiedenis van het fenomenologisch denken.* Utrecht: Het Spectrum.

Boer, Theo de (1989). *Van Brentano tot Levinas.* Meppel: Boom.

Bruggen, Carry van (1919). *Prometheus.* 2 parts. Rotterdam: Nijgh & van Ditmar.

——— (1925). *Hedendaagsch fetischisme.* Amsterdam: Querido.

——— (1985). "Argeloosheid-des-mans" (pp. 218–23) (orig. in *Het Algemeen Handelsblad,* 24 May 1924). In J. Fontijn et al., eds., *Een documentatie.* 's-Gravenhage: Nijgh & Van Ditmar.

Camus, Albert (1942). *L'étranger.* Paris: Gallimard. Eng. translation: *The Outsider* London: H. Hamilton, 1946.

Dreyfus, H., and P. Rabinow, eds. (1983). *Michel Foucault: Beyond Structuralism and Hermeneutics.* Chicago: University of Chicago Press.

Eribon, Didier (1989). *Michel Foucault—(1926–1984).* Paris: Flammarion.

Foucault, Michel (1983). "On the Genealogy of Ethics" (pp. 229–52). In H. Dreyfus and P. Rabinow, eds., *Michel Foucault: Beyond Structuralism and Hermeneutics.* Chicago: University of Chicago Press.

——— (1986a). *The Use of Pleasure.* London/Harmondsworth: Penguin.

——— (1986b). *The Care of the Self.* London/Harmondsworth: Penguin.

——— (1988a) (orig. 1984). "The Ethic of Care for the Self as a Practice of Freedom" (pp. 1–20). In J. Bernauer and D. Rasmusse, eds., *The Final Foucault.* Cambridge, Mass.: MIT Press.

——— (1988b). "Technologies of the Self" (pp. 16–49). In M. Foucault et al., eds., *Technologies of the Self.* Amherst: University of Massachusetts Press.

Gilligan, Carol (1985). *In a different voice.* Cambridge, Mass. and London: Harvard University Press.

Hegel, Georg Wilhelm Friedrich (1978). *Het wetenschappelijk kennen. Voorwoord tot de Fenomenologie van de geest.* Amsterdam: Boom Meppel.

——— (1979). *Grundlinien der Philosophie des Rechts.* Frankfurt am Main: Suhrkamp, Theorie Werkausgabe, band 7.

Hemelrijk, Emily (1988). "Docta Puella. Vrouwen en geleerdheid in het klassieke Rome" (pp. 11–35). In T. Van Loosbroek et al., eds., *Geleerde vrouwen. Negende jaarboek voor Vrouwengeschiedenis.* Nijmegen: SUN.

Ignatieff, Michael (1990). "Why Shouldn't Everyone's Life Be a Work of Art?" *The Observer*, 7 January.

King, Margaret (1984). "Book-lined Cells: Women and Humanism in the Early Italian Renaissance" (pp. 66–90). In Patricia Labalme, ed., *Beyond Their Sex: Learned Women of the European Past*. New York: New York University Press.

Kristeller, Paul (1984). "Learned Women of Early Modern Italy: Humanists and University Scholars" (pp. 91–116). In Patricia Labalme ed., *Beyond Their Sex, Learned Women of the European Past*. New York: New York University Press.

Kuhn, Thomas (1970). *The Structure of Scientific Revolutions*. Chicago: University of Chicago Press.

Labalme, Patricia, ed. (1984). *Beyond Their Sex, Learned Women of the European Past*. New York: New York University Press.

Lévi-Strauss, Claude (1967). *Les structures élémentaires de la parenté*. Paris: Mouton. (1st ed. 1949).

Merleau-Ponty, Maurice (1945). *Phénoménologie de la perception*. Paris: Gallimard.

—— (1948). *Sens et non-sens*. Paris: Les Éditions Nagel.

—— (1955). *Les aventures de la dialectique*. Paris: Gallimard.

Mitchell, Juliet (1975). *Psychoanalysis and Feminism*. New York: Vintage.

Noordenbos, Greta (1987). "Vrouwen in het wetenschapsbedrijf: mogelijkheden en beperkingen" (pp. 20–25). In W. Van Rossum et. al., eds., *Onderzoek naar wetenschap, technologie en samenleving*. Amsterdam: SISWO publikatie (326).

Nussbaum, Martha (1986). *The Fragility of Goodness*. Cambridge: Cambridge University Press.

Pisan, Christine de (1984). *Het boek van de stad der vrouwen*. Amsterdam: Feministische Uitgeverij Sara.

Rang, Brita (1988). " 'Geleerde vrouwen van alle Eeuwen ende Volckeren, zelfs oock by de barbarische Scythen.' De catalogi van geleerde vrouwen in den zeventiende en achttiende eeuw" (pp. 36–64). In Tineke van Loosbroek, ed., *Geleerde vrouwen. Negende Jaarboek voor Vrouwengeschiedenis*. Nijmegen: SUN.

Schiebinger, Londa (1989). *The Mind Has No Sex? Women in the Origins of Modern Science*. Cambridge, Mass.: Harvard University Press.

Stopczyk, Annegret (1980). *Was Philosophen über Frauen denken*. Munich: Matthes & Seitz Verlag.

Vintges, K. (1988a). "Het leven van een vrolijke wetenschapster." *Wetenschap en Samenleving* 40, 4, 29–35.

—— (1988b). "Do We Need Feminist Epistemologies?" *Communication & Cognition*, Special volume: Feminism, Epistemology and Science, 21, 2, 157–60.

—— (1991) "The Vanished Woman and Styles of Feminine Subjectivity. Feminism: Deconstruction and Construction" (pp. 228–40). In J. Hermsen and A. van Lenning, eds., *Sharing the Difference. Feminist Debates in Holland*. London: Routledge and Kegan Paul.

—— (1992). *Filosofie als passie. Het derke van Simone de Beauvoir*. Amsterdam: Prometheus.

Widdnall, Sheila (1988). "Voices from the Pipeline." *Science* 241, 30–39, 1740–45.

Widom, C., and B. Burke (1978). "Performance, Attitudes and Professional Socialization of Women in Academia." *Sex Roles* 4, 4, 549–62.

Williams, Bernard (1985). *Ethics and the Limits of Philosophy*. London: Fontana.

INDEX

Karen Vintges *is Associate Professor of philosophy at the University of Amsterdam. A founder and editor of the journal* Krisis, *she has published essays on Beauvoir, on theories of ideology, on feminism, and on the last work of Michel Foucault and its impact on feminist thought.*

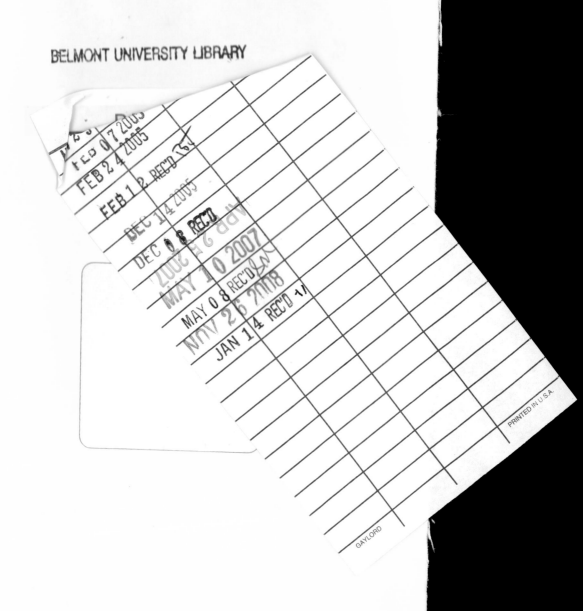